PENGUIN BOOKS

HOW POETRY WORKS:
THE ELEMENTS OF ENGLISH POETRY

Philip Davies Roberts was born in 1938, grew up in Quebec near the
New England border, and spent his formative years in Nova Scotia,
where he now lives. He was educated at Acadia University, Nova
Scotia, and at Jesus College, Oxford. He has worked in Spain as an
English teacher; in England as a schoolteacher, as an editor for Reu-
ters, and as a public relations consultant; in Australia as a university
lecturer, where he specialized in prosody and poetics; and in Costa
Rica as a staff journalist for the *Tico Times*. He has also served as
poetry editor for the *Sydney Morning Herald*, and was founder of the
Island Press, Sydney, which published new collections of work by
many leading Australian poets.

Winner of the Chapman Memorial Prize for Poetry at Oxford, Philip
Davies Roberts has published five collections of poetry, including the
*Will's Dream* cycle, voted poetry book of the year by the *Australian* in
1974. He has also written *Plain English: A User's Guide* (Penguin, 1986)
and a book on the father's role in home birth, as well as an annotated
edition of traditional Mother Goose tunes. His articles have appeared
in *English Studies, Semiotica* and *The Times Educational Supplement*. He is
now working on a new collection of poetry and on a comparative
study of traditional British ballads.

PHILIP DAVIES ROBERTS

# How Poetry Works:
## *The Elements of English Poetry*

*The lyf so short, the craft so longe to lerne*
*— Chaucer*

PENGUIN BOOKS

PENGUIN BOOKS

Published by the Penguin Group
Penguin Books Ltd, 27 Wrights Lane, London W8 5TZ, England
Penguin Books USA Inc., 375 Hudson Street, New York, New York 10014, USA
Penguin Books Australia Ltd, Ringwood, Victoria, Australia
Penguin Books Canada Ltd, 2801 John Street, Markham, Ontario, Canada L3R 1B4
Penguin Books (NZ) Ltd, 182–190 Wairau Road, Auckland 10, New Zealand

Penguin Books Ltd, Registered Offices: Harmondsworth, Middlesex, England

First published in Pelican Books 1986
Reprinted in Penguin Books 1991
10 9 8 7 6 5 4

Copyright © Philip Davies Roberts, 1986
All rights reserved

Printed in England by Clays Ltd, St Ives plc
Set in Aldus (Linotron 202)

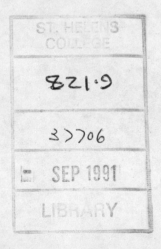

*for my parents*

# Contents

# Preface

First, a warning: this book is *not* about how to create poetry. One of the chief requirements of the poetry of every age is that it should do the unexpected. This effectively makes it quite impossible for anyone anywhere to write a book about how it is to be done. Instead, I try to present an account of the many different effects which may be going on in a poem at any moment, always with the understanding that one should not feel deficient if, in spite of all such effects, the poem still fails to interest and attract the ear. Taste in poetry, as in all the arts, is very much a personal matter.

At the same time, I want to encourage readers who may have been discouraged by previous attempts to develop an appreciation for poetry not to give up hope. This book takes a fresh approach to the subject, one firmly based on the sounds of our language, and I hope that it will make you aware of the many inventive ways in which these may be used. At the end of the book is a brief anthology of poems and selections designed not only to exemplify points I make earlier, but also to attract readers to new fields. If the book does its job properly, you should finally be able to dispense with its text altogether and just concentrate on the poems.

In order to present the printed poem so that you will immediately be able to perceive its rhythmic patterns (a main source of confusion for most readers), I have devised a format in which the opening stresses of the line are set in a vertical column, with any opening weak syllables to the left. (A glance at the poems in the anthology section will demonstrate how this works.) I have to thank the modern poets included for allowing me thus to vary the usual format of their lines. Their willingness may have been prompted by the realization that, nowadays, general public awareness of the rhythms, phonic patterns, and other sound effects of English poetry is at an all-time low. I hope that these new arrangements may do something to change this.

Here I also want to thank the many people who, whether consciously or not, helped me shape this book, most of all Carol Berney for her continual assistance while I wrote it. I would like particularly to mention the generous and valuable help offered by Stephen Knight and Terry Threadgold in Australia; Jüri Gabriel in Britain; Thompson Smith in Canada; and Bruce and Inta Gale Carpenter, Jane Hilberry, and Marcia Kruchten in the USA. I am also indebted to the staffs of the National Library of Australia, Canberra, and the Fisher Library, University of Sydney; the Bodleian Library, Oxford, and the British Museum, London; the Vaughan Memorial Library, Acadia University; and the Indiana University Library and the Monroe County Public Library, Bloomington, Indiana. I am especially grateful to the students of the Language of Poetry course which I gave at the University of Sydney between 1968 and 1980, for their many valuable insights.

The reader of this book may discern that I have a particular interest in the work of the late British poet Robert Graves. I first met Graves when I was a student at Oxford; he took an interest in my early work which became an important factor in the development of my own poetry. Graves held very strong views about the role of the poet and the nature of the poet's inspiration. Although I do not agree with all of these, I feel there can be no doubt about the great and positive influence he had on many young poets of the 1960s and 1970s. I value especially his lifelong insistence that certain visions have to be followed to the end, no matter how long and hard the journey.

# Acknowledgements

Every effort has been made to trace copyright holders of material in this book. The publishers apologize if any material has been included without permission and would be glad to be told of anyone who has not been consulted.

Thanks are due to the following for permission to include works or extracts from works in copyright:

**James K. Baxter**: 'Election 1960' from *Collected Poems*; reprinted by permission of Oxford University Press (New Zealand).

**John Berryman**: No. 40, 'I'm Scared and Lonely', and No. 45, 'He Stared at Ruin', from *77 Dream Songs*; reprinted by permission of Farrar, Straus & Giroux, Inc., copyright © 1959, 1962, 1963, 1964; and Faber and Faber Ltd.

**e. e. cummings**: 'in Just –' (*Chansons Innocentes*) from the *Complete Poems 1913–1962*; reprinted by permission of Collins Publishing Group. Reprinted from *Tulips and Chimneys* by e. e. cummings by permission of Liveright Publishing Corporation. Copyright 1923, 1925 and renewed 1951, 1953 by e.e. cummings. Copyright © 1973, 1976 by the Trustees for the e. e. cummings Trust. Copyright © 1973, 1976 by George James Firmage.

**T. S. Eliot**: 'The Love Song of J. Alfred Prufrock' from *Collected Poems 1909–1962*; reprinted by permission of Faber and Faber Ltd.

**Robert Frost**: 'After Apple-Picking' from *The Poetry of Robert Frost* edited by Edward Connery Lathem. Copyright 1930, 1939, © 1969 by Holt, Rinehart and Winston. Copyright © 1958 by Robert Frost. Copyright © 1967 by Lesley Frost Ballantine. Reprinted by permission of Holt, Rinehart and Winston, Publishers. Reprinted by permission of the Estate of Robert Frost, the editor Edward Connery Lathem, and Jonathan Cape Ltd.

**Robert Graves**: 'Warning to Children' from *Collected Poems 1975*; A. P. Watt Ltd and Robert Graves.

**A. D. Hope**: 'The Death of the Bird' from A. D. Hope, *Collected Poems*; Angus & Robertson (U.K.) Ltd.

**A. E. Housman**: 'Loveliest of Trees' reprinted by permission of The Society of Authors as the literary representative of the Estate of A. E. Housman, and Jonathan Cape Ltd., publishers of A. E. Housman's *Collected Poems*. 'Loveliest of Trees, the cherry now', from *A Shropshire Lad* – authorized edition – from *The Collected Poems of A. E. Housman*. Copyright 1939, 1940, © 1965 by Holt, Rinehart and Winston. Copyright © 1967, 1968 by Robert E. Symons. Reprinted by permission of Holt, Rinehart and Winston, Publishers.

**Langston Hughes**: 'Daybreak in Alabama'. Copyright 1948 by Alfred A. Knopf, Inc., and renewed 1976 by the Executor of The Estate of Langston Hughes. Reprinted from *Selected Poems of Langston Hughes* by permission of Alfred A. Knopf, Inc.

# How Poetry Works

# 1 Beginnings

*Every man will be a poet if he can.*
                                    – H. D. Thoreau

Poetry is with us from our earliest days. A baby's first attempts to make speech sounds are a kind of word-play: sounds like 'ma-ma' and 'da-da' are among the first of these. In the beginning they have no 'meaning' as such, they are just noises the baby likes to make. Soon, however, the child links them with real people or objects, conferring on them what we call 'meaning'.

In this early word-play, the main features of poetry are already present: the use of speech rhythms (as in the way the baby will give the first of the two syllables more prominence: **da**-da), and the use of phonic, or sound, patterns (in this case, just the simple repetition of a single syllable). Soon this play becomes more sophisticated. The one-year-old develops a rudimentary sense of phonic patterns with constructions like '**da**-ba' and '**ba**-ma'. A two- or three-year-old can string more complex patterns together in a way ('ma-ba–**da**-ba–**na**-ba') that shows a grasp of the main principles of English speech rhythms and sound patterns.

Our earliest word-games are based on two-syllable rhythms – a stressed syllable followed by an unstressed one, as in 'monkey' or 'hit it'. These two-syllable units, or *duplets*, are the norm in English poetry. However, other units may also be used: one-syllable *singlets* ('John'), three-syllable *triplets* ('government', 'call for it'), even four-syllable *quadruplets* ('elevator', 'Michael did it'). The child also observes that at any time, one of these units may take the place of another, as in

| Higgledy | piggledy, | my black | hen, |
|----------|-----------|----------|------|
| (triplet) | (triplet) | (duplet) | (singlet) |
| She lays | eggs for | gentle | men |
| (duplet) | (duplet) | (duplet) | (singlet) |

13

and

| **Where** is the | **boy** who looks | **after** the | **sheep?** |
|------------------|-------------------|---------------|------------|
| (triplet)        | (triplet)         | (triplet)     | (singlet)  |
| **Under** the    | **hay**stack,     | **fast** a-   | **sleep**  |
| (triplet)        | (duplet)          | (duplet)      | (singlet)  |

This whole phenomenon, central to the effect of English poetry, is examined more fully in the next chapter.

Until only a few centuries ago, writing and printing were universally regarded as a mere notation for the spoken word. Early in the history of English literature, when each handwritten copy of a manuscript was worth as much as a word processor is nowadays, one book had to be shared among many. So reading was most commonly done as a public or private performance: to a gathering of nobles at the royal court, to a group of monks at their evening meal, to a friend or lover – always aloud.

This approach pervaded even to solitary readers, who would inevitably first pronounce the words in order to comprehend them. In time, experienced readers were able to develop the ability to read and comprehend silently – though at first others looked on this as nothing short of a miraculous gift. Even in our own time, we may still see older people moving their lips as they read.

The accepted notion of writing and print as a transcription of sound worked extremely well for our early poets, of course, all of whom lived and died secure in the belief that if their poems were to be read at all, they would be read out loud. Shakespeare survives his death perhaps not so much because his plays make such marvellous spectacles or because their plots are so fascinating as because his lines *sound* so good – and because, until recently, every reader of Shakespeare would above all *listen* to him. The main magic of Milton's *Paradise Lost* is its majestic sound, something which until recent times would have seemed too obvious to mention. Poets even later than Milton committed their artful sounds to the medium of print secure in the belief that every reader would first of all hear those sounds, if only in the ear of the imagination.

Since the advent of movable type, books have become more

generally available, and we now live in a society which is close to perfectly literate. Our culture now places considerably less importance on the notion of meaning as conveyed by sound, and considerably more on meaning as conveyed by the printed word. In fact, one of the hallmarks of being 'well educated' nowadays is being able to 'speed-read' – to run the eye rapidly over the page of print and perfectly absorb its message without having to hear any of it. But the speed-reader is at a dead loss when it comes to poetry, which cannot be either speeded up or slowed down, and which must be *heard* at its own pace in order to work. It is too bad that those who profess to be most expert on the subject of poetry are, ironically, the most proficient speed-readers of all: the university and secondary-school teachers whose treatment of the subject often turns the young student away from poetry for ever. My main reason for writing this book has been to try to counteract this inappropriate approach.

Spoken English is a stress-based language; and English poetry is a stress-based product of speech and sound, not of the printed word. Indeed, the prominent regularity of speech rhythms is usually the first clue that we may be listening to poetry. Our ears are culturally conditioned in this way. The single most important key to understanding the magic of English poetry is to be found in the rhythms and phonic patterns of our language. Yet the approach of a majority of teachers of English poetry is to concentrate on the more evident aspects of literary study – semantic content (the supposed 'meaning' of the poem), historical background, biographical material, artistic philosophy, or bibliographical data. The result is that most 'educated' readers today approach a poem in the same way as they do a piece of prose: alert to the print, to nuances of characterization, vividness of imagery, aptness of expression, use of striking metaphor and memorable word-combinations – in short, reacting to everything that is evident to the eye. They remain all but oblivious to the sound of the poem's rhythms, to the regular procession of its metre, and to its other patterns of sound. This is indeed a sad irony, considering that for most poets, rhythm and sound are the heart of the poem.

It is natural in any kind of sport that a beginner will seek to improve, to reach ever-higher levels of skills. This is just as true in the play of words as anywhere else. The three-year-old, already a poet of sorts, views the word-games of the two-year-old as *passé*, and is busily working to improve on them in ways which will bring new delight and pleasure. A five- or six-year-old will recite vast quantities of rhymes and jingles: the pleasure these bring is one which demands frequent repetition until the day when the magic is exhausted and the child moves on to something still more novel. Later, she or he is able to create real poems, and may be encouraged to do so by parents and teachers.

At some point, though, for most of us, this creative joy fades. The intensity of our perception of the sounds of language begins to grow dim. Sixteen- and seventeen-year-old students learn how to react to a poem as a piece of print, not as a game of sounds. Most English speakers end up feeling at least indifferent to, and sometimes even alienated by, the sight of a poem on a page. The perennial question, 'What is the poet really saying?' – with its underlying implication that poetry is fully paraphrasable – finally deafens the ear and deadens the heart of the common reader. Long forgotten is the fact that all true poetry is based on the delight of using speech sounds creatively, and that this delight was once common to us all, as children.

As we near the end of the twentieth century, the printed book also appears to be drawing near the end of its five-century career. Soon, verbal and other information, including poems, will be available to us locked into microchips, which will generate printed text, spoken word, or both. Paradoxically, this change may result in a period of resurgence for poetry, particularly if it develops more of an ability in the general public to give the sound of a poem at least as much attention as the printed text receives.

Now, a few words of explanation. We often use the word 'English' somewhat vaguely, so I should make clear that in this book it refers only to the language in which the poems I discuss are written. In speaking of nationalities, I shall use the term 'British' generally to refer to Old World English-speakers (British-English, Irish, Scots, and Welsh) collectively, in order to distinguish them from the residents of New World English-speaking countries such as Australia, Canada, New Zealand, and the USA. When I speak of 'English poetry', then, I mean *all* poetry written in the English language, regardless of country of origin.

For many readers, particularly those with a university education in English poetry, I expect the most difficult chapter in this book will be the next, which deals with the rhythms and metres of English poetry. It is most important that you grasp the material presented in this chapter before venturing further – and, especially, that you can aurally perceive the effects which my examples illustrate. They *must* be read aloud and listened to carefully, as must all poetry.

Don't agonize over poems that don't appeal to you no matter how much you try. Contrary to popular belief, there is no law that you have to appreciate a particular poem because it is by a 'great poet', or is generally acknowledged to be a 'masterpiece', or a 'cornerstone' of English literature. You do need to be patient, however; prepared to wait and listen. Your ears must be able to hear before the poem can speak. Sooner or later, you will find at least one poem, perhaps many, which will ring true for you.

# 2 Stress, Rhythm, and Metre

*They were out of the snow now, but it was very cold, and to keep themselves warm they sang Pooh's song right through six times, Piglet doing the tiddely-poms and Pooh doing the rest of it, and both of them thumping on the top of the gate with pieces of stick at the proper places.*

– *A. A. Milne*, The House at Pooh Corner

The heart of English rhythms and the basis of its metres is *stress*, the emphasis given to certain syllables in spoken English. In the phrase 'Two and two are four', we say that the first, third, and fifth syllables are stressed. Stress is an oral matter, one which is not conveyed by the medium of print. This is why one has to go far beyond the page when considering the effect of a printed poem.

In speech, stressed syllables are differentiated from all others. We shall call these others *weak syllables*, just as stresses may also be called *strong syllables*. How do we show, in speaking, which are the strong, or stressed, syllables? Chiefly, by raising the pitch (that is, the musical 'note') of the vowel part of the syllable. We may also, incidentally, pronounce the stressed syllable more loudly, or prolong it, but neither of these on its own is enough to indicate stress. In fact, in some words ('moment' is an example) the stressed syllable may actually take less time to pronounce than the weak one.

Stress in language is like *accent* in music, and it may be that people with a well-developed sense of musical rhythm will have less difficulty with this aspect of English poetry than those without. However, in the performance of music, accent is conveyed principally by an increase in loudness and, to a lesser degree, duration. Any changes of pitch which may take place at the same time are entirely up to the discretion of the composer, and are not, of themselves, an aspect of musical accent.

In spoken English, a stressed syllable is usually followed by one or two (occasionally three) weak syllables. For example, the phrase 'Wouldn't it?' begins with a strong syllable, and is followed by two weak ones. The whole pattern may be repeated: 'Wouldn't it? Couldn't it?' This repetition of the pattern gives rise to what we call *rhythm*. Note that a single occurrence of the pattern is not enough: for rhythm to exist it must be repeated.

In a poem, a given rhythmic pattern will usually occur a fixed number of times in each line. For example, in the line

**Polly, put** the **kettle on**
●○    ●○      ●○     ●

there are four rhythmic groups, each beginning with a stress. The first three are strong–weak patterns, the last a single stressed syllable. Each occurrence (except the last, which may be taken as a variant) contains two syllables. We'll call this two-syllable rhythm a *duplet*. The duplet is the most basic rhythm in English poetry; most creative rhythmic effects in English poetry involve little more than a substitution of other rhythms, usually triplets or singlets, where duplets are expected.

Now let me explain the dots under the example above. The first dot in each group (printed solid) indicates a stressed syllable. So the first dot in the line shows that the syllable 'Pol-' is stressed. The number of white dots which immediately follow this first dot shows the number of weak syllables in the group. So the total number of dots in a group indicates what kind of rhythm this is: singlet, duplet, triplet, or, occasionally, quadruplet.

The number of times a dominating rhythm occurs in a typical line of a poem is also significant. This is what we mean by *metre*. 'Polly put the kettle on' has four measures of mainly duplet rhythm, so we may describe the metre of its lines as four-duplet. In doing so, we overlook all departures from the dominating rhythm – which means, in this case, that we ignore the fact that the line actually ends with a singlet. This is because metre is an abstraction, a statement of the most common pattern set up by the rhythms of the poem taken as a whole.

The substitution of one rhythmic group for another (a singlet for a duplet in the last measure of this example) is a possibility always open to the poet, who generally tries to keep some balance between regularity and variety of rhythm. Rarely will two lines contain exactly the same rhythmic patterns, even though their metre may be nominally the same. Let's try a few creative substitutions, to see how this works.

First, take a straightforward four-duplet line:

**Come** and **kiss** me, **then** we'll **break**fast
●○       ●○      ●○      ●○

Let's substitute another rhythm in one of the measures. The line

**Sell** the **fur**niture, **pawn** your **neck**lace
●○     ●○○    ●○     ●○

is based on the same metre as the line which precedes it, but a rhythmic change occurs in the second measure, where a triplet has been substituted for the expected duplet. The line

**Come** and get **all** of it, **take** our **trea**sures
●○○      ●○○    ●○     ●○

carries the process one step further. If we continue, we could end up with a whole line of triplets:

**O**ver and **o**ver he **gazed** at her **long**ingly
●○○      ●○○     ●○○     ●○○

Of course, if triple rhythms predominated in the poem, we would have to describe its metre as four-triplet, not four-duplet. Metre is only a generalization about what is most typical in the whole piece. (Triplets can easily gallop away with a poem: they are used extensively only in poems which seek to convey rapidity and excitement, or for comic effect.)

Studies of the way we perceive sounds reveal a good deal about how we hear the speech rhythms of English. For example, it has often been noted that people tend to hear sounds, such as ticks of a clock, in groups of two, the first tick strong and the second one weak. The effect is commonly referred to as the 'tick tock' or 'highlighting' effect, and it seems to be common to all humans, not just English-speaking ones. It may be that the sound of the mother's heart, itself a duplet rhythm, imprints this pattern in the baby's ear before we are born. Certainly, the earliest word-games of children are duple ('**teen**sie **ween**sie'), and even when they start to enjoy triplets ('**higg**ledy **pigg**ledy'), they continue to group them in pairs. This may also explain why the four-stress line (that is, two pairs of duplets) is the most common line in popular English verse – not just in poetry, but in all types of occasional verse: children's songs, 'in memoriam' announcements, greeting-card messages, graffiti and so forth.

Research psychologists have demonstrated that humans tend to perceive isolated sounds as being equally spaced in time whenever it is at all possible for them to do so. One researcher, J. E. W. Wallin, found that subjects continued to hear rhythmic intervals as stable, even when the actual sounds were irregularly spaced.* It seems that people will perceive chronological regularity whenever it is reasonably possible to do so.

The perception of a chain of events as being equally spaced in time is central to the perception of English metres. A technical term, *isochronism*, has been coined to give it a name (the adjective is *isochronous*, and in both words the stress is on the second syllable). The ticks of a clock are isochronous, as is the regular drip of a leaky pipe, or the fixed repetition of the long and short flashes of a lighthouse.

It has often been noted that, from the beginnings of the language, English metres were undoubtedly perceived by their native audience as being based on isochronous rhythms, with stressed syllables falling at regular intervals, and with as many weak syllables as were needed fitted in between the equal stresses. The Old English poet–minstrels probably recited their great epics to the regular strums of a lyre or harp.

|  |  |  | Beornas ge-<br>●○○○<br>warriors, | arwe<br>●○/○<br>ready, |
|---|---|---|---|---|
| on | stefn<br>●○ | stigon.<br>●○ | Streamas<br>●○○ | wundon<br>●○ |
| on to the | prow | stepped. | Streams | mingled |
|  | sund with<br>●○ | sande.<br>●○ | Secgas<br>●○ | bæron<br>●○/○ |
|  | sea with | sand. | Men | bore |

(The

* The actual figure is a '14·5% displacement of temporal reality. In other words, people perceive as roughly the same, intervals in rhythm which are as different in time as ⅐. There is apparently a process of mental equalization at work.' (Chatman, *Meter*, p. 21.)

|        | bearm      | nacan           |     | beorhte     | frætwe          |
|--------|------------|-----------------|-----|-------------|-----------------|
|        | ●○         | ●○              |     | ●○○         | ●○              |
| on     |            |                 |     |             |                 |
| into the | bosom of the | ship          |     | bright      | armour,         |

|        | guth-searo | geatolic.       |     | Guman ut    | scufon          |
|--------|------------|-----------------|-----|-------------|-----------------|
|        | ●○○○       | ●○○○            |     | ●○○         | ●○              |
|        | war-gear   | splendid.       | The | heroes out  | shoved,         |

|        | weras on   | wil-sith        |     | wudu        | bundenne.       |
|--------|------------|-----------------|-----|-------------|-----------------|
|        | ●○○        | ●○              |     | ●○          | ●○○             |
|        | warriors on | might-siege, the |    | wood        | bound [boat])   |

(*Beowulf*, lines 211–16)

Try reading this aloud. A brief guide to Old English pronunciation is offered in Appendix B – but don't be too concerned about this just yet. The important thing is getting the isochronous delivery of the four stresses in each of the Old English lines.

You'll see that there is a good deal of variation in the number of weak syllables in each of the Old English measures. If the strong syllables are going to be delivered isochronously, then it follows that the more weak syllables there are in a given measure, the faster will be their rate of delivery. If you still feel puzzled by all this, you can hear the same thing in a well-known nursery rhyme. Read this out loud, marking the regular stresses by tapping your fingers on something:

|          | Three        | blind        | mice,         |        |
|----------|--------------|--------------|---------------|--------|
|          | ●            | ●            | ●             | *      |
|          | Three        | blind        | mice,         |        |
|          | ●            | ●            | ●             | *      |
|          | See          | how they     | run,          |        |
|          | ●            | ●○           | ●             | *      |
|          | See          | how they     | run,          |        |
|          | ●            | ●○           | ●             | */○    |
| They     | all ran      | after the    | farmer's      | wife,  |
|          | ●○           | ●○○          | ●○            | ●/○    |
| She      | cut off their | tails with a | carving      | knife, |
|          | ●○○          | ●○○          | ●○            | ●/○○   |
| Did you  | ever         | see such a   | thing in your | life,  |
|          | ●○           | ●○○          | ●○○           | ●/○    |
| As       | three        | blind        | mice.         |        |
|          | ●            | ●            | ●             | *      |

This little rhyme does virtually every conceivable thing rhythm can do in English, while still keeping to a regular metre. Notice the effect of the *silent stress,* indicated by an asterisk. This is like a 'rest' in music: a period of silence of specific duration relative to sounds which precede and follow it. A measure containing a silent stress occupies the same amount of time as any other measure. When you recite 'Three Blind Mice' while tapping out the regular stresses with your fingers, you will hear nothing where the asterisks occur except a tap.

A further complexity arises when weak syllables open a line. We may regard these as being part of the measure which ends the preceding line. (I have used a slash mark (/) to indicate a measure which straddles two lines – so the •/∘∘ notation under 'knife' shows that the two weak syllables 'Did you' are also part of the same rhythmic measure.) What we are trying to do is account for the perception of rhythm as it is heard, serially. Whether the listener actually perceives the opening words of line seven, 'Did you', as belonging to the end of line six is of no account metrically; the perceived rhythmic pattern is the same – in this case a triplet, '**knife** / Did you'.

The 'strong versus weak' rhythmic patterns of a line are set up in two different ways. They may occur within a polysyllabic word – say 'farmer' (a duplet) or 'botany' (a triplet). There is nothing a poet can do to alter the rhythms of most polysyllabic words: they are a culturally determined aspect of our language. But rhythms are set up in a second way, by combining individual words into phrases. The meaningful combinations of words which we use are also culturally determined, though here there is much more room for creative manipulation. A poet may choose, for example, between the combinations 'Gone is our nightingale' and 'Our nightingale is gone', depending on whether triplet or duplet rhythms were required. (Certain syllables in polysyllabic words, such as the '-gale' of 'nightingale', may fill either strong or weak rhythmic positions, depending on what metrical expectations have already been created.)

How can we know which are the stressed syllables in a line we are reading for the first time? Generally this is not too difficult. In a line such as

**Close** the **door**, and **pour** the tea!
●○　　　●○　　　●○　　　●

stresses clearly fall on 'Close', 'door', 'pour' and 'tea'. Words such as these – nouns, adverbs, principal verbs and adjectives – are called *lexical* words. Because they carry the main meaning of the phrase, they tend to be stressed. The remaining words – 'the', 'and', and 'the' – are *grammatical* words. They merely modify or specify the relationship between the lexical words, and are normally unstressed. Included in this class are articles, prepositions, auxiliary verbs, and possessive adjectives. We may rearrange the lexical content of the line so that it is transformed into four-triplet metre:

**Shut** up the **door** now, and **pour** me some **tea**!
●○○　　　●○○　　　●○○　　　●

The fact that isochronism is an underlying principle of English metre does not mean, however, that metrically regular lines should be recited in a rigidly punctual fashion, any more than music must be performed in relentlessly strict time. In both arts, isochronism works mainly through the audience's culturally conditioned perception of the regularity of stresses or accents. Of course, isochronous rhythms are not found only in poetry – sermons, political speeches, plays and children's stories all use the effect, particularly at dramatically charged moments. Only in poetry, however, is the effect considered integral to the whole work, underlying it as a system which parallels the meaningful language content of the poem.

I do not mean to belabour the parallels between poetry and music in this chapter. They are clearly distinctive arts, and the contrasts between them far outweigh any similarities. In music a composer may invent any accentual (strong versus weak) pattern which seems appropriate to the needs of the composition; in poetry, rhythm is a product of the stress patterns of specific words and word combinations which the poet appropriates from everyday usage. In the rhythms of music, the composer may also feature durative patterns of long and short notes; in English poetry, we do not normally find patterns of this nature – or, if we do, the delivery will be characterized as 'chanting' or 'sing-song'. In music, the pitch of each note (such as middle C) is fixed; in poetry and spoken English generally, the pitch of a speaker's voice has little to do with what is being said, beyond conveying information about the speaker's age, sex and (perhaps) state of mind. In music, the composer invents new melodic lines and harmonic progressions for each composition; in English poetry, such contours of pitch, the rises and falls of speech, are culturally determined (for instance, the way we say 'Is John here?' differs from the way we say 'John is here.') Only in the matter of isochronism do the two arts have a common feature.

Although the notion of equal-timed stresses is essential to English metre, the timing of weak syllables within the measure is entirely flexible. It is the reader's prerogative to sound the syllables of any measure in the way which seems to accord best with the particular words themselves. A good reader will invariably inter-pose a wealth of nuance within the measure – pausing, maximizing or minimizing stress, and so on – to make the poetry more satisfying and pleasurable, just as any accomplished performer of music will continually introduce similar subtle departures from strict metro-nomic time. These effects may be called interpretational, and their presence (or absence) in what you are hearing can greatly affect your overall reaction to the piece – particularly if you listen with expectations based on someone else's interpretation.

Although the duplet is the rhythmic norm in English, and the triplet its most common variation, there are two other possibilities not so frequently used. One of these we have seen already: the *singlet*, a measure which contains a single syllable only – the stressed syllable – with no weak syllables following. The second measure of this line is an example:

John heard the cry.    Under and over it echoed
●○○            ●        ●○○        ●○○    ●○

For even stronger effect, two singlets may be juxtaposed, as in this line from Wilfred Owen's poem 'Futility' (no. 60 in the anthology section):

Woke, once, the clay of a    cold    star.
●○○        ●○○        ●        ●

An even more radical departure from the usual succession of duplets, triplets, and occasional singlets is the *quadruplet* – a stress followed by three weak syllables. Owen's poem also contains an example of this:

At **home,**          **whispering of fields** un- ,     **sown**.
   •           •○○○         •○           •

Obviously, when you or I read a line of poetry for the first time, we have no idea how many weak syllables there may be in a particular measure until we are sure that the measure has ended. This cannot be confirmed until we have perceived the first stress of the next measure. This is why it's sometimes difficult to work out the best rhythmic pattern in a first encounter with a new poem – and why a reading of a familiar poem is apt to sound more coherent and satisfying.

As we have already seen, the Old English line commonly had four strong syllables and a variable number of weak ones. This state of affairs began to change after 1066 (1100 is generally taken as the end of the Old English and the start of the Middle English period), when Norman invaders and settlers began to introduce French cultural models to the English. Spoken French lacks anything akin to the concept of stress, the basis of spoken English. In French, all syllables are culturally perceived as receiving an equal stress – if stresses seem audible to an English ear, the French ear does not perceive them. When it comes to poetry, the French ear is more in tune with the sound of a regular number of syllables per line, or a metrical pattern of 'long' and 'short' syllables.

Now, eleventh-century English poets were no more able to jettison the stress patterns of their native speech than are poets (or anyone else) today. What attracted them in the French model was the idea of a regular number of syllables per line. They adopted this, while still keeping stress as the basis of English metre – as it must always be – and evolved what we now call *syllable-stress* metre. Stress is still the main uniting feature of a syllable-stress line. But no longer does the poet disregard the number and placement of weak syllables in the line – these are also more or less fixed. The Middle English master Geoffrey Chaucer leaned towards the regularity of syllable-stress metres, and so did many great English poets who followed him.*

---

* Purely syllabic metres have occasionally been attempted in our language, though they are not native to it: an example in the anthology section is Thomas Nash's song 'Adieu, farewell earths blisse' (no. 17) which has no obvious stress pattern but in which every line has precisely six syllables. To the uninitiated Nash's metre merely seems somewhat irregular.

Actually, the main innovation of syllable-stress metre – that the overall number of syllables, both strong and weak, is fixed – may not be all that easy for an English listener to detect. It might be thought that the sound of syllable-stress lines would be more regular than that of pure stress lines, but this is not always so. Take the following passage:

Next, the Texan, an eager-to-please ex-adventurer,
●○      ●○○      ●○○      ●○○         ●○○

Spoke: 'Call the cops.' No-one looked.
●       ●○     ●      ●○      ●

'Fool!' I thought, 'For God's sake, man! Keep quiet!
●○      ●○         ●○          ●○          ●○

Twenty minutes more, and they'll be done for.'
●○        ●○      ●○         ●○       ●○

Each of these lines has five stresses. The first two lines are in the Old English type of stress metre, so the number of syllables in each line is quite variable. (You will see that the first contains a total of fourteen syllables, the second only seven.) The third and fourth lines are in strict syllable-stress metre, and each has exactly ten syllables. How detectable is the shift? Try it for yourself – is there anything which clearly distinguishes the sound of the first two lines from that of the last two?

As the above example is in five-stress lines, now might be a good time to turn to a notable development: the rise of the five-stress line as the fundamental metre of sophisticated English poetry. This happened in the fourteenth century, during the age of Chaucer. By the time of Chaucer's middle period (near the end of the fourteenth century) the idea of syllable-stress metres was well established. The old four-stress line was still popular, but now it always contained exactly eight syllables. (How closely the syllable-stress 'rules' were followed is debatable: modern editors have been known to 'tidy up' the ancient poets to make them look more regular than they may have been.)

A modern reader finds this regularity soporific and even oppressive after a while. This was particularly a problem in Chaucer's time, as most poets had already started to use rhymed line-endings.

Chaucer wrote much of his early work in four-stress couplets, and though he is an acknowledged master of the art, the combination of rhyme with regular stress patterns and fixed syllable-counts can at times be distracting. All the listener's attention is focused on the end of the line and its inevitable rhyme – with the result that other aspects of the poetry are overlooked.

Chaucer paid close attention to the poetry of his Italian and French contemporaries (he visited both countries, and was fluent in their languages), and this may have been where he first got the idea for an English line which would use five, instead of four, stresses. By the time of his most mature works – *Troilus and Criseyde* and the verse parts of *The Canterbury Tales* – he had made the five-stress line his standard. It later became the basic line of Shakespeare, Donne, Milton, Wordsworth, Keats and a thousand other poets, known and unknown, of the English tongue.

It may seem hard to understand why such an apparently asymmetrical line should have become so popular among English poets and their audiences. It seems to violate our desire to hear some kind of duple organization within the line: we expect two-, four-, or even six-stress lines, not five-stress ones. Chaucer seems to have been turning from a line divisible by two to a line which could not easily be split down the middle at all. Yet it was not long before what had begun as an imported fashion was adopted as the standard English line.

If we look at what was written in the five-stress line in English then and during the centuries which followed, we may come up with several reasons for its popularity – though not all of them will be true for all poetry in which it is used. First, the line may be perceived as two balanced halves, each containing five syllables. This results in a kind of bilateral symmetry:

So it passed them by: the summer left us.
●○    ●○      ●○    ●○     ●○

The colon in the above line indicates a pause which falls in the middle of a rhythmic measure, and actually has nothing to do with the way we perceive the metre of the line. The technical word for this kind of pause is *caesura* it is analogous to the fermata ($\frown$) in music. Its main effect is to interrupt the regular procession of isochronous stresses, to suspend the 'time' of the piece – rather like shutting off a motor for a moment, then starting it up again.

After a while, you may discover that the caesura is used in a number of different ways, some particularly characteristic of certain poets or periods. One of the most common effects is to end a sentence or phrase just before the end of a line, and then start a new sentence in the last measure, running it on to the next line:

> To Rose he left a golden purse. But not
> A sausage did he leave his poor old wife.

The caesura is generally indicated through some punctuation stop or pause – a full stop (period), colon, semicolon, dash, or comma. Its position in the line may be constant or variable within the poem; it may be in the middle of a measure (as in the above example), or between two measures. All these factors may be of some interest to the literary analyst, though they have no bearing on the poem's metre.

We have already seen how a poet might use a caesura to divide a five-stress line into two equal halves of five syllables each. Such an exact division is not necessary to create the illusion of two balanced halves, however: the caesura may be used to lend weight to the shorter section of the line, making it seem to balance the larger part:

> He slowed, he stopped.   =   The lady turned aside,
>      2                        3

> We tried and tried to help.   =   But hope died fast.
>          3                   2

Another, more inventive, possibility is for the poet to arrange the rhythms of five-stress lines so that when they are read, four-stress lines are suggested. A good example of this process, taken from William Wordsworth's poem 'The Ruined Cottage', is given in Paul Fussell's book *Poetic Meter and Poetic Form*. The following passage (starting at line 199) is found in a poem written in a five-stress metre, but could well sound, in performance, much more like four-stress lines:

| He | spake with | somewhat of a | solemn | tone |
|----|------------|---------------|--------|------|
|    | ●○         | ●○○○          | ●○     | ●/○  |
| But | when he   | ended there   | was in his | face |
|    | ●○         | ●○○           | ●○○    | ●/○  |
| Such | easy      | cheerfulness, and a | look so | mild |
|    | ●○         | ●○○○○         | ●○     | ●/○  |
| That | for a little | time it     | stole a- | way |
|    | ●○○○       | ●○            | ●○     | ●    |
|    | All recol-  | lection and that | simple | tale |
|    | ●○○        | ●○○○          | ●○     | ●    |
|    | Passed from my | mind like a for- | gotten | sound |
|    | ●○○        | ●○○○          | ●○     | ●    |

instead of the overall five-stress metre of the whole poem:

He spake with somewhat of a   solemn   tone
●○      ●○       ●○   ●○        ●

and so on. Notice the unnatural emphasis we have to give 'of' in order to convey clearly all five stresses of the poem's nominal metre. This is why it is so easy to perform these lines as four-stress ones. Of course, then we come up against the quintuple monstrosity 'cheerfulness, and a' – not only containing more weaks than we would ever normally accept in a single measure, but also the main caesura of the line. If there is anywhere that the four-stress illusion breaks down, it is at this point. As a rule, the ear accepts no more than three weak syllables between stresses – and even three is relatively uncommon.

At this point, some of you may be wondering whatever happened to the old system of scanning metre, the one which treats the line as being divided up into metrical 'feet' which can begin with *either* a strong *or* a weak. Using the notation of this system, the last example above would be:

| Ĥe spáke | wiŧh sóme- | whăt óf | ă sól- | ĕmn tóne |

and would be called 'iambic pentameter' – meaning it has an iambic (˘ ˊ) rhythmic foot, and that there are five of these feet in the line. Unfortunately the system, borrowed from the ancient Greek and Latin theorists, does not reflect the way in which English speech rhythms and, by extension, English poetry, actually work. Furthermore, it involves the ability to bandy about terms like 'trochaic hexameter' and 'anapaestic dimeter', and to speak knowledgeably about 'rising' and 'falling' feet. For most of us, this works as a barrier more than anything else. The stress/measure system and dot notation used in this book demonstrate more accurately and simply what is actually going on in the rhythms of a line. For readers interested in probing a little further into the technicalities of why this is so, I provide some explanation in Appendix C.

Now let's return to the matter of the pervasiveness of the five-measure line in the most sophisticated English poetry. The thought may already have occurred to you that a five-stress line is *not* metrically satisfying in itself at all, and that its main power lies in this very fact in that it is able to merge its rhythms with those of the lines which precede and follow it, combining or linking with others through stretches as lengthy as a Shakespeare play (see no. 18 in the anthology section for an example of this) or *Paradise Lost* (no. 27). The number of ways in which one five-stress line may link up with another is practically infinite.

It must also be acknowledged by anyone involved in English poetry that appreciation of the five-stress line as a basic unit of poetry is an acquired one, which people have to develop, usually for a period of years. It is by no means one which belongs to the majority of English-speakers, for they have probably been put off by having to learn misleading systems of scansion, and to study poetry that offers no appeal – all part of a sadly misguided system of 'cultural education'. Of course, we can enjoy the sound of five-stress lines in Shakespeare or Donne or Dylan Thomas without having to know what their metre is all about. But in all forms of popular poetry, the inevitable norm is not five-, but four-stress lines which commonly end with a singlet – that is, a measure with only one syllable. A frequently heard example is

| Roses are | red, | violets are | blue, |
|-----------|------|-------------|-------|
| ●○○ | ● | ●○○ | ● |
| Sugar is | sweet, and | so are | you. |
| ●○○ | ●○ | ●○ | ● |

This is the basic metre of popular taste, and has been so in English for at least ten centuries.

So far, we have been speaking of poetry with some fixed pattern of line-lengths, poetry which suggests a regular metre. But there is much poetry with no definite metre. Rhythmic patterns are present, of course, as they are in all spoken English; and they are perceived as isochronous. The main difference is that in this sort of poetry (sometimes called *free verse* or *non-metrical poetry*) the content of each individual line dictates its length, its own number of measures. Among such poetry we may include the 'prophetic' books of William Blake, much of Walt Whitman, and such modern works as Allen Ginsberg's *Howl*, to mention a few examples. This kind of poetry often uses some type of linguistic pattern, such as repetition, to replace the regular metrical pattern we usually expect to find.

> Mayhem in the alleys, mayhem!
> ●ooo            ●o         ●o
> Mayhem in the channels laved with bright blood!
> ●ooo            ●o         ●o         ●         ●
> Mayhem in the deadly edges of new angles!
> ●ooo            ●o         ●oo         ●         ●o

In fact, many supposedly non-metrical poems contain passages (often concluding ones) which are metrically quite regular.

Non-metrical poetry depends for its effect on the audience's familiarity with the sound of regular metre. In other words, non-metrical poetry cannot be perceived as such unless the concept of regular metrical poetry is already well established in the listener's mind. To an ear unfamiliar with the sound of metrical regularity, the whole point of 'free verse' is bound to be lost.

Now, a practical matter. If you are listening to a poem being read, without the printed text before you, how can you be sure where the lines end? Generally, most lines will contain some kind of linguistic or phonemic signal: the concluding measure may contain a rhyme, or some other sort of sound pattern. (The next chapter examines these more fully.) So the break between the following lines would be clear to any English ear:

Without a decent motor car
Wilma couldn't stray too far,

because of the rhymed line-endings. An even stronger sign is the presence of a *silent stress* falling in place of the final measure of a line – a feature we have already seen to be common in children's rhymes:

Ding     dong     bell,
•        •       •     *

Pussy's   in the   well,
•○      •○     •     *

The number of stressed syllables in each of the above lines is three – an odd number, which seems to contradict what we have said about our tendency to hear duple organization whenever possible. But the silent stress bulks the line out to an even four measures – and that is, of course, how every English-speaking girl and boy says the lines.

The final measure of a line may also be signalled by some kind of break in the regular pattern already created in the earlier part of the line:

They  hurried here, they scurried there, they ran all over
     •○○○       •○○○       •○○○

       town:
       •/○

'Twas  said by some, 'twas feared by all she'd stained her bridal
     •○○○       •○○○       •○○○

       gown.
       •

Here, three quadruplets (or six duplets, if you prefer to hear them that way) are followed by a final singlet.

At times, a poet may go to great lengths to disguise the metrical scheme, using caesuras and other extra-metrical effects to do this:

He turned. She was still picking spring
flowers. He looked down. 'The thing
of it is this. . . .' It was hard for him
to speak plainly. She sighed, 'Jim . . .'

In a case like this it may be next to impossible for a listener, particularly at first hearing, to decide what the metre of the poem is. (The fact that the lines rhyme hardly helps: the disruptive syntax minimizes the impact of the rhymes to the point where they may not even be heard.) Only reading the printed text will clarify the metre. Analysts of music may also have to resort to a printed score of the piece they are examining for the same reason. This is a perfectly valid approach. Through print, time may be stopped, so that one may then take a better look at the temporal underpinnings of the composition.

Ezra Pound once said that the rhythm of a poem must have meaning. It might not seem that a pattern of stressed and unstressed sounds, taken in isolation, could convey much information. However, it certainly seems true that for most people it is the perception of a regular metrical pattern that provides the first clue that what is being heard is poetry and not some other type of language. Furthermore, cultural conditioning makes most of us hear duplets as 'steady', triplets as 'fast-moving' or 'light-hearted', rigid adherence to a regular metre as 'monotonous', stretches of lines ending with end-stopped singlets as 'heavy', and so forth. These are all in themselves kinds of meaning. Some theorists have amused themselves by constructing 'metrical dummies' made up of nonsense words which follow the rhythmical patterns of a known poem (I. A. Richards's 'dummy' of a stanza from Milton's 'Ode on the Morning of Christ's Nativity' is probably the best-known of these) in order to prove that none of the qualities one takes as being conveyed by these features of the poem are in fact conveyed by them at all. Of course, this may be looking for rhythmic 'meaning' in too narrow a way.

Probably the most important thing to understand about metre as such is that it is an abstract concept, not something you can hear at any one moment while a poem is read. It may be that not a single line in a particular poem will conform absolutely to the nominal metre of the poem. In any good poem some tension will exist between the specific rhythmic irregularities we hear and the abstract metrical regularity we eventually perceive to be underlying these rhythms. This is where much of the richness associated with the interpretation and performance of poetry is to be found.

What is the relation of metre in a poem to the way in which a specific line may be read? Once again, a musical analogy may help. For practising music, performers often make use of a metronome, a mechanical device which produces a series of regular ticks at any predetermined speed. By going over and over the piece in rigorously strict time, using the metronome, practising performers make themselves fully aware of the changing rhythms of the piece, and how they fit into a regular and isochronous metrical pattern. Once they feel confident enough, however, they will then turn off the metronome, and depart from this strictly isochronous regularity in a thousand different ways which combine to make up their personal performing style.

Among jazz musicians, high praise is being told that one knows how to 'read the line' – how to realize the music, make the magic happen, turn the print of the score into a dynamic experience for the audience. This is akin to what the reader of the poem has to do, and every poem requires the same sort of practice. And, as a listener, just as one may judge that the style of a particular musical performance is not in keeping with the composition itself, one may similarly feel that a particular reader's performance of a poem is at odds with the poem itself.

If you are a newcomer to a poem you may have to listen to it several times before you will begin to perceive any metrical organization at all. Some poems begin, or appear to begin, misleadingly with lines which turn out to be metrically atypical. A casual first encounter with the printed text of Hopkins's 'Spring and Fall' (no. 52) may suggest that the poem is in some kind of two-stress metre:

> Margaret, are you grieving
> ●○○○          ●○/○○
>
> Over  Goldengrove unleaving?
> ●○○○          ●○

But Hopkins takes the unorthodox step of using accent-marks in the first line (and elsewhere in the poem) to show us that what he really wants is

> Márgarét, áre you grieving
> ●○    ●  ●○    ●○

Over Goldengrove unleaving?
●○    ●○    ●○     ●○

that is, a four-stress metre. We cannot always rely on poets to make their intentions this clear, however (and indeed some critics have looked askance on Hopkins's unorthodox use of accent-marks as an admission of failure to communicate metre and rhythm through language alone). The best course is to try to relax and let the pattern come to you, instead of straining to identify it at the earliest possible moment. Don't worry if your first guesses turn out to be wrong.

You may be wondering why I should be giving so much attention, in this book, to an aspect of poetry which has little to do with the look of the poem, or its content. The reason is that, for the past two hundred years and more, matters of rhythm and metre have generally either been ignored, or else explained in terms of a system alien to our own language. (For more on this, see Appendix C.) The result has been that this most important aspect of the art of English poetry has been the least understood. This is quite ironic, when we consider that many poems take their first shape in the mind of the poet as isochronous patterns of rhythm, with grammatical coherence and meanings following only later. Poets today can no longer assume that any of the rhythmic effects which are at the heart of a particular poem will be taken in by the average reader.

It's clear that a silent scanning of the text of a poem will reveal nothing of its rhythmic patterns. That is why it is so important that the poem be experienced as sound, not as print. This is the approach I urge throughout this book, and this is why I ask you to become familiar with the material in this chapter before moving on to other matters.

One final point: you may find it helpful to mark your own copy of a poem, with dots or in any other way you like, so as to make its rhythmic patterns clearer. I find that the beginning of the line is where a reader is most likely to go wrong, and so in the anthology I have arranged the lines so that the first stress of each is lined up in a vertical column, on the left side of the page. If you get the first stress right, the rhythms of the rest of the line should follow without too much difficulty.

Nearly all the anthology selections are based on some kind of regular metre. The Old English selection (1) is, of course, in pure stress-based metre. From Chaucer (7, 8) onwards the effect of syllable-stress conventions may be noted. One of the most interesting English poets from a metrical point of view is Gerard Manley Hopkins (51, 52), who was also an accomplished amateur musician. The accent marks which occasionally appear are Hopkins's own, and seem to demonstrate doubts that the reader would otherwise hear the rhythmic patterns he wished to convey. Many of Hopkins's most daring metrical effects descend directly from the conventions of Old English poetry.

# 3 Phonemic Patterns

*The first poems I knew were nursery rhymes, and before I could read them for myself I had come to love just the words of them, the words alone. What the words stood for, symbolised, or meant, was of very secondary importance; what mattered was the sound of them as I heard them for the first time on the lips of the remote and incomprehensible grown-ups who seemed, for some reason, to be living in my world. And these words were, to me, as the notes of bells, the sounds of musical instruments, the noises of wind, sea, and rain, the rattle of milkcarts, the clopping of hooves on cobbles, the fingering of branches on a window pane, might be to someone, deaf from birth, who has miraculously found his hearing. I did not care what the words said, overmuch, nor what happened to Jack and Jill and the Mother Goose rest of them; I cared for the shapes of sound that their names, and the words describing their actions, made in my ears.*

*— Dylan Thomas\**

If we conceive of metre as a separate system which parallels the actual language of a poem, we now must consider an aspect of poetry which is partly a matter of metre, partly a matter of language itself. These are the *phonemic patterns*, the use of different speech-sounds in patterns of repetition and contrast to link together certain of the stressed syllables of a poem's lines. (The term *phoneme*, from which the adjective 'phonemic' is derived, refers to the smallest meaningful units of sound in a language. It is more fully explained in the Glossary in Appendix D.) The best-known phonemic pattern in English is rhyme, which conventionally occurs at line-endings. But there are in all eight different phonemic patterns possible in English, as we shall see.

Rhythm is basically a product of muscle and air pressure, no more. It's clear that the underlying rhythm of the line

**Talk**ing of Mich**ae**langelo

* Quoted in Constantine Fitzgibbon, *The Life of Dylan Thomas* (Boston, 1965) pp. 323–4.

could be as well conveyed by a series of grunts:

UH UH UH **UH** UH **UH** UH **UH**

or even by a binary series of digits:

10010101.

Now let's think about what happens to rhythmic noises such as these after they have passed the vibrating vocal cords. With a little experimenting, you will discover that there are two general ways in which we may particularize these grunts so that they become linguistically meaningful to others who hear them.

First, we may alter the shape of the resonating chamber of the mouth – by opening or closing the jaw, or by holding the tongue in different positions. These vocalic sounds may be produced for as long as the vocal cords continue to vibrate, and one may glide smoothly into another without a break, the shape of the mouth or the position of the tongue being gradually altered from one position to another. We call the single sounds *vowels*, while glides between two vowels are called *diphthongs*. In terms of spelling in the letters of our traditional alphabet, we are taught that the vowels in English are a, e, i, o, u, and, in certain positions, y – though this does not acknowledge the fact that every one of these conventional letters is used for a number of different sounds. (In fact, our conventional alphabet is of limited use in discussing the sounds of English speech.)

The second way in which we may affect our basic vocalic sounds is by altering or interrupting the vowel sounds with other sounds, which we call *consonants*. The tongue, already busy shaping the resonating chamber so that the desired vowels will be produced, does much of the work in producing consonants too, though lips and teeth are also involved.

But before I say any more about vowels and consonants, we need some way for me to communicate the sounds I have in mind. Fortunately, a standard alphabet has been developed for this purpose, using the International Phonetic Alphabet (IPA). For general purposes in English, thirty-four characters are sufficient – twelve vowel and twenty-two consonant sounds. Many of these phonemic symbols are identical to the letters of printed English: /b/ for the sound at the beginning of 'boat', and /t/ for the sound at the end of 'it', for example. (The / / marks indicate that the characters enclosed are intended as phonemic symbols, not conventional letters.) But other of our phonemes have no single character in written English – the consonant sounds at the beginning of 'should' or 'think', for example. For these we need some new characters – such as /ʃ/ for the beginning of 'should' (pronounced /ʃʊd/), and /θ/ for the beginning of 'think' (pronounced /θɪŋk/). The whole of the phonemic alphabet we need is given in Appendix A.

Vowels pose the greatest problem in any discussion of English speech sounds, particularly as there is a great deal of variation in the way they are pronounced in different parts of the English-speaking world. For example, an Australian might pronounce the word 'I' as /ɒɪ/, a Canadian as /ai/, a southern US speaker as /ɒ/, and an upper-class Briton as /ɛi/. Nevertheless, whatever the conventions of our part of the world, none of us needs more than a dozen different vowel sounds in order to differentiate satisfactorily between the different sounds of literary English. Furthermore, rhyme and the other phonemic patterns we'll be looking at are usually (though not always) transferable from one English-speaking culture to another. 'Say' and 'pay' rhyme just as well in Australia, where they may be pronounced /sʌɪ/ and /pʌɪ/, as in Canada, where they will probably sound more like /sɛi/ and /pɛi/.

Now let's return to the consonants for a moment. One feature of English phonemes is that we make a distinction between *unvoiced* and *voiced* consonants. For example, when we produce the sound /p/ at the beginning of 'pin', our vocal cords are still: the sound of /p/ is no more than the sound of air being released from the mouth as the lips are parted. But we can change /p/ to /b/, as in 'bin', by allowing the vocal cords to vibrate at the same time as the mouth is opened. Try it and see. In the same way, the addition of vocalic sound is all which distinguishes /d/ from /t/, /v/ from /f/, /z/ from /s/, /ʃ/ from /ʒ/, and /ð/ from /θ/.

You can test for yourself whether a sound you make is voiced or unvoiced: lay your fingers lightly on your throat so you can feel the cords vibrating when you say 'ahhh'. Then pronounce the consonant loudly – if your fingertips feel a tickle, then the sound you are making is the voiced variety. Try this while pronouncing the following words loudly and clearly: bough, play; thin, then; is, hiss; half, have; pressure, measure; and church, judge. Which of the consonant sounds are voiced, and which unvoiced?

The distinction between voiced and unvoiced consonants is important to the effect of phonemic patterns in poetry. For one thing, it is more difficult in speaking to change from a voiced to an unvoiced consonant and back again quickly than it is to continue using the same sort. Voiced consonants are also easier to pronounce, because the vocal cords are already vibrating for the vowel sound of the syllable. That is why in common speech we often change our /t/s to /d/s, and so forth – we avoid the extra effort.

Most people feel that unvoiced consonants tend to be 'clipped', voiced ones 'relaxed'. This is probably because in syllables which begin or end with unvoiced consonants, the vocal cords have to start and stop more abruptly. They cannot begin to vibrate until after the opening consonant sounds have been heard, and they must be cut short before the closing ones. By contrast, voiced consonants allow the vocal vibration itself to begin and end more gradually. Compare the two unvoiced consonants of 'thought' (/θɒt/) with their voiced equivalents in 'they'd' (/ðɛid/), or those of 'face' (/fɛis/) and 'vase' (/vɛiz/ or /vɒz/). It takes more effort to pronounce the unvoiced consonants clearly – this is why people who habitually voice conventionally unvoiced consonants are termed 'lazy' speakers.

Now, let's go back to our primal grunt to see the kind of thing that may happen to it as it passes through the mouth. Let's take a duplet rhythm as an example:

UH UH

– upon this we may impose a vocalic sound, perhaps the vowels /æ. oʊ/. In itself, this is clearly a cry of pain: 'Ow!' Already we have endowed our vocalic rhythm with meaning. But this becomes raw material for many more words once the tongue, lips and teeth are brought into play. We may perhaps precede it with a /b/ and make it /bæ.oʊ/ ('bough'). Or we may insert another consonant between the vowels – adding an /r/ there would give us /bæ.roʊ/ ('barrow'). We may tack another consonant on to the end – /z/ would give us

/bæ. rovz/ (barrows). Our primal rhythm has taken on very specific meaning indeed! Even a single vowel such as /æ/ may be particularized, with the addition of consonants, into one-syllable words as precisely meaningful as /læθ/ ('lath', a thin strip of wood), /hæsp/ ('hasp', a hinged metal fastening), or even /snæθ/ ('snath', a scythe handle).

A baby's first noises are no more than vocalic sounds. Before the child is a year old, however, distinct vowel sounds are heard – usually /æ/ is the first, and it serves as the basis for later utterances such as 'da', 'ba', and 'ma'. This seems to be the vocalic sound which comes easiest to every baby's mouth; the earliest consonantal additions are usually made by the baby's first birthday.

We saw in the last chapter that one of the main pleasures offered by the phenomenon of rhythm is found in repetition, usually with a certain amount of creative variation to relieve monotony. A baby's first words repeat the entire syllable – 'da-da', 'ba-ba', 'ma-ma'. But the young child soon discovers that it's more interesting to make some change so that the second syllable parallels the first and is not a mere repetition. So such creations as 'da-ba' and 'a-ma' are born. (Notice that nowhere is the essential rhythm altered – phonemic patterns are entirely a product of the mouth.) Or the consonant may remain the same, and the vowel change, as in 'Fee Fie Foe Fum' (/fi fɒi fov fʌm/). The technical words for these two word-sound games are 'rhyme' and 'alliteration', and they are the main phonemic patterns found in English poetry of past ages.

In talking about spoken English, it is common practice to use the term *syllable* to indicate the most basic component of speech. Most people have an understanding of what this word means, and could gladly tell you, if asked, that the word 'dark' contains one syllable and 'obscure' two. Going into more detail, we could say that an English syllable has between one and three constituent parts. There must be a central vowel (or diphthong) – which is the heart of the syllable, and which reveals, in the way it is sounded, whether the syllable is stressed or unstressed. A vowel has to be present: without it there is no vocal sound, and no syllable at all.

The syllable will also contain between none at all (that is, a null) and three distinct consonant sounds before the vowel, and between none and four after it. In other words, there may be no opening consonant sound at all, as in /oʊk/ ('oak') or there may be as many as three, as in /stroʊk/ ('stroke'). Similarly, there may be no closing consonant sound at all, as in /soʊ/ ('so', 'sew') or as many as four, in a word like /sɪksθs/ ('sixths').

*Rhyme** is the best-known of the phonemic patterns that have been used in English poetry. Even a three-year-old child can appreciate the effect of rhyme, as all English nursery songs and chants use it at the end of rhythmically balanced lines. Rhyme has been popular for much more than half the known history of English poetry. All of us can identify the sound of a rhyme, though we may not have a full understanding of how it works.

Phonemic patterns, like rhythmic ones, depend on some kind of parallelism – and parallelism means difference as well as similarity. In the case of rhyme, the difference is one which affects only the opening consonant of the last stressed syllable of the line. The vowel and any following consonants stay the same. So we say that

> /bal/ ('ball') rhymes with
> /kal/ ('call'),
>
> /ai/ ('eye') rhymes with
> /trai/ ('try'),
>
> /**ai**.bol/ ('eyeball') rhymes with
> /**hai**.bol/ ('highball'), and
>
> /**bai**.si.k l/ ('bicycle') rhymes with
> /**ai**.si.k l/ ('icicle').

Furthermore, there must be no change whatever in any weak syllables which may follow the stressed one. It would not do, for example, to rhyme 'eyeball' with 'my fault'.

It seems, then, that complete repetition of all the elements of a stressed syllable is not acceptable as rhyme. Actually, this has not always been the case, which demonstrates that a good deal of cultural conditioning is involved in these matters. Chaucer made

---

* The spelling 'rime', occasionally encountered, particularly among older writers, is etymologically sounder (the word comes from French *rime* and Latin *rima*); moreover, the conventional English spelling 'rhyme' suggests an etymological link with 'rhythm' which in fact does not exist.

frequent use of a convention which went by its French name, *rime riche* ('rich rhyme'). Under this convention, a poet was permitted to write lines such as:

The sun was up, so up I rose
To pluck the lily and the rose,

as long as the repeated word had a different meaning. In this case, /roʊz/ in its first appearance means 'got up' (the past tense of the infinitive 'to rise'), which is a verb; whereas the second /roʊz/ means 'a kind of flower, member of the Rosaceae family' and is a noun. In the Middle Ages *rime riche* was highly regarded, but its use today would probably be perceived as clumsy or inept, especially by readers unaware of the historical convention.

Another odd type of rhyme might best be mentioned here – though in the present sense of the word it is not really rhyme at all. It is called *eye-rhyme* – because to the eye the printed word looks as though it *should* rhyme. The eye-rhyme 'roving/loving' (no. 37) is a good example. It's clear that this is a type of rhyme which can be appreciated mainly in print – by a reader rather than a listener.

Let's leave rhyme and look at some of the other varieties of phonemic patterning possible in English. One which was extremely popular in our earliest poetry works in just the opposite way to rhyme: this is *alliteration*. In rhyme, as we have seen, the opening consonant of the stressed syllable changes, while the rest of the syllable stays the same. In simple alliteration, the opening consonant of the stressed syllable stays the same, and the rest of it changes. Examples of alliteratively linked pairs of words are

/bʊk/ ('book') and
/bait/ ('bite'), or

/brɛd/ ('bread') and
/broʊ.kən/ ('broken').

Furthermore, convention allowed the alliterative poet to write a line of nulls – that is, stressed syllables which open with no consonant at all. For example,

Eager and anxious he eyed the air,

contains four stresses, each opening with a null – in other words, no consonants at all precede the stressed vowels.

Alliteration is the dominant phonemic pattern in our oldest surviving major poem, *Beowulf*. See how it is used in these lines (no. 1: a translation is given in the anthology):

> . . . **mund**gripe **mar**an, he on **mo**de **wea**rth
> **forht** on **fer**the, no thy ær **fram me**ahte
> **Hyge** wæs him **hin**fus, wolde on **heol**ster **fle**on,
> secan **deo**fla ge**dræg**; ne wæs his **droh**toth **thær** . . .

There are four metrical stresses in the typical Old English line, but only the first three alliterate.

Alliteration, then, refers to a repetition of the stressed syllable's opening consonant sound or sounds. This repetition need not be complete: we may also find *partial alliteration* where not all the initial consonants are repeated. An example of partial alliteration is /brʌɪt bidz/ ('bright beads'), where the /b/ of the first syllable is repeated in the second, but the /r/ is not.

The popularity of alliteration as a principle of metrical organization began to wane after the arrival of rhyming poetry from France around the time of the Norman Conquest of 1066. It flowered again in the so-called 'alliterative revival' of the fourteenth century, when *Piers Plowman* and the great *Sir Gawain and the Green Knight* (nos. 5 and 6) were composed. Nowadays, we tend to think of it as too 'easy' to be impressive in extended use; perhaps we feel its sound is somewhat unsophisticated compared with that of rhyme – though this is a culturally conditioned judgement, of course. Nevertheless, the use of alliteration continues, both in poetry and in other forms of spoken English, as a means of artistic emphasis. For example, a recent newspaper interview quotes a musician: 'You're a jazz singer when you can compete with the children of Charlie Parker and the descendants of Dizzy Gillespie.' Clearly, the speaker is using alliteration to give his statement extra weight and memorability.

In order to see more clearly how these phonemic patterns work in English poetry, let's look more at each of the component parts of the stressed syllable. We may symbolize the whole syllable as [C V C], with [C standing for opening consonant, V for vowel, and C] for closing consonant. Bold type indicates those elements of the syllable which do not change.

In the different phonemic patterns of English poetry, some of these elements change, while others do not. For example, in *rhyme*, [C changes, but V and C] do not:

| [C V C] | [C V C] | |
|---|---|---|
| /kl ɒ k/ | /ʃ ɒ k/ | ('clock/shock') |
| /pr ɪ .ti/ | /s ɪ .ti/ | ('pretty/city') |

In *alliteration*, just the opposite happens: [C remains the same, but V and C] change:

| [**C** V C] | [**C** V C] | |
|---|---|---|
| /b ɪ g/ | /b æ d/ | ('big/bad') |
| /**fr**oʊ.zən/ | /**f**aʊn.tən/ | ('frozen/fountain') |

The second example is also a reminder that alliteration may only be partial – not all the members of a group of consonant sounds have to be repeated.

Rhyme and alliteration are the oldest phonemic patterns used in English poetry. But there are other ways in which patterns may be created. In *consonance*, the closing consonant sound (C]) is repeated, while all else in the syllable changes:

| [C V **C**] | [C V **C**] | |
|---|---|---|
| /h ɒ t/ | /s æ t/ | ('hot/sat') |
| /w ɪ n.doʊ/ | /f æ n.tə.zi/ | ('window/fantasy') |

And in *assonance* the central vowel remains the same while the opening and closing consonants change:

| [C **V** C] | [C **V** C] | |
|---|---|---|
| /g ɪ v/ | /h ɪ t/ | ('give/hit') |
| /**h æ** n.dəl/ | /b æ .ləns/ | ('handle/balance') |

The other phonemic patterns in English are all combinations of *alliteration, consonance* and *assonance*. Although in the list below I have given technical names, these three terms, together with *rhyme*, are the most important.

## Alliteration

a. [C V C] (simple): /bʌt//bɛnd/ ('butt, bend')
b. [C V C] (alliteration with assonance): /bʌt//bʌnk/ ('butt, bunk')
c. [C V C] (alliteration with consonance): /bʌt//baʊt/ ('butt, bout')

## Assonance

[C V C]: /bʌt//hʌl/ ('butt, hull')

## Consonance

a. [C V C] (simple): /bʌt//heɪt/ ('butt, hate')
b. C] V [C (reversed): /bʌt//tæb/ ('butt, tab')
c. C] V [C (reversed with assonance): /bʌt//tʌb/ ('butt, tub')

## Rhyme

[C V C]: /bʌt//ʃʌt/ ('butt, shut')

You don't usually need to distinguish between the different types of alliteration or consonance. In general, as with the technical terms of rhythm and metre, it is not so important to use them as it is to realize that English poetry offers great scope for phonemic creativity, and to keep your ears open for this when it happens.

Some of the first rhymed poems in English combined rhyme with the old alliterative patterns. Here are a few lines from the tenth-century piece known today as 'The Rhyming Poem':

> Me lifes onlah   se this leoht onwrah
> ond thaet   torhte geteoh   tillice onwrah
>          glaed waes ic gliwum   glenged hiwum
>          blissa bleoum   blostma hiwum . . .

(I was granted life by [him] who revealed this light and that brightness displayed, graciously revealed. Glad was I joyfully, adorned with the hues, bliss-colours, blossoms' hues . . .)

Notice how, in these lines, the only stressed syllables which are not part of some alliterative pattern are the final ones – those where a rhyme occurs. This is in keeping with the usual alliterative pattern of the stresses in the Old English line:

A    A    A    X

where the As show alliterative stressed syllables, and the X marks a final stressed syllable which does not alliterate.

All the phonemic patterns we have discussed have one thing in common: they affect only stressed syllables. To put it another way, significant phonemic patterning occurs only at the start of a rhythmic measure. The system of phonemic patterns independently parallels the system of rhythm. As in the case of rhythm, it doesn't matter whether the phonemically patterned syllables stand alone as separate words or are part of larger words. The only thing that matters is that they must be stressed. Bearing this in mind, which of the following pairs rhyme?

> inspiration/perspiration
> minute/in it
> treat me/beat me
> I get/forget

And which pairs alliterate?

> rich/respected
> long/unlikely
> sour/insensitive
> superior/singer

In fact, the first and last examples of each group are not valid – can you see why?

One may speculate as to why certain phonemic patterns were so much in vogue in one period, then later faded in popularity. Perhaps, soon after Chaucer, simple alliteration was felt to be too easy – our burgeoning vocabulary at the time meant anyone could string together a lineful of alliteratives. In our own time, rhyme also seems to have fallen out of favour – perhaps for the same sort of reason. It's as though everything that could possibly be done with rhyme has already been done, and done as well as it ever could be. Actually, rhyme, in English, is an extremely demanding pattern. For some sounds the number of possible rhymes is extremely low: one word, /ɒ.rəndʒ/ ('orange') has no rhyming counterpart in English. (Interestingly, in languages where rhyming is easy, such as Italian, in which many words share a few similar endings, rhyme is not much used in artistically ambitious poetry.)

Rhyme held sway from Chaucer's time until our own century, but, except in light and popular verse, seems out of favour now. The old rhymes still charm us, of course, but the sound of rhyming has become a thing we associate with the poetry of bygone days. Since the early years of this century, poets have been experimenting more with other phonemic patterns. Chief among them is the British poet Wilfred Owen; in his poem 'Futility' (no. 60) we find as line-endings in the first stanza the following phonemic patterns:

/sʌn/ ('sun'),
/wʌnts/ ('once'),
/soʊn/ ('-sown'),
/frants/ ('France'),
/snoʊ/ ('snow'),
/naʊ/ ('now'), and
/noʊ/ ('know').

The link between /sʌn/ and /wʌnts/ is one of assonance and partial consonance: the two vowels are the same. Full consonance links the consonants of /sʌn/ to those of /soʊn/ in the third line; and both of these consonants open the fifth word, /snoʊ/, which also is linked by assonance to /soʊn/. The second and fourth sounds, /wʌnts/ and

/frants/, are linked by simple consonance. The last two, /nav/ and /nov/, alliterate, while the latter one, /nov/, rhymes with the fourth, /snov/. A common factor is the consonant sound /n/, which occurs in every one of these syllables. In one short stanza Owen has used five of our eight possible phonemic patterns. The effect is far more complex than the sound of rhyme used throughout would have been.

Before we leave rhyme, we need to touch on one or two other points. We've already seen that the most common rhymes in English involve only one syllable: the line ends on a stressed syllable, which rhymes with the final stressed syllable of a preceding line:

> Know then thy-self, presume not God to scan;
> The proper study of mankind is Man.

(no. 30)

In past centuries, this sort of rhyme was commonly known as 'masculine rhyme', but today *one-syllable rhyme* seems preferable. Similarly, *two-syllable rhyme* is a better term than the old 'feminine rime'. Two-syllable rhyme may be heard in:

> And from this chasm, with ceaseless turmoil seething,
> As if this earth in fast thick pants were breathing,

(no. 33)

*Three-syllable rhyme*, is usually encountered only in verse of a light or humorous nature:

> But this you can't stand, so you throw up your hand,
> and you find you're as cold as an icicle,
> In your shirt and your socks (the black silk with gold
> clocks), crossing Salisbury Plain on a bicycle.

(no. 50)

Phonemic patterning is what transforms the game of poetry from one of purely rhythmic interest into one based on a primary human skill: the act of speech. Modern tastes dictate that a poet's use of such patterning must never be obtrusive; above all, that the reader must never be left with the impression that its demands have forced the poem into becoming something it did not really want to be. Nothing is quite so stultifying as a rhyming poem where the reader can easily guess every rhyme in advance. Pope complained about this nearly three centuries ago:

> Wher·e'er you find 'the cooling western breeze,'
> In the next line, it 'whispers through the trees';
> If crystal streams 'with pleasing murmurs creep,'
> The reader's threatened (not in vain) with 'sleep' . . .
> True ease in writing comes from art, not chance,
> As those move easiest who have learned to dance.
>
> (from *An Essay on Criticism*, ll. 350 ff.)

From a practical point of view, it might be better, given that a poet wishes to use a particular rhyme in a poem, to use the more commonplace word in the second line, taking the greatest possible care that its use sounds natural and unforced. Then if any forcing is required it may be done in the first line before any expectations of rhyme have been raised. If the poet wants a word to rhyme with 'love', for example, there is little choice in English except 'glove', 'shove', 'dove' and 'above' – none of them very close to the sense of 'love'. (You can see why lines such as 'as sure as the stars up above' have been done to death in a hundred commercial English love-songs.) If the poet's choice is 'glove', it would probably be a mistake to use it in the second position:

> How can such tawdry symbols still call up the one I love? –
> A book, a scarf, a comb, and a worn-out glove.

Here, the exigencies of rhyme give the impression of having painted the poet into a corner. Better to use the riskier word first:

> A book, a scarf, a comb, and a worn-out glove –
> How can such tawdry symbols still call up the one I love?

Even though rhyme is no longer much in vogue, anyone who is interested in poetry will benefit from practising its use. Rhyming 'dictionaries', in which lists of words are arranged alphabetically in groups with a common rhyme, are useful for such exercise. Nineteenth-century British literati were particularly fond of a game called *bouts rimés* ('rhymed ends'), in which a series of rhymes was chosen at random to begin with, then the poem created around them. This still makes an entertaining pastime, particularly as a group activity, when quite dissimilar pieces will spring from the same given rhymes. One tip: be sure that the words you choose are not too narrow in meaning (as for example 'transistor' and 'blister' probably would be) and keep mainly to one-syllable rhymes. Before you get too involved in *bouts rimés*, however, you may want to read Chapter 5 to see how rhyme and other phonemic patterns may be used to build up stanzas and conventionally fixed forms, such as the sonnet.

This may be the best time to raise another matter – that of *onomatopoeia* (pronounced /ɒ.nə.mæ.tə.**pi**.yə/). This word comes from the Greek words *onomatos* ('belonging to a name') and *poiein* ('to make'). (*Poiein* is also the origin of our word 'poet' – literally, 'one who makes'.) We use the term onomatopoeia to mean that the sound of a particular word imitates its own meaning, or, in the words of one critic, 'the sound enacts the sense'.

Generally speaking, however, critics and literary commentators have used the term somewhat loosely. Two hundred and fifty years ago Samuel Johnson chided his contemporaries for imagining they heard it when in fact none was present. Johnson allows that there are a few genuinely onomatopoeic words ('thump', 'growl', 'rattle' and 'hiss' are his examples), but points out that other examples frequently used by writers were simply mistaken: 'The fancied resemblances, I fear, arise sometimes merely from the ambiguity of words', he wrote. 'There is supposed to be some relation between a soft line [of poetry] and a soft speech, or between hard syllables and hard fortune.'

In fact, true onomatopoeia would have to convey its meaning to speakers of every language on earth, and very few words do this. Even our words for animal sounds are not the same as those in other languages – Dutch roosters go 'kukeleku', while Spanish ones go 'quiquiriquí', and so forth. Native speakers of other languages find it hard to believe that, in our culture, the selfsame birds go 'cockadoodledo'. So even these words are not truly onomatopoeic.

Some words may be one stage removed from true onomatopoeia: 'whisper', for example, may have been coined because of its use of the unvoiced consonants /s/ and /p/, which sound exaggerated in whispered speech. (In fact, being voiceless, they do not change much in loudness – it's the whispered vowels and voiced consonants which sound *softer* by comparison.) In that way, the spoken word may be said to symbolize its meaning at least partially. This kind of word could be termed 'onomatopoeically derived'.

A much more common effect in any language, however, occurs when the sound of a particular word has certain connotations – not because it imitates the sound of a particular 'meaning' (as in onomatopoeia) but because its sound recalls the sounds and connotations of other words. These then amalgamate and become associated with the meaning of the new word. For example, the words 'nick', 'flick', 'click', 'snick' share certain connotations – sharpness and rapidity. Similarly, words such as 'lump', 'bump', 'clump', 'plump', 'stump', carry connotations of roundness, squatness and mass.

The British linguist J. R. Firth once gave a group of students a simple test to demonstrate this effect. First he showed them two drawings. One was a billowing, clumpy outline, like a plump cumulus cloud. The other looked like a cross between a porcupine and a pincushion. Then he gave them the words 'kikiriki' and 'oombaloo' and asked them to write down which word would be more suitable for each drawing. Firth tells us that only one student matched 'oombaloo' with the spiky drawing and 'kikiriki' with the clumpy one; and that he, when asked why, said he had done it only to enliven what would otherwise have been a boringly predictable response.

The fact is that every person in that room instantly knew which word went with which picture. How? To some degree it may have been visual. The letters of 'oombaloo' itself are full of circles and curves, just like the clumpy drawing. 'Kikiriki' is full of straight lines and sharp angles, like the spiky drawing. But the main reaction in the room would undoubtedly have been to the words as sounds: 'oombaloo' recalls 'billow', 'balloon' and 'ball'; even the lip-rounding associated with pronouncing its 'oos' would reinforce the feeling that this word would naturally be associated with the clumpy figure. Furthermore, 'kikiriki' clearly would *not*: its sound recalls 'spiky', 'prickly' and 'keen'. It's hard to imagine that any native English-speaker could feel otherwise. (On the other hand, it is entirely possible that in other languages the sound of 'kikiriki' could be more associated with clumpy shapes.)

There is no generally agreed name for this effect – meaning conveyed through phonemic connotation limited to the speakers of a particular language. So I shall call it *phonolexis* (from the Greek words for 'sound' and 'vocabulary'). We'll be looking at it again in Chapter 4, which deals more generally with the conventional uses of language in poetry.

Finally, a poet may rely on the sound of one word to recall the associations of an unconnected but similar-sounding word. In T. S. Eliot's line 'The eyes that fix you in a formulated phrase' (no. 56) the world 'formulated' recalls the sound of 'formalin' and 'formaldehyde', and the associations of these words are clearly reinforced by the lines which follow: 'And when I am formulated, sprawling on a pin,|When I am pinned and wriggling on the wall', and by the poet's idiosyncratic treatment of human physicality as detached anatomical specimens: 'Arms that lie along a table, or wrap about a shawl'.

Many people have noted that certain consonant sounds tend to have a predictable effect on readers, an effect which is closely associated with that of phonolexis. For example, the consonant /w/ is often felt to be 'soft' and the consonant /k/ 'hard'. Similarly, as we've already seen, voiced consonants like /m/ and /l/ convey a feeling of relaxation, while unvoiced consonants such as /s/ and /p/ are associated with discipline and fastidiousness (perhaps because of the precision of speech required to pronounce them distinctly). We could locate them on two intersecting 'psychological' axes to show how the soft/hard and relaxed/clipped gamuts interact, as in the diagram opposite.

Of course, this effect is quite subjective and largely a matter of personal interpretation. Generally speaking, it is more helpful to note a poem's frequent use of unvoiced consonants (or of some other discernible effect) than to try to characterize its effect subjectively – your reaction to unvoiced consonants may be quite different from

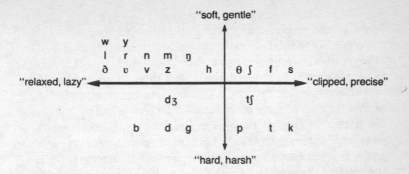

someone else's. Above all, avoid descriptive adjectives such as 'soft', 'flowing', 'harsh' or 'musical' when you try to convey the effect of the sound of a poem.

Phonemic patterns, like rhythmic patterns, are a form of parallelism – and this involves both similarity and difference. We must realize that much parallelism in a poem may not be immediately perceptible to the casual viewer or listener. It all depends on how prominent the parallelism is. We should not expect someone to appreciate the bilateral symmetry of a garden where a rose bush here counterbalanced a similar bush five miles away. Similarly, there must be a relatively short temporal space between parallel occurrences in a poem if they are to be apprehended as such by even the most attentive listener. Two alliterating syllables separated by more than a line of a poetry are apt to go unnoticed. The same is true of rhymes which occur more than five or six lines apart. The greater the gap, the weaker will be the effect of the pattern.

The sound of the poem has always been its primary magic. During the earlier centuries of English, the written or printed page was altogether beyond the reach of the average person, and to most people poetry was sound and sound alone. The Old English bard declaimed his ringing alliterations to the rhythmic sweep of the harp. Chaucer and other medieval poets read their work aloud, often to a courtly audience. The habit of reading poetry silently to oneself developed relatively recently (though poetry readings continue to attract devotees even in our own day). The rise of literacy, so admirable a development in every other way, has led to a common misunderstanding about the nature of poetry, one which has resulted in the alienation of most general, 'non-specialist' readers. Most of the responsibility for this rests with our schools and universities and their patently unsuitable approach to poetry.

More than once, on occasions when I have read some of my poems to people who had previously only seen them in print, I have been told afterwards that my reading made them easier to 'understand', or that they now 'made more sense'. The people had probably read the poems as though they were simply printed messages to be decoded. But poems *have* to be heard to be appreciated. Let me say it again: it is not enough to eye-read a poem. You must at least 'hear' the voice of the poem when you read it. If you have trouble doing this, then read it out loud. If you think this will take too much time, then put the book away and do something else. It is quite impossible to read a poem silently any more quickly than one would recite it, and still do it justice.

You might logically wonder why, if the effect of poetry is so much linked with sound, poets don't write their poems in the phonemic alphabet in the first place and have done with it. That way readers would be continually reminded that this was not to be taken as mere printed language, and also – perhaps even more useful – they would not be tempted into agonizing about the 'meaning' of a poem before at least hearing its sound first. Actually, the 'Dadaists' of the early years of this century did write poems which were purely phonemic constructions. Here's a 'Dadaist' effort of my own:

MEGAN'S LUNCH

/ dæ

  dæ dæ dæ

ə·dæ

ə·dæ

  bʌ bʌ bʌ bʌ bæ

ə·dæ

ə·dæ

ə·dæ

  dæ!/

In the last chapter I pointed out that non-metric poetry could never have existed if metric poetry had not existed first, simply because the concept 'non-metric' would have no meaning unless people had some idea of what 'metric' meant. In just the same way, an avoidance of the most obvious phonemic patterns, alliteration and rhyme, only makes sense if people have an understanding of just *what* is being avoided. Awareness of alliteration and rhyme is so strong among all speakers of our language, whether they have any particular interest in it or not, that poetry which does not use them (especially rhyme, still very much a part of our popular oral tradition today) stands out as 'different'. The other six patterns enable poets to break away from tradition while still not forsaking some kind of audible organization in their work. It is rare to find an accomplished poem in English of any age which does not contain some type of phonemic patterning.

All poets are aware of sound, but some stand out as being particularly innovative in their use of phonemic patterning. Among these are the anonymous author of *Sir Gawain and the Green Knight* (no. 6), who blended alliteration and rhyme in the same poem, and Chaucer (nos. 7, 8), who first showed us the full potential of rhyme. Dryden (no. 29) and Pope (no. 30) are reckoned to be masters of the end-stopped rhyming couplet; after them poets increasingly de-emphasized rhyme. In more modern times, W. S. Gilbert (no. 50), among many humorous versifiers of the Victorian era, milked the laughter inherent in two-, three-, and even four-syllable rhymes; later, Ogden Nash (no. 65) did the same, using non-metrical couplets.

Poets of Celtic extraction have often demonstrated a keen and innovative ear for using phonemic patterning. Ones who come to mind are G. M. Hopkins (nos. 51–2), W. B. Yeats (no. 54), Wilfred Owen (no. 60), Louis MacNeice (no. 67), Robert Graves (no. 68) and Dylan Thomas (no. 71). Hopkins's imitation of a Welsh phonemic pattern, *cynghanedd sain*, which makes the second stressed syllable of a line rhyme with the first and alliterate with the third (as in 'fall/gall/gash', in the last line of no. 51), is especially striking.

# 4 Choosing and Using Words

*Hwat is word bute winde?*
  — Ancrene Riwle

  *One century has words, another century chooses words, another century uses words and then another century using the words no longer has them.*

  — *Gertrude Stein*

Up to now we have mainly been concerned with sounds. Now we turn to the raw material from which the poem is constructed: the vocabulary of our native speech. I want to begin with a brief survey of what authorities on the language of poetry have had to say about the poet's use of words. Throughout, you will see that certain ideas continue to arise: the importance of figures of speech, the overlay of rhythmical patterning, emphasis on economy, directness and vividness of description, and, above all, the concept of the language of a poem as memorable and inviolable. But let the experts speak for themselves.

### Aristotle

Where the historian really differs from the poet is in his describing what has happened, while the other [i.e., the poet] describes the kind of thing that might happen. Poetry therefore is more philosophic and of greater significance than history, for its statements are of the nature of universals, whereas those of history are particulars . . .

For the purposes of poetry, a convincing impossibility is preferable to an unconvincing possibility . . .

In any mode of poetic diction there must be moderation . . . but the greatest thing by far is to have a command of metaphor. This alone cannot be imparted by another; it is the mark of genius – for to make good metaphors implies an eye for resemblances.

Many are the lies of the poets.

*(Poetics*, 335–322 BC)

## Horace

Be brief in what you say, in order that your readers may grasp it quickly and retain it faithfully. Superfluous words simply spill out when the mind is already full . . .

It has always been and always will be allowed to issue words bearing the stamp of the present day. As the forest changes its leaves at the decline of the year, so, among words, the oldest die; and, like all things young, the new ones grow and flourish.

*(The Art of Poetry*, first century BC)

## Longinus

All words united together [in the poem] make a full and perfect organism.

*(On the Sublime*, first century)

## Sir Philip Sidney

One word cannot be lost [from a poem] but the whole work fails . . . every word having his natural seat, which seat must needs make the words remembered.

*(Apology for Poetry*, 1580)

## Samuel Daniel

All verse is but a frame of words confined within certain measure, differing from the ordinary speech, and introduced the better to express man's conceits [i.e. concepts or ideas], both for delight and memory.

*(Defence of Rhyme*, 1602–7)

## Ben Jonson

A poet is that which the Greeks called a *maker*: his Art an art of imitation, of faining: expressing the life of man in fit measure, numbers, and harmony, according to Aristotle . . . A poet . . . writes things like the Truth.

*(Timber or Discoveries, 1641)*

## John Dryden

Wit is best conveyed to us in the most easy language; and is most to be admired when a great thought comes dressed in words so commonly received, that it is understood by the meanest apprehensions, as the best meat is the most easily digested.

*(Essay of Dramatic Poesy, 1668)*

## William Wordsworth

A large portion of the language of every good poem can in no respect differ from that of good prose . . . There neither is, nor can be, any *essential* difference between the language of prose and metrical composition.

(Preface to *Lyrical Ballads*, 2nd edn, 1798)

## S. T. Coleridge

[The poem is marked by its] untranslatableness in words of the same language without injury to the meaning. Be it observed that I include in the *meaning* of a word not only its correspondent object but likewise all the associations which it recalls.

*(Biographia Literaria, 1814)*

## William Cullen Bryant

[Language is] limited, and imperfect, and, in point of comprehensiveness, distinctness, and variety, falls infinitely short of the mighty and diversified world of matter and mind of which it professes to be the representative. It is however to the very limitation of this power of language . . . that Poetry owes her magic.

*(Lectures on Poetry, 1825–6)*

## Ralph Waldo Emerson

The poet is the Namer, or Language-maker, naming things sometimes after their appearances, sometimes after their essence, and
giving to every one its own name and not another's . . . The poet
made all the words . . . For though the origin of most of our words is
forgotten, each word was at first a stroke of genius, and obtained
currency because for the moment it symbolised the world to the first
speaker and to the hearer. The etymologist finds the deadest word to
have once been a brilliant picture.

('The Poet', 1844)

## T. E. Hulme

The great aim is accurate, precise, and definite description. The first
thing is to recognise how extraordinarily difficult this is. It is no mere
matter of carefulness; you have to use language, and language is, by
its very nature, a communal thing; that is, it expresses never the
exact thing but a compromise – that which is common to you, me,
and everybody. But each man sees a little differently, and to get out
clearly and exactly what he does see, he must have a terrific struggle
with language, whether it be with words or the techniques of other
arts. Language has its own special nature, its own conventions and
communal ideas. It is only by a concentrated effort of the mind that
you can hold it fixed to your own purpose.

(*Romanticism and Classicism*, 1913–14)

## T. S. Eliot

Poetry must not stray too far from the ordinary everyday language
which we use and hear . . . While poetry attempts to convey
something beyond what can be conveyed in prose rhythms, it
remains, all the same, one person talking to another.

(*The Music of Poetry*, 1942)

Is there any way in which we may accurately sum up such a
diversity of views on one subject? Is there really a special 'language
of poetry', as some of these writers seem to be claiming, or is there
not? We know already that part of the answer lies in matters of
rhythm and metre, and phonemic patterning. Of course, we are also

conditioned by our cultural background to expect the vocabulary of a poem to be striking, well chosen, both graceful and powerful, and above all memorable, making us apprehend some aspect of our existence in a new and pleasurable way. But are there certain words, certain phrases, which are *in themselves* 'poetic', or which give us the feeling that what we are hearing is poetry and not some other form of language?

Let's return to the oft-expressed view of the pundits already quoted that the language of a poem should be 'memorable'; that is, that it should beg to be re-created again and again, without change. Already we know that part of this memorability is the result of rhythm, metre, and phonemic patterning. We certainly cannot change any of the words of a poem without destroying some of these sound effects.

But there is more. Unlike other language, the language of poetry is not simply and solely a vehicle for meaning. Ordinary language may always be paraphrased – that is, its meaning may be expressed in different words without anything essential being lost – but the language of a poem may not. A poem is exactly what it sounds like and says. It has no larger paraphrasable 'meaning' than this. Archibald MacLeish puts this truth memorably in the last lines of his 'Ars Poetica' (no. 62): 'A poem should not mean | But be.'

How is this done? Leaving aside matters of rhythm, metre, rhyme and other phonemic patterns, what makes the vocabulary of a poem *seem* poetic? One interesting answer to the question has been suggested in Suzanne Langer's fascinating book, *Philosophy in a New Key*. In this work, Langer compares the effect of music to that of poetry. '*What music can actually reflect is only the morphology of feeling*', she writes. By 'morphology', or the shape of feeling, we mean not this or that particular feeling, but feeling in itself, the essence or structure of feeling. In the same way, 'though the *material* of poetry is verbal, its import is not the literal assertion made in the words, but *the way the assertion is made*.' What the poem articulates is, in the end, itself.

Linguists sometimes use the term *referential* to describe the most basic quality of everyday language. What this means is that our speech-sounds usually refer to, or symbolize, something else. For example, the sound /meɪ.pəl tri/ refers to a large plant (a tree), one whose springtime sap may be boiled down into syrup and whose leaves turn red or yellow before falling every autumn.

In contrast to referential language is a more specialized variety, *performative* language. In performative, or ritualistic, language, the mere act of speaking certain words is generally perceived as causing some sort of change to occur. For example, the spoken words, 'I now pronounce you man and wife', coming from a minister, justice of the peace, or other legally empowered person, is generally perceived by English-speakers to cause a change in the marital status of two people. The spoken words cause no physical change, but a change in public attitude. It's as though the pronouncement had put into effect one of those 'search and replace' operations which word processors do so nicely – everyone concerned merely replaces 'George is a bachelor' and 'Mary is a spinster' with 'George and Mary are married'.

Obviously, then, any use of performative language demands unanimous social acceptance if it is to work. We may think of it as a kind of agreement that what has been said to have happened will now be perceived by all as in fact having happened. Performative language, for this reason, cannot be treated referentially, in the way we treat ordinary language. The referential observation 'John is happy' may ordinarily be countered with 'Is he?', or 'No he isn't, really.' But what sort of conversational response can 'I now pronounce you man and wife' elicit? 'You do?' 'No you don't, really!' – the thought of such rejoinders to a performative pronouncement is laughable. In fact, even the response 'I don't understand', spoken at such a time, would sound ridiculous to the ears of the community.

As poetry is spoken performance, its language too is performative. Ignorance of this may be the main source of confusion over the elusive 'meaning' of poetry. Because performative language has a great deal in common with referential language (access to the entire English lexicon, for one thing), it is often assumed that it may be treated as referential. Nothing is further from the truth. Rejecting a poem because it's not the way you speak is no more valid than rejecting an artist's painting because it's not the way you would paint a wall. (On the other hand, it *is* quite acceptable for you to reject a poem or a painting simply because you don't like it.)

In all ages, one of the poet's main efforts has been to use language in a performance which will make people listen, not simply because of what the poem says, but because of *how* this is said. In other words, the language must strike the listener as different from everyday language – if it does not, then it is of little lasting interest. The poem has to be more than a straightforward and neutral bearer of meaning.

It follows then that the language of poetry must have an extremely high information content. In ordinary conversation, many of our words, even whole phrases and sentences, carry little real information. This is especially true of such openers as 'How are you?', and 'Fine, thanks, and you?', and closers like 'Have a good day', and 'See you later'. They are simply ways in which we mark the beginning and end of friendly conversation. In a poem, on the other hand, all words, even phrases as semantically empty as these, are information bearers. Even if a particular word in a poem does not carry a great deal of semantic weight, it is as important to the performance of the poem as any other word is.

As a matter of fact, a poet may well choose to use 'empty' conversational phrases in a poem, in order to contrast them with its more weighty passages. T. S. Eliot does this in *The Waste Land*, when he includes, in the context of a serious poem, a garrulous conversation among the *habitués* of a London pub. Their final inebriated 'Goonight. Goonight.' merges to chilling effect with an echo of the mad Ophelia's wail: 'Good night, ladies, good night, sweet ladies, good night, good night.' (*Hamlet*, IV.v.69–70) Another example is this line from Robert Lowell's 'Grandparents' (no. 74):

They're all gone into a world of light; the farm's my own.

which incorporates a quotation from the seventeenth-century poet Henry Vaughan. This kind of verbal collage is an extremely effective poetic technique, and well demonstrates how, in all ages, poets have been able to draw on all preceding eras and types of English for the language of a single poem.

In a poem all words may carry lexical information. In prose and other written forms of language, a pronoun such as 'I' has no independent meaning – it depends on the reader's knowing to whom it refers. But in a poem even a word like 'I' may be made to take on its own independent meaning. The French poet Rimbaud exploited this fact in his famous line 'Je est un autre' ('I is another'). A poet knows that a statement like this will be taken to carry meaning, if for no other reason than that it occurs in a poem and not in some purely referential piece of language. Another good example of this effect is Matthew Arnold's 'Dover Beach' (no. 43), where we encounter unexplained yet still meaningful references to 'I', 'you', 'us' and 'we'.

One problem you may encounter in the poetry of earlier times is that the meanings of certain words and phrases have changed since the poetry was written. It is inevitable that this will happen in any language; the more distant the origins of the poem, the greater the potential for misunderstanding. In order fully to understand even the shortest Old English poem, a reader may have to spend weeks or months studying not only the language, but also the social institutions of the time, the relationship of the poem to others of the same period, and so forth.

With a fourteenth-century poet, such as Chaucer, the difficulties may not seem as formidable, but many traps still lie in wait. Chief among these is assuming that such familiar-looking Middle English words as 'inspired' (breathed) or 'fowl' (bird of any kind) or 'summer' (spring) had the same meaning for Chaucer as they have for us today. Even with Shakespeare and his contemporaries, the problem is still a major one. The best we can do is to make ourselves as familiar as possible with poetry of all periods, to try to become aware of changes of meaning that have occurred in particular words, and to learn as much as we can about the literary and social background. All this takes time. Fortunately, some helpful books are available: I have listed a few in the reading list at the end of the book.

Most contemporary English poets show a good working knowledge of the history and present range of meanings of their vocabulary. The majority of English words come from one of three general classes: Germanic (words derived from Old English via the old Germanic and Scandinavian tongues of Europe); Latinate (words adapted from Latin, French, and other Southern European languages); and newly formed (words created from elements already in the language). For example, the word 'book' is Germanic (German *buch*), 'volume' is Latinate (French, from Latin *volumen*, 'roll of sheets'), and 'paperback' was newly coined (following the advent of the first such books) from 'paper' (French *papier*) and 'back' (Old Scandinavian *bak*).

Of the one thousand most commonly used words in Modern English, 62 per cent come from Germanic sources, and 38 per cent from Latinate ones. The proportion changes in favour of the Latinate ones as our vocabulary expands, however. Moreover, the distinctive styles of many poets and writers depend on their use of markedly atypical proportions. In particular, the use of words taken directly from Latin (as opposed to Latinate words borrowed from French) can give a writer's language a markedly bookish flavour. In Shakespeare, only one word out of ten is a direct Latin borrowing, while Samuel Johnson typically uses three times this number. The work of most writers falls somewhere between these two stylistic extremes.

New-coined words have not made up a particularly large proportion of our poets' vocabulary at any one time – possibly because of the danger of their being misunderstood, or because poets prefer to use words which have stood the test of time and which are not going to disappear in a year or two, as so many once-lively slang words have done. Coining their own words has appealed greatly to certain poets, however. A good example is Lewis Carroll, whose delightful 'Jabberwocky' (no. 46) makes extensive use of such purely non-sensical inventions as 'burbled', now a part of standard English. Other coinages can be the result of sound repetition ('walkie-talkie'), compounding ('dugout'), derivation ('laundromat' from 'laundry' and 'automatic'), or back-formation 'enthuse' (from 'enthusiasm').

It is important, then, that poet and reader share some understanding of the *etymology* (origins and history) of the words in a poem if they are to work with full effect. Both should also have some understanding of the various *connotative* overtones which particular words may have in addition to their *denotative* function. 'Empty', 'blank' and 'vacuous' all denote approximately the same idea – 'lacking contents'. However, 'blank' also suggests 'vacancy, monotony, lack of interest', and 'vacuous' has further connotations of 'stupidity' and 'inanity'. The poet must be alert to these over-tones to be able to make the 'right' choice. To make things even more difficult, some words or phrases may have varying meanings or connotations in different English-speaking countries. Possibly this is one of the reasons that most modern English poets are not read much beyond their own dialectal regions.

Of course, these are matters common to all language, not just poetry. But let's now take a look at some particular uses of language which we associate mainly with poetry. Foremost among these is *metaphor*, first quantified by Aristotle (see his remarks at the beginning of the chapter). 'Metaphor' comes from the Greek, meaning 'to carry over'; Aristotle describes it as 'the application of an alien name by transference'. A poet who writes 'the lake was a quicksilver mirror' or 'the hostess wafted into the room' is using metaphor, describing one thing (the lake, the way the hostess moves) in terms of another (a mirror, a gentle breeze). An example of metaphor cited by Aristotle from the poetry of his times is one in which old age is called 'the evening of life', and evening 'the old age of day'. 'Good metaphor implies an eye for resemblances', Aristotle observes.

In ordinary metaphor, the resemblance is stated directly, without any explanation. A variation of metaphor, *simile*, makes the comparison more explicit, however, by using the words 'like' or 'as' in stating the resemblance: 'the lake was like a quicksilver mirror' or 'the hostess moved as gently as a breeze'. Simile leaves rather less to the imagination of the reader. Other types of metaphor include *synecdoche* (from the Greek 'a receiving together'), in which a part of something stands for the whole thing. 'She was a lass of twenty summers' uses synecdoche to say that the person in question was twenty years old. *Metonymy* (Greek for 'other name') transfers the name of something to take the place of something else with which it is associated. 'A White House spokesman' really means 'a spokesman for the executive branch of the government of the United States of America'. The Old English poets used a kind of metonymy known as *kenning*: 'bound wood' (meaning 'ship') and 'whale's way' (meaning 'sea') are examples.

Metaphor has been the basis of a great deal of figurative language in English poetry from the fifteenth century onwards. It's not hard to find examples in the anthology section. The whole first stanza of 'They Fle from Me' (no. 15) is an extended metaphor, comparing the poet's past lovers to deer who once 'put theimself in daunger | To take bred at my hand'. Other extended metaphors occur in 'Crossing the Bar' (no. 53), 'Because I Could Not Stop for Death' (no. 49) and 'Uphill' (no. 47). Here are some other shorter examples:

> Beauty is but a flowre
> Which wrinckles will devoure
>
> (no. 17)

> Like as the waves make towards the pibled shore,
> So do our minuites hasten to their end
>
> (no. 20)

> O My Luve's like a red, red rose,
> That's newly sprung in June
>
> (no. 32)

> . . . I wheel'd about
> Proud and exulting, like an untired horse
> That cares not for its home.
>
> (no. 34)

> Turn the key deftly in the oilëd wards,
> And seal the hushëd Casket of my Soul,
>
> (no. 39)

> . . . then off, off forth on swing,
> As a skate's heel sweeps smooth on a bow-bend
>
> (no. 51)

> . . . my skin
> Bright as a Nazi lampshade
>
> (no. 76)

Many poets and philosophers have argued that a metaphorical response to the world is a very primitive one: it shows a desire to explain new things in terms of things already understood, or to bestow new ways of looking upon old things. The eighteenth-century Italian philosopher Giambattista Vico argued that in the beginning *all* language is metaphor. The modern linguist M. A. K.

Halliday similarly conceives of grammar (the rules of combination which govern language) as metaphor. Underlying both views is the idea that metaphor serves as a means of experiencing and understanding the facts of the world about us.

Metaphor is a form of parallelism; it deals with resemblances, not replications. The poet must be sensitive as to how far the reader or listener will be prepared to go to grasp the declared resemblance. When A. E. Housman linked cherry-tree blossoms to snow via their whiteness (no. 55), he used a metaphor which was not difficult for his readers to understand. But when, a scant fifteen years later, T. S. Eliot compared 'evening' to 'a patient etherised upon a table' (no. 56), he was asking a good deal more of his contemporaries' imaginative abilities. (Further, Eliot's simile additionally develops the persona of the poem's speaker, whereas Housman's depends wholly on a conventional social response from the reader.)

In considering metaphor and its variants, we may ask the question: 'How unlikely is this comparison?' On a rough scale from 1 to 10, with 10 standing for the most unlikely comparison, we might give Housman's metaphor a 1 or 2, and Eliot's an 8 or 9. Geoffrey Leech shows how Dylan Thomas's metaphor 'a grief ago' (from his poem 'This Bread I Break') may be placed on a scale running from 'many moons ago', (which Leech places at 1 on the scale) through more unusual but still comprehensible parallel constructions such as 'three overcoats ago' and 'two wives ago', and ending with 'a humanity ago' (he gives this a 10, adjudging it even more deviant than Thomas's metaphor).

It's evident that there must be some kind of background or norm against which we may compare the terms of the poet's new metaphor. The more unusual or unexpected these are, the more attention the metaphor will receive from the reader – up to a point. When we first encounter Housman's snow/cherry blossom metaphor we may feel it to be a suitably 'artistic' close to a well-wrought lyric. But how are we to react to a line which compares the evening to an etherised patient, when we have no precedent for such a comparison? Remember, though, that the language of a poem is not being used primarily to communicate a message, but to draw attention to the act of expression itself – and this Eliot's etherised patient clearly does.

Metaphor and its variants are commonly known as 'figures of speech'. Let's look at some other varieties, beginning with two which are often confused: *personification* and *anthropomorphism*. Their effects are actually quite different. *Personification* occurs when the poem addresses an inanimate or abstract object (love, the west wind, the Brooklyn Bridge) as if it were a person:

A · dieu, farewell earths blisse

(no. 17)

Earth, let not thy envious shade
Dare it selfe to interpose

(no. 21)

Goe lovely Rose,
Tell her that wastes her time and me,
That now she knowes,
When I resemble her to thee
How sweet and fair she seems to be.

(no. 25)

*Anthropomorphism*, on the other hand, endows non-human objects with human physical and emotional qualities:

. . . But Patience, to prevent
That murmur, soon replies

(no. 26)

Be · cause I could not stop for Death,
He kindly stopped for me

(no. 49)

Next your pillow resigns and politely declines to remain at
its usual angle!

(no. 50)

The kind old sun will know

(no. 60)

He stared at ruin. Ruin stared straight back.

(no. 72)

the  Pierce Arrow clears its throat in a horse-stall

(no. 74)

Generally, personification uses the second person (you, thou), while anthropomorphism favours the third (he, she, it, and they).

There is little a poet can do to alter the common denotative meanings of English words. 'Apple' means what it means whether it occurs inside a poem or outside. However, there is much scope for creativity in the use of 'poetic licence' – language which does not make literal sense or is not literally truthful. These include *pleonasm* (which means 'to be excessive'), a self-evident phrase like 'round circle' or 'the necessary essentials'; and *tautology* (which means 'the same word'), the same as pleonasm except that it is made as a statement: 'The circle is round', or 'These essentials are necessary'. (Many writers make no distinction between pleonasm and tautology.) *Oxymoron* (which means 'extremely silly') occurs when a phrase is incompatible with fact; for example, 'a square circle' or 'the unnecessary essentials'. Finally, *paradox* (which means 'beyond belief') is like oxymoron, except that, as in the case of tautology, a statement is made, one which seems self-contradictory: 'The circle is square', or, 'These essentials are unnecessary'. An example of paradox occurs in Wallace Stevens's line 'It was evening all afternoon' (no. 59). Paradox usually calls for a conventional explanation, however: a circular object may somehow have been squashed into an angular one, the 'essentials' may have been so-called by someone else, or, in the case of the Stevens line, it *felt* like evening all afternoon.

These are all varieties of what we might call 'factual nonsense' – the words make perfect sense, but what they state does not. Poetry may also make use of what we may call 'lexical nonsense' – that is, expressions which in themselves make no literal sense: 'brassy history', 'a purple breakdown', 'contrapuntal sausages', and the like. It is important to distinguish between the two effects. 'The fat lady is underweight' is a statement quite different in essence from one such as 'Blue spaghetti enforces love'.

Any kind of absurdity, factual or lexical, has the effect of causing the reader to put aside considerations of literal meaning in order to consider a figurative interpretation. We should be able, then, to distinguish between *literal* and *figurative* language; most of us will have been aware of the difference since primary school. The main purpose of literal language is to communicate conventional meaning. Figurative language, on the other hand, is not to be interpreted in this way: we do not expect blood to flow after a 'cutting remark', for example.

A poem may occasionally contain statements which are neither wholly true nor wholly false. Perhaps they might better be understood as artistic misrepresentations of truth. The ancient conventions of 'poetic licence' have occasionally caused confusion and even pain to readers not familiar with them. The two most common of these are *hyperbole* and *litotes*. Hyperbole (from Greek words meaning 'throwing beyond') denotes subjective exaggeration of objective fact:

> The blisse fulest notes he harpëd there
> That even ani man yherd with ere
>
> > [There he harped the most joyful notes that any man
> > has ever heard]
>
> > > (no. 3)
>
> And I will luve thee still, my dear,
> Till a' the seas gang dry.
>
> > (no. 32)
>
> > > . . . Five
> > green shaded light bulbs spider the billiards-table,
> > no field is greener than its cloth . . .
>
> > > (no. 74)

Litotes ('simple, plain'), on the other hand, *understates* the facts, or presents a positive fact by denying a negative one:

> 'If thou crave batayl bare,
> Here faylez thou not to fyght.'
>
> > ['If you crave bare battle you won't fail to (find a)
> > fight here.']
>
> > > (no. 6)

Her  lothely lere
  Is  nothynge clere

[Her  loathsome complexion is not at all clear . . .]

(no. 13)

. . . I thence
In · voke thy aid to my advent'rous Song,
That  with no middle flight intends to soar
A · bove th'Aonian Mount . . .

(no. 27)

The special sorts of language we have been looking at were at one time all included under the general heading of *rhetoric*. In medieval English universities the study of rhetoric was an important one, one which stressed the best and most vivid way of communicating ideas or facts. Today, the term tends to be used pejoratively – it suggests falsehood or phoniness (whence such expressions as 'mere politician's rhetoric'). Chaucer frequently used a variety of rhetorical conventions. Most of these are no longer so commonly employed – at least not consciously – though two remain well known: circumlocution and the rhetorical question. *Circumlocution* denotes exactly what its name suggests: roundabout speaking. A well-known example of this occurs in Coleridge's 'Kubla Khan', where, instead of a plain 'ten miles', the poem has:

. . . twice five miles of fertile ground
With  walls and towers were girdled round

(no. 33)

A *rhetorical question* (the technical term is *quaestio*) is one which presupposes a particular response on the part of the reader or listener:

The  shepherds sing; and shall I silent be?
My  God, no hymne for thee?

(no. 22)

Was it for this the clay grew tall?

(no. 60)

Spotting figures of speech and rhetorical conventions in poetry is in itself a somewhat pointless occupation. Observing that a certain phrase contains metaphor, or personification, or rhetorical questioning or anthropomorphism does not in itself offer any additional pleasure to the reader. Still, these are useful code words for relating certain expressions to a tradition as old as poetry itself.

Be careful not to conclude that a poet really has a simple and even prosaic 'message' to offer, and that any figurative or rhetorical colouring is added after the event, as a kind of spice to make the 'message' more 'poetic'. Use of these effects only works when they seem organically germane – like Arnold's metaphor of the Sea of Faith, or Dickinson's anthropomorphic presentation of Death as a coachman. Keats's remark still holds true: 'If Poetry comes not as naturally as the Leaves to a tree it had better not come at all.' Most experienced readers of poetry have an unconscious awareness of the effect of these figures when they occur, but this does not mean that they bear them in mind constantly while reading or listening to a poem. Pleasure must come first; a microscopic analysis of a poem may add very little to your enjoyment, especially if it is done as a mechanical and aimless exercise.

One more special effect needs to be mentioned – I have kept it till now, as it is perhaps the most difficult to perceive, and may often be mistaken for something else. This is *irony*, the statement of a fact or a truth in terms of its opposite. Irony in an everyday context may be fairly easy to perceive – for example, an individual who is obviously depressed may be greeted with the ironic words, 'You certainly look happy today!' when in fact the opposite is clearly the case. It takes maturity and experience in using a particular language to appreciate irony, however, which is why it does not usually work on young children or on foreigners whose English is not extensive.

The use of irony in poetry presents further difficulties. First of all, the language of the poem may be far removed from everyday language. Second, the social context may not be clear to the reader. Third, in spoken speech, irony is usually conveyed clearly enough by the use of a certain intonation. 'You certainly look happy today!' spoken ironically sounds quite different from the same words spoken as a straightforward observation of fact – the ironic version stresses the opening 'you', whereas the straightforward observation would stress 'certainly'.

The importance of its context to irony can be seen in Christina Rossetti's 'Uphill':

> Will there be beds for me and all who seek?
> Yea, beds for all who come.
>
> (no. 47)

Here, of course, the irony depends on the reader's knowing that what is being talked about is the inevitability of death. Without this realization, the irony will be missed – likewise the point of the whole poem. Here are two more examples:

> And I have leve to goo, of her goodenes
> [And I have permission to go, through her kindness]
>
> (no. 15)

> Dying
> Is an art, like everything else.
> I do it exceptionally well.
>
> (no. 76)

The majority of the terms discussed in this chapter have their origins in Greek rhetoric. As a result, many may appear alien and difficult, especially to a newcomer. Some English literary critics in the past have tried to coin English equivalents, but these have never caught on. The virtue of maintaining the old terms is that they link English poetry to other European literary traditions, and that they are more or less equivalent in all European languages. We have seen that English poetry has little in common metrically with the poetry of Latin and Greek, and that the terms of quantitative scansion are misleading when applied to our poetry. In the matter of figurative language, however, we have much in common with other European cultures, and a discerning use of these terms may demonstrate this.

In the last part of this chapter I want to look at the poet's use of distinctive *syntax*. This word (coming from the Greek, 'to join together') refers to the way in which we string words together to form phrases and sentences, following certain conventional 'rules' of grammar. For example, in normal English syntax we put the subject of a sentence (usually a noun or pronoun) first and the predicate (main verb) second. We say 'John runs', not 'Runs John'. If the sentence contains an object (another noun or pronoun which is affected by the action of the subject), we usually put the object after the verb: 'John hits Henry', not 'John Henry hits'. Other conventional syntactic arrangements in everyday English put adjectives before nouns, adverbs after verbs but before adjectives, and so on.

English poets have usually felt quite free to play around with the conventions of syntax. Perhaps the most common type of syntactical alteration involves the adjective/noun order. A simple example of this occurs in Yeats's line:

> While I stand on the roadway, or on the pavements gray
>
> (no. 54)

We should probably think it very strange if someone in ordinary conversation made a reference to 'pavements gray' or a 'tree green'. In Yeats's line, however, the demands of the metre and the rhyme scheme make the inverted syntax seem acceptable. Nevertheless, this kind of adjective/noun inversion now sounds as distinctively old-fashioned to our ears as do antique archaisms such as 'thee' and 'quoth'; Yeats may have been the last major English poet to be able to get away with this kind of 'poetic' alteration of conventional syntax (and this particular line occurs in one of his earliest published poems).

A larger aspect of syntax has to do with the kinds of sentences and phrases the poet creates. Are they short and simple?

> Bring me my bow of burning gold!
> Bring me my arrows of desire!
> Bring me my spear! O clouds, unfold!
> Bring me my chariot of fire!
>
> (no. 36)

Or long and convoluted?

> But   Adeline was not indifferent: for
>     (*Now* for a commonplace!) beneath the snow,
>     As a volcano holds the lava more
> With · in – *et caetera*.

(no. 38)

(See also Keats's sonnet 'To Sleep' (no. 39), which consists of one highly complex sentence.) Many of a poet's more unusual syntactic choices are enjoined by rhythmic, metric, and phonemic considerations. This is especially true in the case of less-accomplished versifiers who slot lexically empty words into their lines to keep the rhythm going:

> Now   let me just tell you of what he did say
> All   as I was passing his door that fine day . . .

Here the words 'Now', 'just', 'of', 'did', 'All', and 'fine' contribute little to these lines other than making them rhythmically regular. A little of this padding goes a long way. An accomplished poet will usually try to come up with better ways to handle the form.

Certain ages made extensive use of syntactic regularity as a literary device. The Blake lines above, with their repeated 'Bring me', do this. Such regularity was especially favoured in the eighteenth century, when ostentatiously balanced phrases were judged to be the hallmark of fine craftsmanship:

> With   too much knowledge for the Sceptic side,
> With   too much weakness for a Stoic's pride,
>   He   hangs between; in doubt to act, or rest,
>   In   doubt to deem himself a God, or Beast,
>   In   doubt his mind or body to prefer,
>     Born but to die, and reas'ning but to err . . .

(no. 30)

However, syntactic parallelism, particularly that of repetition, has been a feature of poetry of all ages in English:

Awë bleteth after lomb,
Louth after calvë cu,
Bulluc sterteth, buckë verteth,
Murie sing, cuccu!

(no. 2)

For fourthly he sharpens his paws by wood.
For fifthly he washes himself.
For sixthly he rolls upon wash.
For seventhly he fleas himself . . .

(no. 31)

Ah, did you once see Shelley plain,
And did he stop and speak to you
And did you speak to him again?
How strange it seems and new!

(no. 42)

In the parcel a small island,
On the island a large tree,
On the tree a husky fruit.

(no. 68)

A cake of soap,
A wedding ring,
A gold filling.

Herr God, Herr Lucifer
Be·ware
Be·ware.

(no. 76)

As with the other forms of parallelism we have met so far
(rhythmic, metric, phonemic, figurative), the features involved in
syntactic parallels must be relatively close together in order to be
perceived. The parallels in the examples given above could hardly be
missed, even at first hearing. Larger-scale parallels, such as those
which unify MacLeish's 'Ars Poetica' (no. 62), are a little more
subtle. However, we may find trivial the syntactic parallels of a line
such as 'He found his key and opened the gate'; they bestow no
particular memorability upon it.

Parallelism, as we've already seen, always implies both similarity and difference. Two phrases with no similarities would of course show no parallelism whatever. Two absolutely identical phrases would not be parallels either – the second one would be merely a repetition. (Actually, a repeated line *is* different from its forerunner in that it is an echo, something the first line clearly is not.) Parallelism operates in other arts too – above all in music, where large-scale repetition and recapitulation is a common feature. It satisfies one of our most basic desires: to perceive some kind of symmetry in things that bring pleasure.

People who have been exposed to a fair amount of English poetry often come to feel that each century seems to have produced its own kind of poetic diction and forms. Indeed, it often appears that the turn of the century itself marks the watershed between one style and another. Can it be that there is something in this? Or are we merely imposing subjective impressions on the actual facts?

In the 1950s an American scholar, Josephine Miles, carried out a study to try to isolate some objective evidence to account for this common impression. She took a sample of 1,000 lines of poetry (from different poets) for every decade from the sixteenth century to the middle of the twentieth, then analysed the contents of these lines to see whether any kind of pattern could be seen. Her findings showed that the turn of each century was indeed marked by a noticeable change of style. In all centuries but the eighteenth, the first sixty years or so were generally marked by styles which leaned towards adjectives and away from verbs. Then during the last forty years of each century the balance between adjectives and verbs was about equal. In the eighteenth century alone, the balance tipped the other way: the first sixty years were generally dominated by styles in which verbs predominated and adjectives were scarce; then, once again, the final forty or so years showed a shift to a more balanced style.

Miles also discovered that poetry which favours adjectives, as most English poetry since the sixteenth century has done, tends to be organized in *stanzas* (groups containing a fixed number of lines), whereas poetry which favours verbs leans towards a line-by-line style of writing, one in which the content dictates the progression and organization of the poem.

If history repeats itself, the twentieth century should end with a 'balanced' period, as all other centuries since the sixteenth have done. My own subjective feeling has been that for at least the last thirty years most English poets have been at pains to avoid a heavily adjectival style. A well-chosen noun often makes an adjective redundant, of course. It is generally felt that heavily adjectival styles are 'weak' and that verbal ones, particularly if active verbs are favoured, are 'strong'. However, this may simply be a natural reaction against the adjectival style which Miles shows predominated during the first six decades of this century.

One of the pleasures of poetry is that to create it all you need is a voice. Of course, if your memory is not the best, pen and paper can be a great help. But the earliest English poets composed their poems in their heads, some of them epics which were memorized and passed along orally for centuries. (*Beowulf* is our only surviving Old English epic, but we must assume there were many more that never got written down before being lost.) The Old English poets used as raw material what poets have always used, something there in the air for all who have ears to hear – the sounds of our native speech. The art of poets of all ages has been to take these sounds, and so work them that people will be struck by them and get pleasure from them.

Unfortunately, few people know how to read poetry any more, and many others who do treat it as though it were a newspaper article or a short story that somehow got garbled. But I hope that this chapter has made one thing clear: a poem is chiefly a performance. So if you are not attracted by the sound and words of a particular poem (in the way you might feel unmoved by the sound of a particular piece of music), then move on and look for another. The search itself is a large part of the pleasure that art brings.

# 5 Lines into Forms

*He's a Blockhead that can't make two Verses; and he's a Fool that makes four. – Thomas Fuller*

Now we are going to leave 'ordinary' English behind, and turn our attention to how metrically regular lines may be combined into larger *forms*, in ways found only in poetry. Every major poetic form in English since the fourteenth century has been the result of two factors, often working together: metre and rhyme.

Young children soon learn how to combine lines into *couplets*, rhythmically regular pairs of lines which rhyme. A line such as

The grass is green, the sky is blue

has only to be followed by another with the same (or roughly the same) rhythm pattern, and ending with a word which rhymes with /blu/, the last stressed syllable of the first line. For the line above, we need something which goes

DA **DA** DA **DA** DA **DA** DA D/u/

– so we need words which fit into this four-measure metre, and which give us a final stressed syllable with a /u/ sound. Any number of lines could be invented:

The horses neigh, the cows go 'Moo!'
I wonder what there is to do.
If I pass by, will I see you?
But we are going to the zoo.
The buttercups are blooming too.
And yet this day I'll surely rue.
They say you're leaving – is it true?

and so forth. In each of these, the rhythmic pattern of the first line has been duplicated, and an acceptable rhyme-word found.

The first uses of rhyme in English do not go much beyond simple couplets – and the couplet has always remained the basic building-block of most English poetic forms. Here is a two-couplet stanza from the twelfth-century 'Hymn of Godric':

| | |
|---|---|
| Saintë Maryë, Christës bur, | shelter |
| Maidenës clenhad, moderës flur, | purity flower |
| Dilie min sinnë, rix in min mod, | remove merge heart |
| Bring me to winnë with the self God. | joy |

Now a two-couplet lyric from the early thirteenth century:

| | |
|---|---|
| Now goth sunnë under wode – | wood |
| Me reweth, Marië, thy fairë rode. | I rue face |
| Now goth sunnë under tree – | |
| Me reweth, Marië, thy Sone and thee, | |

and, from the same period or earlier, a rhyming tag which is still part of our oral tradition:

Thirty days hath September,
April, June, and November.

The first long rhyming poem of any note in English is the early-thirteenth-century *The Owl and the Nightingale*, a long Valentine's Day discussion between birds about different types of love – all in couplets. Not long after, at the start of the fourteenth century, comes *Sir Orfeo* (no. 3), a considerably livelier work, also in couplets. Then, only a generation or so after that, we find a complete mastery of the couplet form in the work of Geoffrey Chaucer:

| | |
|---|---|
| The Cook of Londoun, whil the Revë spak, | |
| For joye him thoughte he clawed him on the bak. | |
| 'Ha ha!' quod he, 'for Christës passion, | |
| This millere hadde a sharp conclusion | |
| Up·on his argument of herbergage! | lodging |
| Wel seyde Salomon in his langage, | |
| "Ne bryng nat every man into thyn hous"; | |

> For  herberwynge by nyghte is perilous.                    lodging
> Wel  oghte a man avysëd for to be                            cautious
>     Whom that he broghte into his pryvetee . . .'
>
>     (*The Canterbury Tales,* lines 4325–34)

Note the easy use of conversational idiom, run-on lines and poly-syllabic rhymes. In *The Canterbury Tales,* Chaucer anticipated most of the ways in which the couplet would ever be used. Here are some examples from poets who followed him:

> Kinde  pitty chokes my spleene; brave scorn forbids
> Those  tears to issue which swell my eye-lids;
>     I  must not laugh, nor weepe sinnes, and be wise –
> Can  railing then cure these worne maladies? . . .
>
>     – John Donne

>     But at my back I alwaies hear
> Times  wingëd Charriot hurrying near;
> And  yonder all before us lye
> De · sarts of vast Eternity . . .
>
>     – Andrew Marvell (no. 28)

> Time,  place, and action may with pains be wrought,
> But  Genius must be born, and never can be taught.
>     This is your portion, this your native store:
>     Heav'n, that but once was prodigal before,
> To  Shakespeare gave as much; she could not give him
>     more . . .
>
>     – John Dryden

> Of  these am I, who thy protection claim,
> A  watchful sprite, and Ariel is my name.
>     Late, as I ranged the crystal wilds of air,
> In the  clear mirror of thy ruling star
>     I  saw, alas! some dread event impend,
>     Ere to the main this morning sun descend;
> But  heav'n reveals not what, or how, or where:
>     Warn'd by the sylph, oh pious maid, beware!
>
>     – Alexander Pope

Some few in town observed in Peter's trap
A boy, with jacket blue and woollen cap;
But none inquired how Peter used the rope,
Or what the bruise, that made the stripling stoop;
None could the ridges on his back behold,
None sought him shiv'ring in the winter's cold;
None put the question, – 'Peter, doest thou give
The boy his food? – What, man! the lad must live:
Con · sider, Peter, let the child have bread,
He'll serve thee better if he's stroked and fed.'
None reason'd thus – and some, on hearing cries,
Said calmly, 'Grimes is at his exercise.'

           – George Crabbe


How pleasant, as the sun declines, to view
The spacious landscape change in form and hue!
Here, vanish, as in mist, before a flood
Of bright obscurity, hill, lawn, and wood;
There, objects, by the searching beams betrayed,
Come forth, and here retire in purple shade;
Even the white stems of birch, the cottage white,
Soften their glare before the mellow light . . .

           – William Wordsworth


A ship is floating in the harbour now,
A wind is hovering o'er the mountain's brow;
There is a path on the sea's azure floor,
No keel has ever ploughed that path before;
The halcyons brood around the foamless isles;
The treacherous Ocean has forsworn its wiles . . .

           – Percy Bysshe Shelley


As the husband is, the wife is: thou art mated with a
        clown,
And the grossness of his nature will have weight to drag
        thee down.

He will hold thee, when his passion shall have spent its
        novel force,
Something better than his dog, a little dearer than his
        horse.

What is  this? His eyes are heavy: think not they are
        glazed with wine,
   Go  to him: it is thy duty: kiss him: take his hand
        in thine . . .

                                          – Alfred, Lord Tennyson

    The  bear puts both arms around the tree above her
    And  draws it down as if it were a lover
  And its  chokecherries lips to kiss good-by,
    Then  lets it snap back upright in the sky.
    Her  next step rocks a boulder on the wall
 (She's  making her cross-country in the fall).
    Her  great weight creaks the barbed wire in its staples
 As she  flings over and off down through the maples . . .

                                          – Robert Frost

You may feel you can detect, in this brief survey, a progression away from lines in which the rhythmic pattern is fixed (as in a solidly five-duplet line, for example), and towards lines of mixed rhythms, such as Frost's:

Her great weight creaks the barbed wire in its staples
●      ●    ●○    ●○○○       ●○

(this being only one of several different ways in which the line might be performed as a five-stress one). However, even Chaucer, in the fourteenth century, could feel free to create a line such as

Pekke hem up right as they growe and ete hem yn
●○○    ●○○    ●○    ●○    ●
[Pick them up, just as they grow, and eat them up.]

within the context of a poem based on a five-duplet metre. (The line is from 'The Nun's Priest's Tale', *CT* 2967, *4157.)

The couplet is the most widely used form in English poetry, still the most frequent in all types of popular verse. The main problem in using rhyme as deliberately and frequently as this is that the listener may easily be able to guess the rhyme in advance, and end up listening more for the rhymes than for the rest of the poetry – particularly if they are obvious, or, even worse, forced. Some poets have taken great pains to draw the listeners' attention away from the rhyme. A favourite solution is to use lines in which the meaning and syntax lead the ear quickly past the rhyme. The seventeenth-century poet Francis Quarles carried this device to its probable limit in these lines from 'Christ and Ourselves':

> I wish a greater knowledge, than t'attain
> The knowledge of myself: a greater gain
> Than to augment myself: a greater treasure
> Than to enjoy myself: a greater pleasure
> Than to content myself . . .

The same effect was used by Keats with far greater skill. Many who have heard quoted, but have never read, the familiar lines which open his poem 'Endymion', may not have realized that they rhyme:

> A thing of beauty is a joy forever:
> Its loveliness increases; it will never
> Pass into nothingness; but still will keep
> A bower quiet for us, and a sleep
> Full of sweet dreams, and health, and quiet breathing . . .

Both lines of a couplet may have a mid-line pause (a *caesura*):

> He called to her. She turned away.
> He scratched his head – was this in play?

in which case the poet might decide to treat them as a four-line group instead (such mechanical matters usually get decided early in the working-out process):

> He called to her.
> She turned away.
> He scratched his head –
> Was this in play?

The couplet has been transformed into a *quatrain*, a group of four lines. Now, if the poem is a long one the poet may decide to compose the whole thing in one repeated form – quatrains, for example – with a line-space between each repetition. We call each of these repetitions a *stanza*. (The term 'verse', which is often heard, has other meanings too, so I prefer to avoid it altogether. 'Stanza' is Italian for 'room', and nicely conveys the idea of the stanzas of the poem as a series of rooms of identical dimensions but quite different décor and contents.)

In describing the stanza form of a given poem we are interested in two things: the metre (including the dominant rhythmic pattern), and the arrangement of the rhyme, if any. We have already discussed the vocabulary for describing the poem's rhythms and metre in Chapter 2. So now we have to devise a way to describe its *rhyme-scheme* (that is, the order and arrangement of rhymes in a typical stanza or a whole poem). The usual way is to give the first occurrence of each rhyme-sound a letter, beginning with *a*, then proceeding in alphabetical order. If the second line ends with a sound which rhymes with the first, then it too is an *a*. If it doesn't, use a new letter. The rhyme-scheme of a simple couplet,

> Know then thy-self, presume not God to scan;  *a*
> The  proper study of mankind is Man.  *a*

(no. 30)

then, must be *aa*, the first *a* standing for 'scan', and the second for the rhyme, 'Man'.

In the case of a quatrain with only one rhyme (that is, between the ends of the second and the fourth lines),

> As  fair art thou, my bonnie lass,  *x*
> So  deep in luve am I;  *a*
> And  I will luve thee still, my dear,  *x*
> Till  a' the seas gang dry.  *a*

(no. 32)

the rhyme-scheme is *xaxa* (*x* stands for 'non-rhyming line'), as only the second and fourth lines rhyme.

Another quatrain form is no more than a grouping of two separate couplets into one four-line stanza: *aabb*. An example of this two-couplet quatrain is:

| And since to look at things in bloom | a |
| Fifty springs are little room, | a |
| A·bout the woodlands I will go | b |
| To see the cherry hung with snow. | b |

(no. 55)

Now, you will see that beyond *xaxa* and *aabb* there are two further ways in which the rhymes of a quatrain may be arranged. In one of these, the rhymes are *interlaced*; that is, the first line rhymes with the third, and the second with the fourth:

| How the chimney-sweeper's cry | a |
| Every black'ning church appals; | b |
| And the hapless soldier's sigh | a |
| Runs in blood down palace walls. | b |

(no. 35)

in an *abab* rhyme-scheme. In the other, the *closed quatrain*, the first line-ending rhymes with the last, and the second with the third:

| How do I love thee? Let me count the ways. | a |
| I love thee to the depth and breadth and height | b |
| My soul can reach, when feeling out of sight | b |
| For the ends of Being and ideal Grace . . . | a |

– Elizabeth Barrett Browning

– so the rhyme-scheme is *abba*. The form (which in this example is the opening of a sonnet) is called 'closed' because the *a*-rhymes enclose the *b*-rhymes.

Conventionally, our description of the rhyme-scheme ends with the end of a stanza. Usually the poet will maintain the same rhyme-scheme for the whole of a poem. This does not mean that the *a*s and *b*s of one stanza will rhyme with the *a*s and *b*s of another – simply that throughout a poem in *abba* quatrains the first line of each stanza will rhyme with the last line, and the second with the third. (It is not common for the same rhyme-sounds to occur throughout any whole poem of more than four lines.)

We may place the rhyme-schemes we have looked at so far on a scale running from informal/popular to formal/sophisticated, showing the kinds of poetry for which they are most generally used. The top two on the list demand only one pair of rhymes, but the rest call for two separate pairs to be combined.

**INFORMAL/POPULAR**

| | |
|---|---|
| *aa* | (couplet) |
| *xaxa* | (couplet rearranged as open quatrain) |
| *aabb* | (two-couplet quatrain) |
| *abab* | (interlaced quatrain) |
| *abba* | (closed quatrain) |

**FORMAL/SOPHISTICATED**

The couplet and the quatrain are binary forms, which may explain why they are the most popular forms of English poetry. Even for the largest and most complex 'fixed' forms, these remain the basic building-blocks. We may, however, build outwards from the couplet in another way: by adding a third line to make a *tercet* (sometimes spelled 'terzet'). In the simplest tercet form, a non-rhyming line is inserted in the middle of a couplet:

| | | |
|---|---|---|
| | Old Mother Hubbard | *a* |
| | just for a joke | *x* |
| | went to the cupboard. | *a* |
| But | when she got there | *b* |
| the | whole thing backfired: | *x* |
| the | cupboard was bare . . . | *b* |

A more ambitious tercet rhyme-scheme uses a third line which rhymes with the first two, in an *aaa* pattern:

| | | |
|---|---|---|
| The | wrinkled sea beneath him crawls: | *a* |
| He | watches from his mountain walls, | *a* |
| And | like a thunderbolt he falls. | *a* |

(no. 44)

I say 'more ambitious' because, while it is difficult enough in English to find two words which rhyme, fit well into a given metre, and do not appear to be forcing themselves upon what the poet is saying, it is at least doubly difficult to find a third which will do all of this so close to the other two. Because of the vastly increased difficulty of finding suitable rhymes, then, and also because of the uneven nature of three-line groups, the tercet is never found in popular poetry.

There is another way in which tercets may be somewhat more easily formed, however: this is by using an interlaced *aba bcb cdc* (and so on) rhyme-scheme. Technically this is known as *terza rima* ('third rhyme'); and it has the advantage of giving increased distance between the rhymes – more time to arrive at a suitable rhyme:

|  |  |  |
|---|---|---|
| | Over and over | *a* |
| she kept | asking us all | *b* |
| why she | needed a lover, | *a* |
| till | one day a tall | *b* |
| | dark lovely stranger | *c* |
| took her | off to a ball. | *b* |
| Sus · | pecting no danger | *c* |
| she | left us all waiting | *d* |
| like | dogs at a manger . . . | *c* |

*Terza rima* has been used sporadically in English since the fifteenth century – if not before – and is seen at its best in poetry which has a constantly advancing narrative style.

One way of producing three-line groups which requires only pairs of rhymes is to write one group of lines that don't rhyme with each other at all, then follow it with another three-line group which contains all the rhymes for the first (*abc abc*):

|  |  |  |
|---|---|---|
| The | keen stars were twinkling | *a* |
| And the | fair moon was rising among them, | *b* |
| Dear | Jane. | *c* |
| The gui · | tar was tinkling | *a* |
| But the | notes were not sweet 'till you sung them | *b* |
| A · | gain. – | *c* |

(no. 40)

This has the undoubted advantage that only two pairs of rhymes are required – what we have, in fact, is three interlacing couplets.

Couplets, quatrains and tercets are the basic forms of all open-ended poetry in English. But around Chaucer's time, interest began to develop in larger and more complex stanza forms, the so-called *fixed forms* in which the smaller forms combine into larger groups using a set rhyme-scheme. The oldest of these fixed forms is the one known as the *carol*. It is also notable because, unlike the other fixed forms we'll see in a moment, the carol seems to have been a genuinely popular poetic form, comparable to the traditional ballad, which flowered a little later.

Today, the word 'carol' has come to mean a song mainly linked with Christmas. This sense of the word is more recent, however. Its origins, in early medieval times, are in dance, and the word comes from the French *caroler*, to dance in a ring. In time, words began to be associated with the music for the dance, and a common form evolved in which a leader sang the stanzas of the song, then the rest of the participants joined in with an unchanging *burden*, or chorus, as they danced round. What many of the carols have in common is a shift of rhyme in the last line of the leader's stanza – a shift to the rhyme of the burden. The rhyme-scheme of a typical carol, then, might be *aaab bb* (in which *bb* denotes the lines of the burden).

| | | |
|---|---|---|
| While  thou haste be within oure house | | *a* |
| We  ete no puddings ne no souse, | | *a* |
| But  stinking fishe not worthe a louse – | | *a* |
| Fare · wele fro us both alle and some. | | *b* |
| *Burden:* | Fare · wele, Advent! Christemas is come; | *b* |
| | Fare · wele fro us, both alle and some! | *b* |

Another rhyme arrangement occurs in the carol 'Bring Us in Good Ale' (no. 11):

| | | |
|---|---|---|
| | Bring us in no egges, for ther ar many shelles; | *a* |
| But  bring us in good ale, and give us nothing elles, | | *a* |
| And  bring us in good ale. | | *b* |
| *Burden:* | **Bring us in good ale, and bring us in good ale,** | *b* |
| | **Fore our blessed Lady sak, bring us in good ale.** | *b* |

From contemporary evidence it seems that in the typical carol dance the group chorus stood still while the leader sang each of the successive stanzas of the song. At the end of each stanza, all would join in the burden, linking hands and dancing round in a ring. The change of rhyme at the end of each of the leader's stanzas not only alerted the chorus to its entry, but also, by its sound, served as a cue to the rhyme of the burden.

Although each carol was undoubtedly the creation of one or two inventive minds in a particular community, carols stand out from all other forms of English poetry in that their expression is always popular and communal. Typically, the pronouns found in a carol are first-person plural ones: we, us, our. In no other common form of English poetry is this the case. The content of a carol may be serious, but more usually it is entertaining and jocular, an outburst of good spirit. Even the most serious carols express themselves in terms understandable to all – see 'The Corpus Christi Carol' (no. 12), for example. This carol does not have the usual shift of rhyme at the end of each stanza, but it does have the typical burden, and uses extremely simple language to convey matters of great depth and mystery.

Since the carol had its origins in France, although its content is popular and communal, its form was probably brought to England after 1066 by people in the service of the Norman-French invaders. Other, more complex, forms which caught on in England were imported in the same way, but their appeal was to a more upper-class audience. The first of these forms, *rime royale* (the term is French for 'royal rhyme', which gives a good indication of its intended audience), may have been first used in English by Geoffrey Chaucer. It was by far the most popular form among ambitious late-medieval poets. Chaucer's longest completed poem, *Troilus and Criseyde*, is in *rime royale* throughout. The form uses seven-line stanzas, rhymed *ababbcc*: in effect, an interlaced quatrain (*abab*) overlapping, by one line, a two-couplet quatrain (*bbcc*). Thomas Wyatt's 'They Fle from Me' (no. 15) is a good example of a shorter poem in this most popular of courtly stanza forms.

The appeal of *rime royale* is twofold. First, except for the three *b*-rhymes, only single pairs of rhymes are required. Second, the stanza opens with the advancing sound of an interlaced quatrain (*abab*), but closes much more deliberately with that of two couplets (*bbcc*), comparable to the effect of a perfect cadence in music. The main technical demand of the form is in finding and using suitable triple *b*-rhymes. The weakest point is the rhyme in line five, which is not only the third of the *b*-rhymes (hence, potentially the most forced-sounding), but also the final line of the 'couplet' formed by lines four and five. Obviously, this is a rather exposed position. The characteristic flavour of the *rime royale* stanza is the result of its overlapping of two quatrains, strengthened by its closing couplets (perhaps inspired by the burden of the popular carol).

A similar form, but this time with eight lines, is *ottava rima* ('octave rhyme'). This is another Italian import, not used commonly in English until some centuries after the advent of *rime royale*. This stanza merely inserts an extra *a*-rhyme into the old *rime royale* stanza after line 4: *ababababcc*. To my way of thinking, *ottava rima* offers nothing that *rime royale* does not except the difficulty of having to find two sets of triple rhymes, *a* and *b*, instead of only one. Perhaps this is why its main appeal has always been to poets of whom we think primarily as consummate rhymesters. Lord Byron is an example: his *Don Juan* (no. 38) is one of many nineteenth-century poems to make use of the form. Here are two other stanzas from the same poem to show the discursive style for which Byron is noted:

> The  coast – I think it was the coast that I
> Was  just describing – Yes, it *was* the coast –
>    Lay at this period quiet as the sky,
> The  sands untumbled, the blue waves untossed,
> And  all was stillness, save the sea-bird's cry,
> And  dolphin's leap, and little billow crossed
>  By  some low rock or shelve, that made it fret
>  A · gainst the boundary it scarcely wet . . .

> They  look'd up to the sky, whose floating glow
>    Spread like a rosy ocean, vast and bright;
> They  gazed upon the glittering sea below,
>    Whence the broad moon rose circling into sight;
> They  heard the waves splash, and the wind so low,
> And  saw each other's dark eyes darting light
>    Into each other – and, beholding this,
> Their  lips drew near, and clung into a kiss . . .
>                        (Canto II, stanzas 181–2)

The sixteenth-century poet Edmund Spenser used a nine-line stanza for his great epic *The Faerie Queene* (two stanzas are included in the anthology): it is known as the *Spenserian stanza*. It opens with the interlaced quatrain (*abab*) used in *rime royale* and *ottava rima*, but continues with a second interlaced quatrain (*bcbc*), then concludes with a final line, another *c*-rhyme. The effect, then, is of two interlaced quatrains, the second overlapping by one line (line 8) a final couplet: *ababbcbcc*. The demands of this form are Herculean: *four b*-rhymes are required, in addition to three *c*-rhymes and two *a*-rhymes. The only relief is that the *a*-rhymes are used first, so at least the opening of the stanza need not appear forced.

Whereas the carol (like the folk ballad and the lyrics of modern songs) uses the traditional four-measure line, all the other larger forms we have discussed – *rime royale*, *ottava rima* and the Spenserian stanza – use the more sophisticated five-stress line, the line imported into English by Chaucer. A number of other five-stress forms of lesser importance also have French origins, and were also brought to England in medieval times. Foremost among these are the rondeau, rondel, ballade, and villanelle: we'll look at each one briefly now.

Poetic forms whose names begin with the syllable 'rond-' are linked to the rondo forms of classical music. The root itself means 'return', and what all these forms have in common is that they continually circle back to material first presented in their opening lines – just as the musical rondo form continually returns to themes stated at the outset. It seems likely that these forms grew out of such leader-and-chorus dances as the carol, though they ultimately developed into poetic forms now associated more closely with courtly, sophisticated audiences.

The *rondel* (also spelt 'roundel') is one of the rondo forms much favoured by Chaucer and other poets of his day. It has fourteen lines, and uses only two rhymes throughout, repeating two of the opening lines halfway through, and closing with a repetition of the poem's first three lines. The *rondeau* is similar, but has ten or thirteen lines. Like the rondel, it has only two rhymes, and uses one of each of them in its repeated two-line refrain. A good example of a rondeau is Chaucer's 'Nowe welcome, Somor' (no. 7), from *The Parlement of Foules*.

Another attractive medieval form which uses patterns of line repetition is the *ballade*. This form is in eight-line stanzas, rhymed *ababbcbc*, with the same line appearing at the end of each stanza, as a kind of burden. This means that the *c*-rhymes in a ballade have to be the same for the whole poem. Here is a stanza from Chaucer's 'Ballade to Rosamund':

> Ma · dame, ye ben of allë beaute shrine,
>  As fer as cercled is the mapamounde,
> For as the crystal glorious ye shine,
> And likë ruby ben your chekës rounde;
> Ther · with ye ben so mery and so jocounde,
> That at a revel, whan that I see you dance,
>  It is an oinëment unto my wounde,
> Thogh ye to me ne do no daliance.

[Madam, you are the shrine of all beauty the world over, for you shine like the glorious crystal, and your round cheeks are like ruby; withal you are so merry and joyous that when I see you dance at a revel (ball), it is balm to my wounds, even though you do not play the game of love with me.]

Other fixed forms such as the *villanelle*, which has five tercets and a concluding quatrain, parallel the effects of the rondel, rondeau and ballade, returning to one or more lines which function as a kind of burden. All of them come from medieval French song-and-dance forms. To anyone contemplating using one of them for a new poem, I offer one very large reservation: modern readers can find enough of the most skilled rhyming and interweaving of lines into fixed forms in any historical anthology of English poetry. Use of these forms today may have the effect of turning the reader's attention away from the other aspects of the poem. Skilful rhymes are no longer enough: we look for something more subtle.

In James Joyce's *A Portrait of the Artist as a Young Man*, the hero—artist, Stephen Daedalus, writes a poem in the form of a villanelle. It takes some work, and the reader gets a look over the artist's shoulder during the process. Here is the poem that results:

> Are you not weary of ardent ways,       *a1*
> Lure of the fallen seraphim?       *b*
> Tell no more of enchanted days.       *a2*

95

| | |
|---|---|
| Your eyes have set man's heart ablaze | *a* |
| And you have had your will of him. | *b* |
| Are you not weary of ardent ways? | *a1* |
| | |
| Above the flame the smoke of praise | *a* |
| Goes up from ocean rim to rim. | *b* |
| Tell no more of enchanted days. | *a2* |
| | |
| Our broken cries and mournful lays | *a* |
| Rise in one eucharistic hymn. | *b* |
| Are you not weary of ardent ways? | *a1* |
| | |
| While sacrificing hands upraise | *a* |
| The chalice flowing to the brim, | *b* |
| Tell no more of enchanted days. | *a2* |
| | |
| And still you hold our longing gaze | *a* |
| With languorous look and lavish limb! | *b* |
| Are you not weary of ardent ways? | *a1* |
| Tell no more of enchanted days. | *a2* |

It's hard to believe this poem is by the author of *Ulysses* and *Finnegans Wake*. What has puzzled literary critics most about it is this: did Joyce intend the poem as a successful artistic statement? If he did, its use of the villanelle form seems to work against it. Or is this twentieth-century 'artist's' use of the form an ironic comment on his own self-deluding character? Whatever your view, Joyce's attempt to use one of the old fixed forms in a modern way may have been the last of any significance in English letters – and its main significance is that it just does not work.

It is curious that Chaucer, who recognized the potential of so many southern European forms, missed the greatest of them all: the *sonnet*, often referred to as the 'king' of English verse forms. The sonnet sprang up in Sicily, possibly from popular shepherds' songs. The earliest recorded sonnets are by Giacomo de Lentino (who flourished between 1230 and 1240), but the first great sonneteers came a century later, from hundreds of miles to the north: Cavalcanti, Dante, and Petrarch – perhaps the greatest of all. We know that Chaucer read at least one of the sonnets of Petrarch, because he translated it into English – but not as a sonnet. (Instead, he expanded it into three stanzas of *rime royale*.)

Let's look at an example of the Italian model, a sonnet by Petrarch, one which Chaucer might well have read:

| | |
|---|---|
| I'vo plangendo i miei passati tempi | *a* |
| i qual posi in amar cosa mortale, | *b* |
| senza levarmi a volo, avend'io l'ale | *b* |
| per dare forse di me non bassi esempi. | *a* |
| Tu, che vedi i miei mali indegni ed empi, | *a* |
| re del cielo, invisibile, immortale, | *b* |
| soccorri all'alma disviata e frale, | *b* |
| e 'l suo difetto di tua grazia adempi: | *a* |
| al che, s'io vissi in guerra ed in tempesta, | *c* |
| mora in pace et in porto; e se la stanza | *d* |
| fu vana, almen sia la partita onesta. | *c* |
| A quel poco di viver che m'avanza | *d* |
| ed al morir degni esser tua man presta. | *c* |
| Tu sai ben che 'n altrui non ho speranza. | *d* |

[I keep weeping over my past which I spent in loving a mortal thing, without lifting myself to flight, although I had wings to give perhaps no mean proof of myself. You, who see my unworthy and wicked ills, king of heaven, unseen, everlasting, help this soul, lost and frail, and make good its infirmity with your grace:
so that, if I have lived in war and tempest, I may die in peace and in port; and, if my sojourn was vain, my leave taking at least may be just. May your hand deign to be near in that little of life which is left to me and in my death. You know full well that I place no hope in any other being.]
– from *The Penguin Book of Italian Verse*

The Italian sonnet had many qualities common to all our main sonnet forms: fourteen lines, a regular metre, a fixed rhyme-scheme. However, the difficult rhyme-scheme of the Italian sonnet was not widely used by English poets until Milton. The first English sonneteers of any note were of the fifteenth and sixteenth centuries: Wyatt, Surrey, Drayton, Sidney and Shakespeare. These poets used a different rhyme-scheme for the sonnet, which became known as 'English'. In this form, the first twelve lines, the *douzain*, are made up of three quatrains. The douzain is balanced by a concluding couplet. Shakespeare's 'Like as the waves make towards the pibled shore' (no. 20) is a good example of an English sonnet.

The hallmark of the English sonnet form, then, is the structural division into the opening douzain and the closing couplet, perhaps derived from the close of the *rime royale* stanza. Unfortunately, this arrangement is rather disproportionate – some critics have likened it to a mouse chasing an elephant, or a balloon being punctured with a pin. Shakespeare's sonnets are frequently admired for their strength of language, or their vivid imagery or memorable expression – but scarcely ever for their organic balance. Indeed, if you read a number of English sonnets at a stretch, the clinching effect of these final couplets may come to seem predictable and even (dare it be said?) irritating. English sonnets are perhaps better savoured one at a time.

It was left to John Milton to return to the original Italian sonnet model to see whether it could be used to good effect in English. The major appeal of the Italian sonnet was its more useful structural arrangement: an opening *octave* (eight-line section) balanced a closing *sestet* (six-line section). The English poets had already converted Petrarch's regular ten-syllable lines into English five-duple metre. The only remaining problem was that of the Italian rhyme-scheme. Petrarch's octave rhymes *abbaabba*, so *four a-*rhymes and *four b-*rhymes are needed, as well as rhymes for the sestet. This demand is not too great for Italian, where rhyming sounds are abundant, but in English it is extremely difficult, and calls for great inventiveness on the part of the poet. There is a very real danger of resorting to what Keats (one of the greatest exponents of the Italian sonnet in English) called 'pouncing' rhymes – rhymes which are snatched at and used out of pure desperation, because the language offers nothing better. It is noticeable that Milton uses other devices, such as *run-on lines* (lines which are not end-stopped syntactically, but which carry the reader on quickly past the rhyme), to draw attention away from that particular weakness.

Other English poets came up with different ways of reconciling Italian and English sonnet forms. Edmund Spenser, for example, used an English rhyme-scheme, but made a major syntactical break after the eighth line, as the Italian sonnet does. John Donne also on occasion used a combination of the two traditions, making an even clearer break (through both rhyme and syntax) after line eight, as in the Italian model, but nevertheless concluding with a couplet. In his

'At the round earths imagin'd corners' (no. 24), he uses traditional Italian quatrains for the octave, then ends the sonnet in an English style: *abba abba cdcd ee*. English poets have found other ingenious ways to get round the rhyme's demands but still preserve the Italian sonnet's structural balance of octave and sestet. Wordsworth, for example, keeps the enclosing *a*-rhymes in the first two quatrains, but changes the internal rhyme of the second quatrain: *abba acca*. Four *a*-rhymes are still needed, but only two of all the others. Other poets use new rhymes for the second quatrain: *abba cddc*, or else an open or interlaced form of quatrain: *abab cdcd*. Each of these 'solutions' takes us a further step from the Italian original, but each nevertheless preserves the quintessential 8:6 proportion of the Petrarchan model.

Although the conventional sonnet line is a five-stress one based on duple rhythms, many poets nearer our own times have felt free to experiment with other metres and forms. Chief among these is Hopkins, whose 'Windhover' (no. 51) is in a highly original Italian-based sonnet form. Hopkins maintained that all his sonnets were in five-stress lines. In actual practice, it is at times impossible to guess which five syllables in a line are the stressed ones. For example, a line such as: 'Of the rolling level underneath him steady air, and striding', might be stressed

Of the  rolling level underneath him steady air, and striding,

or

Of the  rolling level underneath him steady air, and striding,

– to mention only two possibilities. Hopkins's measures are typically quite elastic, stretching to take in any number of extra syllables (and even, some critics have claimed, extra-metrical stresses).

Hopkins invented another sonnet form – the *curtal* (from the French *court*, 'short') *sonnet*. The curtal sonnet has the same proportions as the standard Italian sonnet, but is abbreviated. Its first section consists of two tercets (which Hopkins usually rhymes *abc abc*), while the remainder is made up of four and a half lines (rhymed *dcbdc*). Each section, then, is reduced by one-quarter, so the essential proportions of the Italian sonnet, 8:6, are preserved in the

curtal sonnet as 6:4½. There is one significant compromise however: it would be difficult to split a five-measure line into two equal
halves (which the poet must be able to do, for the sake of the final
line). Hopkins gets round this by using six-stress lines throughout,
and making the final line a three-stress one:

PEACE

When will you ever, Peace, wild wooddove, shy wings
    shut,     *a*
Your  round me roaming end, and under be my boughs?     *b*
When,  when Peace, will you, Peace? I'll not play hypocrite     *c*

To  own my heart: I yield you do come sometimes; but     *a*
That  piecemeal peace is poor peace. What pure peace allows     *b*
A·larms of wars, the daunting wars, the death of it?     *c*

O  surely, reaving Peace, my Lord should leave in lieu     *d*
Some  good! And so he does leave Patience exquisite,     *c*
That  plumes to Peace thereafter. And when Peace here does
    house     *b*
He  comes with work to do, he does not come to coo,     *d*
He  comes to brood and sit.     *c*

The curtal sonnet remains more of a curiosity than anything else; it
is hard to imagine that anything further will ever be done with it –
but of course one never knows. Even more aberrant is the *reverse
sonnet*, a humorous creation of the early-twentieth-century British
poet, Rupert Brooke. As far as I know there is only a single example
of this genre. Brooke took the main weakness of the English sonnet,
its disproportionate balance of douzain and couplet, and turned
them to comic effect by reversing the usual order of things. First
comes the couplet, then follows the backwards-working douzain.
This progression is paralleled by the content of the poem, which
begins at its climactic point, then closes with inconsequentiality.

Hand trembling towards hand; the amazing lights     *a*
Of  heart and eye. They stood on supreme heights.     *a*

Ah, the delirious weeks of honeymoon!     *b*
Soon they returned, and, after strange adventures,     *c*
Settled at Balham by the end of June.     *b*

| | |
|---|---|
| Their money was in Can. Pacs. B. Debentures, | *c* |
| And in Antofagastas. Still he went | *d* |
| Cityward daily; still she did abide | *e* |
| At home. And both were really quite content | *d* |
| With work and social pleasures. Then they died. | *e* |
| They left three children (besides George, who drank): | *f* |
| The eldest, Jane, who married Mr Bell, | *g* |
| William, the head-clerk in the County Bank, | *f* |
| And Henry, a stock-broker, doing well. | *g* |

Brooke underscores his joke with continual rhythmic variation. A standard English sonnet might commonly begin with five-stress lines of more or less regular duple rhythm, working towards greater freedom and irregularity as the conclusion is reached. Brooke, however, places his most rhythmically irregular lines at the beginning, then gradually works towards lines of increasing regularity, such as the splendid:

With **work** and **social pleasures. Then** they **died.**
  ●○          ●○      ●○              ●○              ●

The bathos of the final lines is underlined by rhythms which seem deficient. The last line, in particular, has to be given a most unusual syntactical stress if it is to have a full five measures:

And **Henry, a** stock-**broker,** doing **well**
  ●○      ●○          ●○            ●○      ●

In normal speech, of course, the line would have only four measures, beginning with two of rather light-sounding triple rhythm:

And **Henry, a** stock-**broker,** doing **well**
  ●○○        ●○○              ●○      ●

The fact that Brooke chose the English sonnet form to parody is interesting, as it points up the essential weakness of the douzain–couplet division. It would be far more difficult to write a reverse sonnet parodying the Italian form, which is considerably more amorphous and diverse in its potential.

Finally, another sonnet curiosity, the *submerged sonnet*, or sonnet contained within a larger form. A notable example occurs in a larger work already mentioned, T. S. Eliot's *The Waste Land*.

Here is the stretch of lines in which it is found. I leave it to you to determine where it begins – and how it ends.

> . . . I too awaited the expected guest.
>    He, the young man carbuncular, arrives,
> A small house agent's clerk, with one bold stare,
>    One of the low on whom assurance sits
> As a silk hat on a Bradford millionaire.
> The time is now propitious, as he guesses,
> The meal is ended, she is bored and tired,
> En · deavours to engage her in caresses
> Which still are unreproved, if undesired.
>    Flushed and decided, he assaults at once;
> Ex · ploring hands encounter no defence;
> His vanity requires no response,
> And makes a welcome of indifference.
> (And I Tiresias have foresuffered all
>    En · acted on this same divan or bed;
>    I who have sat by Thebes below the wall
> And walked among the lowest of the dead.)
> Be · stows one final patronising kiss,
> And gropes his way, finding the stairs unlit . . .

We must not leave this brief consideration of the sonnet without mentioning sonnet sequences – so popular in Elizabethan times, and still surviving in various forms today. Shakespeare's sonnets make up the best-known of all English sonnet sequences, yet between the years 1591 (with Sidney's *Astrophil and Stella*) and 1597 (Tofte's *Laura*) we know of seventeen others – and there were probably many more which have not survived. (Shakespeare's were published a little later, in 1609.) Some of these sequences were arranged as a *corona* (from the Latin, 'crown'), in which the last line of one sonnet is repeated as the first line of the next, the closing line of the whole sequence being the same as the opening one. Even more fiendishly ingenious was the *sonnet redoublé* ('redoubled sonnet'), a corona of precisely fifteen sonnets in which all the linking lines of the first fourteen sonnets appear *in order* as the fifteenth sonnet. Presumably one wrote the last sonnet first, then proceeded to fill in the rest of the sequence.

The popularity of the sonnet form has continued to our own day, reaching fine flowerings in the work of Donne, Milton, Wordsworth, Keats and Hopkins – though many other poets wrote excellently in the form and might be added to this brief list. Modern poets who have written sequences of sonnets, sometimes departing from traditional models to develop their own unique forms, include John Crowe Ransom ('Two Gentlemen in Bonds'), Edna St Vincent Millay ('Sonnets from an Ungrafted Tree'), Dylan Thomas ('Altarwise by Owl-light'), W. H. Auden ('Sonnets from China'), John Berryman (*Berryman's Sonnets*) and Robert Lowell (*Notebooks*). Lowell's speciality is unrhymed sonnets which preserve only the essential metre and 8:6 division of the traditional Italian sonnet. Berryman's *Dream Songs* (see no. 72 for two examples) have often been loosely compared to sonnets in their use of a fixed rhyme and stanza form, though Berryman has three stanzas of six lines each, instead of one of the traditional fourteen-line sonnet forms. Finally, the poem which concludes the anthology section, 'Married Love' by Sherod Santos, also has many of the attributes of an unrhymed sonnet, though the main structural break occurs at the end of the ninth line, and some of the lines have six or seven, rather than five, stresses.

The notion of unrhymed sonnets leads us on to the subject of unrhymed poetry in general. We saw earlier that non-metrical poetry can be perceived as such only if a well-established tradition of metrical poetry already exists. The same holds true of non-rhyming poetry, which comes at the end of a long tradition of rhyming poetry. Many listeners today still expect poetry to rhyme; and in all periods of English poetry some kind of phonemic patterning has been used – either alliterative or rhyming – to link the lines and stanzas of the poem. Phonemic patterning in poetry is a well-established cultural norm – and poetry which avoids it for effect depends on the audience's awareness of this norm.

Many examples of how this works may be found in the plays of Shakespeare. By his time, rhymed five-stress couplets had been the norm in poetry for two centuries. Shakespeare continues to use five-stress lines, but typically does not rhyme them (this is known as *blank verse*). None the less, he may still – particularly in his earlier-to-middle works – use rhyme to round off a speech (particularly before the speaker exits) or a scene, as in the conclusion of this dialogue from *Richard II* (II.iv):

*Captain:*

> 'Tis thought the King is dead. We will not stay.
> The bay trees in our country are all wither'd,
> And meteors fright the fixed stars of heaven.
> The pale-fac'd moon looks bloody on the earth,
> And lean-look'd prophets whisper fearful change.
> Rich men look sad and ruffians dance and leap,
> The one in fear to lose what they enjoy,
> The other to enjoy by rage and war.
> These signs forerun the death or fall of kings.
> Fare·well. Our countrymen are gone and fled,
> As well assur'd Richard their king is dead.

[*Exit.*]

*Salisbury:*

> Ah, Richard! With the eyes of heavy mind
> I see thy glory like a shooting star
> Fall to the base earth from the firmament.
> Thy sun sets weeping in the lowly west,
> Witnessing storms to come, woe, and unrest.
> Thy friends are fled to wait upon thy foes,
> And crossly to thy good all fortune goes.

[*Exit.*]

Shakespeare's lines of blank verse are not closer to 'ordinary language' than are rhymed couplets, but actually one step further away from it. In any case, the success of the effect depends on the audience's familiarity with earlier poetry in couplets.

Finally, we should look at one particularly English fixed form which still survives, and which seems as healthy as ever: the *limerick*. Invented, as far as we know, by a Victorian, Edward Lear, the limerick is usually printed as a five-line stanza, rhymed *aabba*:

| | |
|---|---|
| There once was a young man from Sheen | *a* |
| Whose musical ear was not keen. | *a* |
| He said, 'It is odd, | *b* |
| But I cannot tell "God | *b* |
| Save the Weasel" from "Pop Goes the Queen".' | *a* |

This is what the eye sees. But the limerick above all depends on its sound – its lolloping rhythm and its comic rhymes. And what we perceive when we *hear* a limerick is the old traditional nursery-rhyme stanza: four lines, each having four stresses (the first, second, and fourth close with a silent stress*), and with an internal rhyme, such as 'odd/God', in the third line:

| There | once was a | young man from | Sheen | |
|---|---|---|---|---|
| | ●○○ | ●○○ | ● | */○ |
| Whose | musical | ear was not | keen | |
| | ●○○ | ●○○ | ● | */○ |
| He | said 'It is | odd, but I | cannot tell | "God |
| | ●○○ | ●○○ | ●○○ | ●/○○ |
| Save the | Weasel" from | "Pop Goes the | Queen".' | |
| | ●○○ | ●○○ | ● | * |

The comic appeal of the limerick lies in the challenge of finding rhymes – three *a*-rhymes, and two *b*-rhymes in close proximity. The usual solution calls upon some degree of forcing, which in itself may contribute to the humour. Double and triple rhymes are often used to exaggerate the effect, as in a well-known example by Dixon Lanier Merrit:

A wonderful bird is the pelican,
His bill will hold more than his belican.
He can take in his beak
Food e·nough for a week,
But I'm damned if I see how the helican.

There is much more to the limerick than I have mentioned here – for example, it is virtually mandatory that it first of all introduce a person or thing, often from a named town or country, and then expound on one or more of its peculiar characteristics. The audience for the limerick is also a fairly limited one. But all this comes under the heading of cultural conventions, which we'll look at more closely in Chapter 7.

---

*See Chapter 2, pp. 22–3 on the silent stress as a common feature of English folk metres.

This survey has clearly taken us a long way from the first crude couplets of Old English. Yet the development of practically all our most complex forms took place within two or three centuries of that time. By the sixteenth century all the standard poetic forms of English poetry were being used. Any departure from them since has been a matter of individual experiment, creating no fashions.

It is curious, as Josephine Miles has pointed out, that certain periods were more given to fixed forms, while others took more pleasure in poetry which relied on a line-by-line development, as with couplets or the *blank verse* (unrhymed five-stress lines) of Milton (no. 27) and Wordsworth (no. 34). Present-day taste shies away from all but the most 'informal' of forms. Even such a gifted poet as Robert Lowell suffered a considerable decline of critical esteem with the publication of his unrhymed sonnets. Most poets now would probably avoid forms as grandiose as the traditional sonnet, rondel or ballade; or schemes as complex as *ottava rima*, *rime royale*, or the Spenserian stanza. The poet's approach today seems to accord with the words of the twentieth-century Greek poet, George Seferis: 'All I want is to speak simply, for this grace I pray.'

# 6 The Poem on the Page

*He does not write whose verses no one reads.*
*– Martial*

In its beginnings, with the dawn of human language, poetry was simply an oral art – an entertainment, a communicative and demonstrative game of skill based on socially recognized speech-sounds. We have no idea how many thousands of years passed before people tried to record their word-sounds in some permanent form. The earliest writing we know of is from the thirtieth century BC, and this is only a kind of representational shorthand – its shapes symbolize external objects, not speech-sounds. (The same is still true of certain scripts today – such as that used by the Chinese.) Only much closer to our own times, around the ninth century BC, do we find the first use of symbols to represent the actual sounds of speech. The most ancient surviving written poem, the *Odyssey* of Homer, is a mere twenty-eight centuries old.

Until very recent times script and print were the only ways in which the sounds of speech could be preserved. What we know of our earliest poems depends wholly on the survival of written records. We may speculate all we like about the nature or the performance or the sound of the earliest English poetry, but these speculations are no more than educated guesses based on the chance survival over many centuries of a few pieces of stone or skin or paper. We have no better way to put together a credible picture. And though the evidence is dim and imperfect, it does offer a number of suggestive clues.

A complicating factor is that many single poems, and even whole genres of poetry, did not survive because the people of the times when they were popular did not consider them worthy of preservation. In the Old English and Early Middle English periods all written records were hand-copied. The people who did the copying were clerics employed by the scriptoria ('writing-rooms') of the medieval monasteries. It must be assumed that only material approved by the governing officials of these institutions would generally have been recorded in manuscript form. This is why religious, moral, and didactic poetry bulks so large in the annals of our early literature, and why secular material plays so small a part. Not until the thirteenth and fourteenth centuries is there a relaxing of this attitude; only after that time does secular material begin its gradual ascendance to the dominating position it holds today.

It is difficult for us to grasp the full implications of this, particularly as far as the art of poetry and its performance are concerned; to do so, we must make a considerable effort of imagination. We might compare early poetry with improvised jazz today, which is seldom written down (though it is recorded on disc and tape). People ten centuries from now will form quite an erroneous picture of the sound and performance of improvised jazz if all they have to go by are the few written transcriptions of live performance which exist. This is not only because so few performances are recorded in this way, but also because of all that can *not* be transcribed in conventional notation – particularly the unique way in which jazz 'swings'. Furthermore, we can easily think of many other kinds of extraneous but highly pervasive oral material today which may not survive at all – the obsessive dogmas of radio and television ads, schoolchildren's game-chants and songs, the intonations of broadcast racing commentaries, a fundamentalist preacher's pitch, the spiel of an auctioneer – all of which may play some part in the creation of poetry today. To most of us, a good deal of this material is so familiar and insignificant that it would probably never occur to us to bother trying to record it, especially in a medium as far removed from sound as print.

If we speculate about the sound and performance of Old English poetry, we have to deal with sketchy and incomplete evidence. Most scholars generally agree on the pronunciation of Old English (see Appendix B for a short guide to this) – but it would be illuminating (and possibly quite amusing) if we could waft these worthies back into the Dark Ages and let them put their theories to the test. Even their most polished pronunciations might well turn out to be incomprehensible to the people of those times.

By the time we get to Chaucer, we are on firmer ground. Most former English students can intone the opening lines of *The Canter-*

*bury Tales* (and many do so in the most unlikely places). The knack, of course, as in any public performance, is to appear confident, and consistent, in your pronunciation – and to pray that there aren't any other 'experts' in the crowd. In any case, any reading of Old or Middle English is very much a reconstruction, based on internal evidence – sound patterns such as alliteration and rhyme – together with occasional references in the literature to specific matters of pronunciation which occasionally come up. Obviously, no one alive today has ever heard real Middle English spoken – nor the English of Shakespeare, Donne, Milton, nor even Wordsworth. Not until a century ago, with the invention of sound recording, could the sounds of speech, including poetry, be preserved with any fidelity.

Our twenty-six-letter Roman alphabet is a crude way to record the sounds of our speech. When Irish missionaries introduced it to England and began to use it for recording English speech-sounds, they tried to be consistent in the way they did this, and to render these sounds in a more or less phonetic way, with certain letters or combinations of letters consistently standing for certain speech-sounds. This worked fine through the Middle English period, as every scribe and copyist could be his own orthographer, spelling each word in what seemed the best way to convey its pronunciation. Uniformity of spelling was not an important consideration, as long as a reader could 'hear' the written word and know what it was. Even as late a writer as Shakespeare could sign his own name in a variety of ways – Shakspear, Shaxpere, and so on – without eyebrows being raised. The important thing was always the speech-sounds the letters symbolized. The letters were only a means to this end.

Problems began to develop after the introduction of printed books to England by William Caxton in the late fifteenth century. All at once, people all over the nation could encounter the same work at the same time, as multiple copies of a single work became available. Caxton's books were read in areas of the British Isles where pronunciation and even vocabulary were quite different. People in such areas would have found reading these books as difficult as we might find reading a modern book in Dutch today. But Caxton's shop was in London, and this became the centre of British publishing, which it still is. This fact, together with the influential location of the royal court in London, meant that people in other parts of Britain had to get used little by little to the standards of London vocabulary and spelling, even where these did not reflect the sounds of their own speech. Moreover, the influence of print now meant that spelling conventions became more widespread and fixed, even though regional pronunciations were still quite different.

Thus began the gradual split of sound and script which has persisted until the present, when English orthography is one of the most difficult aspects of our language. English today is heard all over the world, in numerous different dialects and pronunciations which continue to evolve. The idea of one standard 'phonetic' English spelling, so often raised by idealists, is for this reason alone quite impracticable. Even moderate spelling reforms, such as those introduced in the USA in the nineteenth century ('color' for 'colour', 'meter' for 'metre', and the like), have only made the global problem more complicated – particularly in a country such as Canada where both forms are commonly used, and consistency in spelling (at least as between 'UK' and 'US' spelling) is now out of the question.

We have rambled some distance from the subject of poetry, but it is important to be aware of all the difficulties raised by the poem in print. First, in the case of our older poetry, we must be aware that what we have of the poem on a page may only be the vaguest approximation of the sound it actually made when it was first conceived. The written record may not have been made until centuries after the poem was created (as was the case with *Beowulf*); furthermore it may be loaded with accretions, deletions and other overlays to confuse us further. Second, and just as important, the written record gives us little idea of the performance of poetry at the time – a matter which is examined more fully in the next chapter.

As far as we know, few people in Old English times actually read poetry, at least in the sense that one 'reads' a book of poetry today. The poet (or 'scop', to use the term of the times) declaimed the alliterative lines of an epic such as *Beowulf* or shorter poems such as 'The Seafarer' or 'The Wanderer' to an audience, possibly as part of the celebrations at a midwinter feast or other entertainment. Some sort of musical accompaniment, a reinforcement of the regular stresses of the lines, may have been part of this performance. The mainstay of the Old English poet's art was the memorized formula through which prefabricated sequences (for example, dealing with such topics as the arming of a warrior or the architecture of a hall) were slotted in to bulk out the story. The version of *Beowulf* which we know today was probably the result of a single recitation by a single poet – but the Beowulf story must have been told by tens, even hundreds, of different singers, each of them reciting the tale a little differently every time. There was no *one* authentic version of an Old English epic, just as, a few centuries later, there was no *one* authentic version of a traditional ballad.

By the time of Chaucer this picture had changed considerably. Manuscript production was more sophisticated and systematic; there are, for example, ten surviving manuscripts of *The Canterbury Tales* from Chaucer's time or soon after it, which indicates that there must have been a much larger number of them at the time. Interestingly, an illustration in one of the surviving manuscripts of Chaucer's *Troilus and Criseyde* appears to show Chaucer himself reading his poem (from a manuscript copy) to an assembled audience. It is quite possible that some of Chaucer's audience would have been able to read and write, but many others would have been more or less illiterate. Reading and writing were skills still very much limited to the clergy and to scholars. Moreover, a single handwritten copy of a literary work was extremely expensive – so a large personal library was not a common thing.

With Caxton's press and the start of mass production of books, the price of reading material began to decline markedly. As more and more people could afford books, so more and more were motivated to learn to read and write. By Shakespeare's time, a century later, an avid general readership had already come into being. This explains the burgeoning popularity of poetry, essays and plays in printed form at that time.

Now, although poetry had already begun its move away from the area of a strictly oral art form to that of one founded on print, this process was not as sudden as we might suppose. For one thing, printed paper books, particularly in the first two or three centuries after Caxton, were still generally treated as records of speech-sounds – rather as we would treat a music score today. Well beyond Shakespeare's time, most people were in the habit of reading their books aloud, even when they were quite alone. Indeed, until comparatively recent times, it was common that readers would still move their lips to 'pronounce' the words they were reading, even though they did not speak them aloud. The few readers skilled enough to be able to read silently and without lip movements were greatly admired by others – rather as we today might be impressed by the ability of someone trained in music to 'hear' the polyphonies and harmonies of a piece of music while silently reading the printed score.

Not long after Caxton, though, began the process in which printed speech was to become something important in itself, something separate from the sound of speech. This is the point at which the traditional nature and aims of poetry began to be forgotten. The development of modern reading habits, which call for visual recognition of printed symbols rather than aural perception of spoken symbols, made (and continues to make) it difficult for most readers to react to the medium of poetry as encountered in the form of a printed record.

However, poetry is still primarily an oral art, in spite of mass-produced books and widespread literacy. In a world where print-based literary genres – the novel, the short story, the essay, the autobiography – dominate the marketplace, the only hope now for the survival of poetry is that it be perceived above all else as oral performance, even though most people's main source of poetry will continue to be the printed page. Ultimately, if the reader has enough familiarity and experience in hearing a certain poem, it should leave the page and enter the memory. Only then may it be fully savoured. (Similarly, in a practised performance of a piece of music, the printed score is usually not needed.) This is why so much emphasis has traditionally been placed on memorizing poetry in schools. Memorizing certainly does have the advantage of causing us to hear, speak, and remember the sounds of a poem instead of just eye-reading them, but the idea usually backfires in a schoolroom because not everybody likes the same poem. And, ideally, memorizing a poem should be something one *wants* to do. A more sensible and realistic approach might be for each individual first of all to find a poem that pleases, and only then to reread, comprehend, and finally memorize the poem for its most effective realization.

Caxton's press brought another change in the public attitude to poetry, a significant one. Until printed books, the majority of people who had come into contact with poetry would only have *heard* it – like the majority of people who come into contact with music today. If any underlying structural patterns were to be perceived, they would have to be perceived aurally. This is why, until the time of Caxton, poetic forms are fairly simple. Alliteration linking two halves of one line, couplets linking two lines – these were the standards of poetic form. It takes a dull ear not to be able to perceive them, or not to be able to form, in a short while, some sort of conception of the 'line' of a given poem, even when this line is something in the air rather than something visible to the eye.

By the time of Chaucer, a taste for more complex forms had already begun to develop, as the surviving poetry shows. On one hand, for example, we have the skilful combination of alliteration and rhyme in a single stanza form, found in *Sir Gawain and the Green Knight* (no. 6), created by a poet living somewhere near present-day Liverpool. (This explains why the language is so different from Chaucer's, even though the two poets were contemporaries.) On the other, we have the adoption into English of such fixed forms as the rondeau, ballade and *rime royale* stanza (all mentioned in Chapter 5) – forms which demand a much larger conceptual grasp, and a complete familiarity with earlier forms, of the audience.

None the less, the most complex fixed forms in English were not possible until the advent of the printed book. After it came the rise of *terza rima*; the Spenserian stanza, with its most demanding rhyme-scheme; the first popular English sonnet sequences, culminating in Shakespeare's; and ultimately the *ottava rima* stanza of Byron's *Don Juan* (no. 38) – a form which in this case uses the appeal of sound for its wit and humour, but depends on its visual appearance for a full appreciation of its intricate craftsmanship. *Don Juan* may be seen as the simultaneous peak of the oral and the printed traditions of English poetry.

Since Byron's time, even though many people continued to read poetry out loud (indeed, some still do so), the dominance of print has brought widespread confusion over how to approach and read poetry for best effect. Performing poetry is an act which seems alien to our own times. Even passively listening to a recording of a poem is not an activity which is likely outside a classroom. Yet, as I have argued consistently throughout this book, if we do not hear the poem we read, its main magic is bound to be lost on us.

However much poetry may be an oral art, the odds are that the first time we encounter a poem it will be in the form of a printed text. If we are literate, we should encounter no difficulty in visually apprehending the words of this text. Beyond the words, however, we run into a number of more or less arbitrary printing conventions peculiar to poetry which distinguish it in appearance from other forms of printed language. Some of these may cause difficulties, as we shall see.

Here is a well-known poem by Robert Burns as it is usually printed (it appears, with stress column, as no. 32 in the anthology section):

### A Red, Red Rose

O My Luve's like a red, red rose,
   That's newly sprung in June;
O My Luve's like the melodie
   That's sweetly played in tune.

As fair art thou, my bonnie lass,
   So deep in luve am I;
And I will luve thee still, my dear,
   Till a' the seas gang dry.

Till a' the seas gang dry, my dear,
   And the rocks melt wi' the sun:
O I will love thee still, my dear,
   While the sands o' life shall run.

And fare thee weel, my only luve,
   And fare thee weel awhile!
And I will come again, my luve,
   Though it were ten thousand mile.

Now, leaving aside all questions relating to rhythm and metre, sound patterning (in this case, rhyme), choice of words, and stanza organization – in other words, leaving aside most of the primary effects of the poem – what strikes us most about the way it looks on the page?

First of all, the printed poem enables us to see line and stanza divisions clearly and as a whole. A quick look is enough to show us that it is in quatrains and that there are four stanzas in all. If we were listening to this poem for the first time and had never seen it in print, we might not be absolutely certain it was in quatrains until after the end of the second stanza, and of course we wouldn't know how long it was until it had come to an end. So the first glance at any printed poem immediately acquaints us with these two kinds of information.

Next, we can easily see that rhyme is of structural importance in the organization of the quatrain stanzas of the poem, and that the rhyme-scheme is a relatively informal one, *xaxa*. It may also strike us as interesting that each of the lines begins with a capital (upper-case) letter, even though it does not necessarily mark the start of a new sentence or occur in a place where we would normally expect a capital to be used. The convention of beginning each line with a capital was not firmly established until the time of Caxton, and many poets then and since have felt perfectly free to disregard it as unnecessary and irrelevant.

A further convention in the poem as printed above is that the second and fourth lines of each stanza are indented. Why is this? We might take it as an indication that the second and fourth lines are in some way different from the first and third – and this turns out to be true: lines one and three contain four stressed syllables, but two and four have only three, ending with a silent stress. However, the metre of all the lines is the same: four duplets, the main metre of English popular poetry.

Another piece of information conveyed by the indentations is that the second and fourth lines rhyme. But it would make more sense, if one wanted to show the rhyme-scheme as clearly as possible, to line up the ends, not the beginnings, of the lines, like this:

        *x*          *a*

O My Luve's like a red, red rose,
    That's newly sprung in June;

  O My Luve's like the melodie
    That's sweetly played in tune.

and so forth. In fact, in earlier times typographical conventions such as these often reflected an editor's rather than a poet's views. If Burns's poem had been composed in Old English and recorded by a contemporary scribe it might have looked more like this:

O My Luve's like a red red rose that's newly
sprung in June O My Luve's like the melodie
that's sweetly played in tune As fair art thou
my bonnie lass so deep in luve am I and I will . . .

and so on. As I have already said, eight or ten centuries ago written poetry was viewed as no more than a recording of a sound art. But by Burns's time the *look* of the poem on the page is as important a feature as the *sound* it happens to make – at least on one's first encounter with it.

Before we leave the matter of the printed appearance of conventional poetry, I need to raise a thorny problem, one which takes us right back to matters of rhythm, metre and phonemic patterning. It has to do with our conception of what a poetic line is – where we conceive of the line as beginning and ending. Let's look at a more complex example of conventionally printed poetry, a short lyric by Byron (no. 37):

### So We'll Go No More A-roving

So we'll go no more a-roving
　So late into the night,
Though the heart be still as loving,
　And the moon be still as bright.

For the sword outwears its sheath,
　And the soul wears out the breast,
And the heart must pause to breathe,
　And love itself have rest.

Though the night was made for loving,
　And the day returns too soon,
Yet we'll go no more a-roving
　By the light of the moon.

The metre of this poem is the same as that of the Burns poem above. However, let us lay the first lines out in more detail, using the notation explained in Chapter 2:

| So we'll | go no | more a- | roving | |
|---|---|---|---|---|
| | ●○ | ●○ | ●○ | */○ |
| So | late in- | to the | night | |
| | ●○ | ●○ | ● | */○○ |
| Though the | heart be | still as | loving, | |
| | ●○ | ●○ | ●○ | */○○ |
| And the | moon be | still as | bright | |
| | ●○ | ●○ | ● | */○○ |
| For the | . . . | | | |

Right away we may note a kind of overlap between the poem's printed lines and its rhythmical groups. Each of these lines begins with one or two unstressed syllables which, metrically speaking, are part of the last measure of the preceding line. At the same time, each of these final measures itself lacks a spoken stress (this is indicated by the asterisk). We have seen the same effect in nursery rhymes such as 'Three Blind Mice' (see p. 22). In the case of Byron's poem, a clearer picture of the rhythmic organization of the lines might be given if they were printed so that each of the final measures appeared all in one place, at the end of each line:

| So we'll | go no | more a- | roving | \| So |
|---|---|---|---|---|
| | ●○ | ●○ | ●○ | *○ |
| | late in- | to the | night, | \| Though the |
| | ●○ | ●○ | ●○ | *○○ |
| | heart be | still as | loving, | \| And the |
| | ●○ | ●○ | ●○ | *○○ |
| | moon be | still as | bright. | \| For the . . . |
| | ●○ | ●○ | ● | *○○ |

The obvious drawback of treating the line in this way is that the rhyming syllables no longer come at the end; and traditionally rhyme which is used as a structural principle has always been heard as marking the end of the line. There is no neat way to resolve the conflict between line organization by rhythm and line organization by rhyme (or other sound patterning), though our ears have long since become used to accommodating it.

Byron's poem is more troublesome than most in that every line, as I have indicated, may be thought of as ending with a silent stress, equivalent to a musical rest, followed by one or two weak syllables which open the following line. Even in a more regular four-measure line, such as that found in Housman's 'Loveliest of trees' (no. 55), however, we may note the same clash between the rhyme-ended lines (as they are conventionally printed):

> And since to look at things in bloom
> Fifty springs are little room,
> About the woodlands I will go
> To see the cherry hung with snow

and the rhythmical measures of the metrical line:

| And | since to | look at | things in | bloom |
|-----|----------|---------|-----------|-------|
|     | ●○ | ●○ | ●○ | ● |
|     | Fifty | springs are | little | room, \| A- |
|     | ●○ | ●○ | ●○ | ●○ |
|     | bout the | woodlands | I will | go \| To |
|     | ●○ | ●○ | ●○ | ●○ |
|     | see the | cherry | hung with | snow. |
|     | ●○ | ●○ | ●○ | ● |

There is no easy answer to this problem. In fact, the conflict of print and sound may be seen as one of the main factors contributing to the particular richness of poetry. You should try to be continually aware of these two opposing demands when you read a poem – whether its organizing principle is alliteration or rhyme, whether it is in the form of blank or non-metrical verse. And you should be aware of them as two independent effects which work at the same time. This takes some skill, especially if you are going to hear them both clearly. By and large the typographical format of a poem *is* arbitrary, simply a guide to the sound it makes. This is why I have had no qualms about rearranging the lines of the anthology selections in a way which highlights the first stress of each line. In a way, this approach reflects the increased attention which twentieth-century poets have given to the visual appearance of their poems. A pioneer in this was the American poet e. e. cummings. (The unconventional absence of capital letters in his printed name is public homage not only to his role as a poet, but also to the importance of his views on typography.) In fact, many of cummings's poems turn out to be quite rhythmically regular when read aloud. The words and sounds of much other recent poetry are sprinkled randomly over the field of the page, with no easily perceptible method at work. Arrangements of this sort are usually taken as mere intuition and idiosyncrasy on the part of the poet, simply one more way to make the language of the poem as different from ordinary English as possible.

Certain writers, among them the American theorist Charles Olsen, have argued that typographical arrangement should be used as a guide to performance; and, in particular, that the regular spacing of typewriter print lends itself to use as a precise guide to pauses and other effects of timing in performance. John Cage, an American musician and theorist, has even published lectures in a quasi-metrical form, in which stress-groups are arranged in vertical columns. To show how Cage's notation works,

| I could continue | writing this chaper | just like this, and |
| thereby hope | all of you reading would | follow it through. |

This underlines the isochronous nature of the delivery of stresses in ordinary English speech. The reader's eye supposedly spends roughly the same amount of time on each group of words, so that the opening stresses of each group are heard as equally spaced in time. (Actually, each of the above groups contains two stresses.)

Even as early as medieval times, some poets and scribes had begun to experiment with striking ways in which to arrange written or printed poems on a page. This tradition reached a peak with some of the poems of George Herbert (seventeenth century), which he laid out in the shapes of wings, altars, communion chalices, and so on. More modern poets primarily noted for the sound of their works – such as G. M. Hopkins and Dylan Thomas – also composed works in which the shape of the printed stanza is part of the appeal. In all of these, however, the pleasure offered by recognizing the symbolic shape of the printed stanza, and the poet's cleverness in devising it, declines markedly after the initial impact. If you do continue to enjoy the poem it is more likely to be because of its sound than its

Fury said to a
mouse, That he
met in the
house,
"Let us
both go to
law: *I* will
prosecute
*you*. – Come,
I'll take no
denial; We
must have a
trial: For
really this
morning I've
nothing
to do."
Said the
mouse to the
cur, "Such
a trial,
dear Sir,
With
no jury
or judge,
would be
wasting
our
breath."
"I'll be
judge, I'll
be jury,"
Said
cunning
old Fury:
"I'll
try the
whole
cause,
and
condemn
you
to
death."

striking shape. The only exception to this, in my view, is Lewis Carroll's tale of a cat and mouse, written in rhymed four-stress lines (it appears in Chapter III of *Alice in Wonderland*), which was, is, and always will be a printed 'tail' above all else.

In recent decades, however, a new kind of printed poetry has appeared, one which depends primarily on visual appearance, and little, if at all, on sound. Indeed, much of this poetry cannot be read out loud at all. I use the term *eye-poetry* to refer to it, though other labels, such as 'visual poetry' or 'optic poetry', have also been used. The first eye-poetry appeared in the early 1950s in Switzerland (Eugen Gomringer) and in Brazil (the Noigandres group). Most of its first exponents had some grounding in the visual arts (painting, sculpture, typography, architecture) as well as literature, and were avowedly liberating poetry from the confines of traditional grammar and the linear conventions of the printed page. Eye-poetry conceived this liberation in visual, rather than aural, terms. The symbols used to communicate the sound of the traditional poem were made the sole point of interest, and sound was treated as of little or no consequence.

Eye-poetry, then, is non-literary in emphasis. It follows that most literary comment about it is likely to be at least inadequate, if not completely off the mark. It is a medium which has sprung from the widespread public perception – increasing with the spread of universal literacy – of the poem as a mainly printed object, rather than a speech-sound performance. Eye-poetry depends totally on visual appeal, except to the degree that all literate people may to some degree 'hear' the phonetic potential of any conventional typographic symbol they see. Unlike the traditional poem, which, at least in performance, has to be perceived serially as sound revealed in time, the eye-poem comes across as a whole piece, all at once.

The genre of eye-poetry is usually included in the larger category of *concrete poetry*: creative works which highlight single aspects of language other than the usual referential ones of every day. In the case of eye-poetry, emphasis is on the medium of the printed letter or word only. Another field of concrete poetry, more closely related to the traditional bases of English poetry, is *ear-poetry*, also known as 'phonic poetry' or 'sound poetry', in which emphasis is on the spoken sound only. In an ear-poem, certain patterns of sound are

*April Diver*

**SPRING!**

board board **board** board **board** board board

**SPLASH!**

*waterwaterwaterwaterwaterwaterwater*     *waterwater*

used to create a temporal and linear design which may also have little to do with the referential aspects of ordinary language (though it may depend on phonolexis for some of its effects). For example:

*The History of My Uncle's Monocle*

**oh my** eye my eye my my
**oh** eye my **eye** my eye eye
eye **oh** eye my eye my eye
**my oh my** eye eye my eye

The modern ear-poem had its beginnings in the French Dadaist movement of the early twentieth century. One of the most noted ear-poems in English is Louis Zukofsky's 'Julia's Wild' (no. 79), which rearranges the words from a line of Shakespeare's *Two Gentlemen of Verona* over and over, until the sound of its ten-syllable line reverberates in the mind as an independently living thing, far removed from the referential sense of Shakespeare's original line.

Part of the effect of an ear-poem may be communicated to a reader who only looks at the lines on the page (we may call this the 'concrete' effect), but, as in all traditional poetry, the full impact can only be found in the hearing. This is also true of the *action-poem*, in which two or more voices are used in a sound performance as closely related to drama as it is to traditional poetry, though the printed action-poem too may incidentally offer some secondary appeal to the eye. As in all traditional poetry, the main attractions of action- and ear-poetry are those of rhythm and metre, sound patterning, phonolexis, and any literary and other cultural overtones that may be present.

What all concrete poems have in common is that, although they grow out of language, they make us put aside our everyday ideas about what language (even creative language) is and what it may be used for. The eye-poem is analogous to sculpture or painting: it must be viewed, without any artistic preconceptions, for its effect. The ear-poem is analogous to music: it must be heard, without any linguistic preconceptions, to work. And the action-poem is analogous to drama: it must be experienced in acted performance, as a dialectical interaction of forces. In all cases, concrete poetry is something which must be perceived, absorbed non-linguistically, rather than *read*, in a literary sense. This asks a lot of the reader (whether viewer, listener, or audience participant) who may have to sacrifice many of the preconceptions of what poetry is and what it is likely to do. Of course, there is nothing new about such a demand in general – all innovative poetry of every age has made it, and it is the basis of all art.

Before we quit the territory of the typography of the poem, let's look for a moment at the importance of the printed book to our cultural conception of poetry – what it is and what it does. As we have seen, the Old English audience perceived poetry as a kind of word-juggling – a performance in which a story was told, but in language far-removed from that of simple reportage, language drawing attention to itself, and, by reflection, to the skill of the poet, for the entertainment and edification of all. To its audience, the poem itself had no more permanent existence than a whistled tune. Its attraction was evanescent, and linear – like a tune, all the more compelling because of its transience.

Since Caxton, however, the printed text of the poem has taken on its own independence. Ten centuries ago, an answer to the question, 'What is the language of poetry?' might have been: 'Speech-sounds which give pleasure and demand repetition for their own sake.' Today, our answer to the same question is more likely to be: 'Any literary text found within the context of a "book of poems".' This second definition may seem tautological or even facetious, but think about it for a moment. Generally speaking, the attention we give to the language of a poem is like the attention we may bestow on a screwdriver displayed in an art museum – quite different from the way we react to the same object in its everyday location in a toolbox or a kitchen drawer. The context in which we find the object determines our approach and attitude, the cultural conventions and expectations we bring to bear on it. The same is true of the poem: if we understand that it *is* a poem, our approach and reaction to it will be vastly different from our reaction to the same language in an everyday context. In the end, to paraphrase an old remark, the essence of the magic of poetry is in the ear of the reader or listener. Language cannot *be* a poem unless it is perceived so by its readers or listeners.

An interesting demonstration of this fact is the recent rise of another form, the *found poem*, which became popular for a time in the 1960s and 1970s. A found poem is linguistic material (usually printed language) taken from another context and presented in the context of a 'book of poems'. Here is an example, based on the words of a story which originally appeared in the sporting pages of an Australian newspaper:

> Pymbal shook his head with dismay,
> wrapped both hands around his throat
> as he walked from the final green.
> 'I have fingerprints all over my throat,'
> he said, 'I choked with fright.'
>
> Shoddy approach shots to the greens
> cost him strokes. Back on home soil
> he wondered 'how stupid a man can be'
> after his round. (He has had
> a year of misery on the greens.)
>
> Hailstorms & rain caused the first round
> of the tournament to be abandoned.
> 'I threw the putter back in a corner
> and used it again for the first time today.'
> (The e·vent will end on Sunday.)

Some poets, particularly in the last hundred years or so, have made use of the *epigraph*, a short quotation from earlier literary works printed at the head of a poem. It is often difficult to know whether an epigraph should be viewed as part of the poem itself, or as something more akin to an emotional stage direction for the reader's benefit. T. S. Eliot uses a six-line quotation from Dante's *Inferno*, in the original fourteenth-century Italian, as an epigraph for 'The Love Song of J. Alfred Prufrock' (no. 56). What is a modern reader, particularly one who speaks no Italian and may know no Dante, to make of this? Is it essential to our appreciation of 'Prufrock' that the source and the meaning of this epigraph be understood? If so, one would suppose that Eliot might have provided a translation, or at least a reference to the work from which it is taken – but he does neither. Perhaps, then, it is to be taken as an indirect assertion of the poet's wide-ranging and multilingual literary background, or as a kind of password between poet and a reader of similar background: 'If you recognize this as Dante and are able to understand the Italian and to appreciate why I have used it as an epigraph, then you and I will understand each other.'*

Although the importance of the printed poem has grown steadily during the past ten centuries – even to the point where it has largely usurped earlier social perception of the poem purely as a speech-sound performance – still the print itself must always be something secondary. We can't deny that easy access to print for an ever-wider audience has been a main condition of the creation and subsequent popularity of much great poetry of the last three or four centuries – from the sonnet sequences of the Elizabethans to the irregular typographical 'arrangements' of such twentieth-century poets as cummings. But we are also aware that the printed book must certainly be superseded by new media in the near future. It may be

---

* A literal translation of the Dante is: 'If I thought my answer were to someone who might ever return to the world, this flame would quake no more. But since no one has ever returned alive from this depth, if what I hear be true, I answer you without fear of infamy.' The words, which are in *Inferno*, Canto 27, lines 61–6, are spoken to the character of Dante by Guido de Montefeltro, one who is being punished for fraud. (Dante perceives him as a quaking flame.) The relevance of the quotation to 'Prufrock' is not immediately clear: it may have something to do with a personal confession of acts felt to be shameful or at least (in Prufrock's case) unworthy. Guido makes his confession under the mistaken belief that Dante too is condemned to hell for ever, and that he has nothing to lose in being frank. Eliot's epigraph may indicate that Prufrock's frankness is also based on false security proceeding from a mistaken assumption about the reader.

that poetry will then begin to communicate itself more effectively, to return to its traditional basis as a serial art based on the sounds of speech arranged in time. The more traditionally based poems of the past will survive the change with no trouble; the appeal of many will be strengthened by it, in fact. The actual sound of the poem, rather than its appearance, may once again become the primary reality of the art.

A final point: most poets working in the past four or five centuries (at least) have used written language as a means of working on and recording particular poems, even though these poems probably began in their creators' heads as sound – sometimes only as rhythms to which words were gradually fitted, sometimes as evocative phrases which were moved round on the paper until they combined effectively with others. Paper and ink (or typewriter or line printer) are an effective adjunct to memory, then, so that even though the end results may be speech-sound constructs, their creation is greatly facilitated by the written forms of language. Exactly the same sort of thing occurs in the composition and orchestration of music. Paper or other writing surfaces enable us to record our thoughts, to view them later, and to rearrange them without regard to confines of time. When the composition is complete and it is performed, time is reintroduced as its most vital component.

# 7 Society, Culture and the Poet

*The audience is the reward of the speaker.* – *Babylonian Talmud*

No poem can exist independently: it must be perceived as one to be one. The greatest works of Chaucer, Shakespeare, Donne, Milton or Keats live only as long as living audiences continue to enjoy them. In this chapter we'll look at the different social groups that poets of various periods have addressed, as well as some of the cultural attitudes of the audiences.

In the eighteenth century, Vico argued that in the beginning all language must be poetry. The first time that someone somewhere pointed to a rock and made some kind of speech-sound intended to symbolize the reality of that rock, we assume there must have been someone else there listening. Moreover, something in that sound must have appealed to that listener enough for the usage to become fixed, first for that listener, then for the community, and ultimately for the whole of that society. The appeal of the first sound was like the appeal of poetry: it was pleasurable and fit for what it was supposed to symbolize.

In a short time, however, the novelty of the sound of this new-born word would have begun to fade, just as the novelty of the sound of new words and expressions today soon does. Before long, their use becomes more utilitarian than pleasurable. This is the basis of everyday referential language: no longer do we have to point to or draw a likeness of an object: a mere sound will suffice. In time, most people will no longer remember the first poetic impact of the word, nor can they comprehend just why the sound seemed so 'right' to its first hearers, why it seemed to symbolize something else so well.

Sometimes, of course, we can guess at the origins of certain words. Obvious examples are the /æ.mæ/ and /æ.dæ/ (or /æ.bæ/) sounds, which in many languages evolve into symbols for mother and father respectively. These are the first sounds babies make, so it is an easy matter for attentive parents and siblings to reinforce and gradually condition the infant into hearing them as 'words' of a specific language, whether the final versions be 'ima' and 'abba' (Hebrew), 'maman' and 'papa' (French), 'mam' and 'tad' (Welsh), 'mom' and 'pop' (US English), or 'mum' and 'dad'. Many primitive words may have arisen in this way, through an initial process of oral experimentation followed by wider social acceptance of specific sound combinations as symbolizing certain things.

By the time of the tenth century a wide and sophisticated English vocabulary was well established. The origins of most everyday words would have been long forgotten by the average person. In such circumstances, a poet will still try to use everyday language in such a way that it draws attention to itself as the first spoken word sounds must have done. The Old English scop did this in a variety of ways: by making the sound pattern of alliteration the basis of the line; by a frequent use of kennings ('whale's way' and 'bound wood', in place of 'sea' and 'ship', have already been mentioned); by artful arrangement of syntax so that long, convoluted sentences are balanced by short, direct ones; and, above all, by employing regular, isochronous, stress-based speech rhythms.

Behind all this, as in every age, is the desire to make the language of poetry sound different from everyday language. Only by sounding different will it be perceived as 'poetic' by its audience. Furthermore, in all ages, the language of a new poem, if it is a true and worthwhile one, must be different in effect from the language of an old one. This is because, whatever else it may or may not do, the language of the poem has to draw attention to *itself* in order to exist, to be perceived as poetry. A new poem which does not sound essentially different from an old one does not do this.

The Soviet linguist Yury Lotman has described the way we perceive everyday language as 'automatic'. This parallels T. E. Hulme's illuminating comparison between ordinary language and algebra: reality is transformed into abstract functions (words) for the purposes of speech communication, and then reconverted into a modified reality, the modification being based on what operations the functions have performed, at the end of the process. This is what Lotman means by 'automatic perception': we do not question or think about the actual words, only what they communicate about external reality. He refers to an interesting experiment carried out by the Hungarian scholar Ivan Fónagy to show how this works. Volunteers in this experiment listened to a poem (by Hungarian poet Endre Adi), a newspaper article, and a conversation between two young girls – but they were given only one phoneme at a time. After each phoneme, they were asked to predict the phoneme that would follow. As one might expect, the young girls' conversation was the easiest to predict: 71 per cent of its phonemes could be correctly guessed in advance. In the case of the newspaper article, 67 per cent of the phonemes were correctly guessed. But the poem was not so easy: the subjects were able to guess only 40 per cent of its phonemes correctly in advance. *

This relative unpredictability of the language of poetry means that the listener must pay close attention to every sound. One cannot allow oneself to slip into the automatic perception of language with which everyday conversation or news items are taken in. Poetry prevents this automatic perception from taking place by continually arresting the listener's ear with novelty: the surprise of striking imagery, the inventiveness of phonemic patterning, the motor effect of metre, as well as the interest inherent in the fresh views of reality conveyed by the poem. It follows that any new poem, or any poetic language, that sounds as though it has been heard before, allows the listener to begin perceiving it automatically, as though it were conventional language, and then to react to the piece as if it were no more than some kind of referential communication and not a poem at all.

The main effort of the poet in every age has been to strike some kind of middle ground between too much novelty and invention, which would lead to the audience's rejecting the poem as incomprehensible, and not enough, which would lead to its being judged not sufficiently 'poetic'. This demand is impossible to meet in an absolute sense: poets continually fall on one side of the fence or the other. Wallace Stevens conveys the dilemma well in these lines from 'The Man with the Blue Guitar':

* Ivan Fónagy, 'Informationsgehalt von Wort und Laut in der Dichtung', *Poetics, Poetyka, Poètika* (Warsaw, 1961), p. 592.

A man bent over his guitar,
A shearsman of sorts. The day was green.

They said, 'You have a blue guitar,
You do not play things as they are.'

The man replied, 'Things as they are
Are changed upon the blue guitar.'

And they said then, 'But play, you must,
A tune beyond us, yet ourselves,

A tune upon the blue guitar
Of things exactly as they are.'

These lines may be interpreted in a number of ways, but, for present purposes, let's assume that the 'shearsman' is the poet, and that the 'blue guitar' symbolizes the medium of language – not just ordinary language ('things as they are') but the language of poetry ('changed upon the blue guitar'). The demand of the audience seems to be self-contradictory and impossible to meet ('A tune beyond us, yet ourselves'): they are explicit that while they want 'a tune upon the blue guitar' (a poem, let us say), it must be 'of things exactly as they are'. This brings us right back to the shearsman's inescapable truth: 'Things as they are | Are changed upon the blue guitar.' There is no escape from the dilemma. Yet, paradoxically, its statement in this poem is itself aesthetically satisfying.

In every age, audiences and spectators have tended to resist artistic innovation. Any half-educated person can feel at home with yesterday's art; it is difficult to be as self-assured with new art, especially as each new production seems to overturn all that went before. 'Why this obscurity?' people complain. 'Why are poets (or painters, or composers) of today so incomprehensible? Give me a good old-fashioned nineteenth-century poem (or painting, or symphony) any day!' In fact, this conflict is the basis of all art and will never change unless, of course, we completely alter our notions of what art is and what it does. Without novelty, without innovation and experiment, without a continual move away from the old and a relentless desire to 'make it new', we lose the very basis of art.

Let me give an example. Readers today are often puzzled when they encounter the *Lyrical Ballads* of Wordsworth and Coleridge.

How could they have caused such a furore at the time of their first publication in 1798? They seem innocent enough – sometimes even archaic in phrasing and expression, sometimes over-sentimental in subject matter – but on the whole not at all difficult to understand nor even, for that matter, particularly striking. To understand their impact on the audience of the time, you must look at the rest of the poetry which was being published. It's like leaping fifty years backwards, into the heart of the eighteenth century. Most of the poems published in literary magazines when Wordsworth and Coleridge were young are in couplets, phrased in a style little changed from the neoclassical traditions of Dryden and Pope. Much of the old formulaic poetic diction of the eighteenth century (circumlocutions such as 'enamelled fields' and 'feathered choirs', for example) continues to appear. Of course, the editors, publishers and readers of that time had little doubt that this *was* the language of poetry – the fact had been well established for at least fifty years.

Wordsworth and Coleridge's book was a dash of cold water in the face of this cultural smugness. Gone were the formulaic couplets, gone the stilted poetic diction, gone the prevalent notion that poetry was no more than elegant ways of saying commonplace things – 'what oft was thought, but ne'er so well expressed'. The new poetry swept aside all such preconceptions.

The function of Wordsworth and Coleridge's new poetry was, as always, to prevent their audience from perceiving it automatically. The British public found it profoundly discomforting (this is borne out by the defensive Preface which Wordsworth penned for the second edition of the book). Still, before long it became the norm, and poets who followed – Byron and Keats, Tennyson and Browning, Whitman and Hopkins – each in turn had to come up with further radical innovations, all to keep one step ahead of the audience's automatic assumptions.

The language of poetry can never be static, never predictable on first hearing. If it succeeds, it should be as a challenge to the hearer, who will then want to hear it again, to know it better, to savour the new sound. Even though the perception of it will in time become more familiar, the poem will never lose the aura of novelty which was there from the beginning. This is the basis of all art.

One notable development in the history of English poetry was the shift of its appeal from public group to private individual. As we saw in the previous chapter, this was paralleled by, and was to a very large degree a result of, the spread of literacy and the advent of print from the late fifteenth century on. The Old English poet recited his work by heart to a community audience; only later may some scribe have written it down. In medieval times, much popular poetry is also communal in its appeal. But from medieval times onwards we find more and more poetry addressed from one individual to another. The chances are that many of these poems may still have been read to a group; nevertheless, their tone is essentially private and intimate. By the time of Shakespeare's sonnets, the growth of general reading skills meant that it was no longer necessary for a poet to write as though the poem were going to be publicly broadcast (even though much intimate poetry can still survive this kind of treatment). Poems could be addressed from one individual to another in a way that implied that they would be read in private by a single reader.

This development removed certain obstacles for the poet but presented others in its place. When poetry was more of a community activity, the poet had to limit material and references to what would be of interest to the majority. The poet's views on conduct, morality, religious belief, and so forth, had to meet with general approval if the poetry were to be heard at all. On the other hand, as poetry became more personal, addressed to an individual rather than a group, it increasingly ran the risk of alienating other readers with counter-cultural views or general obscurity.

In our own day, with most poetry making its first appearance in print, distances between poet and reader may be immense – perhaps stretching over many thousands of miles and hundreds of years. The Old English poet had a very clear idea of the intended audience, perhaps knowing its every member by name. The twentieth-century poet's view is more likely to accord with that of Gertrude Stein: 'I write for myself and strangers.' Social pressure would never have allowed the Old English poet to maintain such a stance in public for a moment.

A major problem presented by the poetry of bygone ages is that it may draw on all manner of material which is obscure to us today but which would have been quite familiar to the poet's audience when it was written. An obvious example of this in English poetry is the matter of Christianity. From the time of the arrival of the first Christian missionaries in Britain, the stories and symbols of Christianity permeated every level of society. In the Middle Ages, religion was a matter of paramount importance, of far greater concern than any matters of the secular world. By the same token, a person's status and emotional nature were of chief interest, not his or her physical characteristics. A modern reader may become irritated with these emphases – modern tastes, after all, favour physical detail; and matters of religion are something most of us prefer to keep private. Furthermore, it may be next to impossible for us today to appreciate fully the symbolic richness which even such a short phrase as 'bloudie crosse' (no. 16, line 10) had for its first audience. Even such biblical allusions as 'pillar of salt', or 'eyeless in Gaza', or 'the cock crew thrice' may need explanation. Much of this material has become so unfamiliar that we have to rely on annotated editions and reference books for enlightenment. But, of course, the works of those times were not written for us, any more than books and poetry of today are likely to meet the expectations of an audience five hundred or a thousand years from now.

Literary commentators often use the term *genre* to mean a certain class of literature – the elegy and the detective novel are two literary genres, for example. Although genres popular in the past may seem to us today to be unnecessarily confined to conventional boundaries, in reality all genres have their fixed limits, even if they are frequently redrawn. One must develop an educated historical imagination to be able to appreciate them: this is just as true for poetry as for any other art.

In medieval England, starting in the thirteenth century and continuing past the fifteenth, a genre of poetry which is now known as the *medieval lyric* was extremely popular. Medieval lyrics are usually short (less than 100 lines), deal with a single subject, and are conventionally addressed to an individual (so the pronouns 'I' and 'you', rather than the communal 'we', predominate). Most are highly formulaic, following the patterns of similar poems from France and other parts of Europe. For example, the *chanson* (the French terms are usually used even for the English poems) is a love-lyric. So is the *chanson d'aventure*, but it is more particularized, in that it always opens with a formulaic line: 'As I rode out last evening', or 'As I went out the other day', followed by a description of what the narrator encountered along the way.

Another very popular medieval lyric genre was the *reverdie* (literally, 're-greening'), which celebrates the joys of spring. It usually opens with a reference to spring or April, and nearly always has a reference to the birds seeking their mates, with, typically, 'each one singing in his own tongue'. This may be followed by a statement about how all this has the effect of turning the narrator's thoughts towards love, or towards a specific person – the beloved, who is the main focus of attention in most medieval lyrics.

It is important to appreciate the popularity of a genre such as the *reverdie*, in order to understand why poems on this subject are so common, of course. But it's even more important to be aware of what was conventional in them and what was innovative. By and large, the medieval audience did not prize innovation or originality as highly as we do today, putting much greater social pressure on the poet to conform to the traditional limits of a particular genre. This social pressure, however, did not prevent certain poets from introducing marked departures from convention. The old round 'Sumer is icumen in' (no. 2) is the oldest preserved *reverdie* in English, but it contains phrases that are quite unique to it, particularly the rustic realism of 'Bulluc sterteth, buckë verteth'. Furthermore, it does not proceed to become a love song; a celebration of the simple joys of spring is enough in this case. 'Lenten ys come with love to toune' (no. 4) is perhaps more conventional, though its language and sentiment are appealingly direct by comparison with many other *reverdies*. A much more conventional and courtly *reverdie* is Chaucer's 'Nowe welcome, Somor' (no. 7), cast in the form of a rondeau. (The novelty here is one of context: this rondeau is actually being sung *by* the birds, not about them.)

Armed with even this little understanding of the *reverdie* genre, we are in a far better position to consider the effect of other poetry which plays on its conventions – such as the opening lines of Chaucer's *Canterbury Tales* (no. 8): 'Whan that Aprill with his shoures soote . . .' The very word 'Aprill' would have sent a clear signal to Chaucer's audience: this must be a *reverdie*. The familiar progression unfolds: there are the usual references to new green growth, and the birds singing. But this is where Chaucer pulls off a major surprise: 'Thanne [then, in spring] longen folk to goon on pilgrimages.' This is something altogether new for what started out sounding like a traditional *reverdie*. Undoubtedly Chaucer's audience, expecting the development of some kind of love poem, would have been amused at being so taken in.

This little joke, so obvious to the audience for which the poem was written, today has to be laboriously explained if it is to be appreciated at all. Unfortunately, such explication is apt to kill the humour of it – in the way that comic strips no longer seem quite so funny when you've finished explaining their 'jokes' to a three- or four-year-old. Yet the alternative, not to say anything at all about it, may lead a modern audience to miss the whole essence of Chaucer's wit.

An understanding of past literary conventions may be important for a full appreciation of modern poetry, too. Poets of every age have always felt perfectly free to make use of echoes from past conventions in order to create something new. An example of this, also based on the medieval *reverdie*, is in T. S. Eliot's *The Waste Land*: 'April is the cruellest month . . .' This opening effectively stands the whole convention on its head, linking 'April' with 'cruellest month'. Although separated by five centuries, Chaucer and Eliot use a single convention for their own original, and quite different, ends. In both cases, the full effect depends on the reader's being aware of the conventional limits and expectations of an established genre.

Another convention of medieval times has to do not so much with any particular poetic genre, though it too is very much a part of medieval poetry: it concerns the conventional poetic description of a lady. After reading a number of poems which include such a description, you might well end up thinking that all beautiful ladies of the Middle Ages were clones: they inevitably had broad foreheads, thin eyebrows, bright eyes ('grey as glass' was the usual simile), white skin, a long thin neck, small but shapely breasts, and so on. Chaucer turns this to humorous effect in a later passage from the 'General Prologue' of *The Canterbury Tales* when he describes the Prioress using much of this conventional description ('hir nose tretez, hir eyen greye as glas . . .') – quite comically out of place when applied to a supposedly chaste and pious nun. Some decades later, Thomas Hoccleve tacitly invokes the whole convention when he describes *his* love as having grey skin, a narrow forehead, a body shaped like a football, black eyes, and so forth (no. 10). Something of the same kind occurs in the passage from John Skelton's 'The Tunnynge of Elynour Rummyng' which appears in the anthology section (no. 13). As always, the joke is much funnier if you are aware of the conventions.

Many reference books are available to supply the essential background information needed to appreciate effects such as these. A good historical dictionary, such as the *Oxford Etymological Dictionary*, or the old but still indispensable thirteen-volume *Oxford English Dictionary* (now available in a two-volume micrographic edition) will explain the meanings of words in earlier periods, and how they have changed. The *Oxford Guide to English Literature* offers much information on the literary background of specific British poets and their work, as well as further information on poetic forms, genres, and so on. Companion guides to Australian, Canadian, New Zealand and US literature are also available. An excellent book for unravelling proverbial and mythological references is *Brewer's Dictionary of Phrase and Fable*. A. J. Waldron's *A Reference Guide to English Literature* lists other similar works which may be of use, explaining what areas they cover. Beyond this, check your local library shelves – a wealth of helpful information is close at hand. The real danger is in spending too much time on digging up background information and not enough on the poem itself.

It may not be so difficult for us to appreciate the cultural conventions of more recent poetry, though we should always be aware that what we read must reflect *some* aspect of convention – even if, as in the case of the *Lyrical Ballads*, the main point is that an earlier convention is being roundly rejected. We cannot appreciate the significance of this if we do not know *what* is being rejected.

I have not said much about the role of the poet in all this. Let's assume, for now, that the function of society in conceiving such a role is roughly similar to that of its function in creating and shaping a community view of poetry and its effects. Every young child of normally lively mind enjoys playing with words, just as most enjoy various kinds of physical exercise and games. As we grow older, we play word-games less and less. If we continue to be interested in words, especially in word-games, our interest seems to become not only more sophisticated but also more serious. In general, society perceives poetry as it perceives religion – as something to be approached with reverence and difficulty. Poets are the priests of this religion. (This may not be my own view of poetry and poets, but that is of little account if the rest of society sees it that way.) Robert Graves claimed that one should never refer to oneself as a poet, that 'poet' is a kind of honorific title that only others can bestow. Others feel that poets, like saints, are born only after dying.

In each of the four English-speaking countries where I have lived (Canada, the UK, Australia and the USA, in that order) poets and poetry have markedly differing functions. It can be enlightening to watch the confusion that results when poets of one of these cultures encounter those of another. The British poet Ted Hughes found himself mobbed by fame-hungry young Australian poets when he flew in to read at the Adelaide Festival of the Arts a few years ago – something that would have been far less likely to happen to him in decorous England, where the fame of a poet is a much more subdued matter. The Canadian writer Margaret Atwood attended the same festival, and later wrote an article for her fellow Canadians expressing some shock at the aggressive heckling that greeted some poets performing at readings there – something that would have violated all Canadian rules of poetry etiquette. On the other hand, poetry readings in Australian cities are usually well attended and very lively, appealing to a wide variety of social types – something that cannot be said for readings in other English-speaking societies – and new poetry is routinely published in Australian daily newspapers and weekly current-affairs magazines (a fact which causes poets in other English-speaking countries to gasp with amazement and envy).

Canadian poets have always been much less strident than their Australian counterparts, like most Canadians, taking themselves perhaps every bit as seriously, but in a more understated way. On the other hand Canadians, unlike Australians, generally pay little public attention to their poets. Nor is there much social backing for a specifically 'Canadian' poetry yet. In general, the work of Canada's poets – if one ignores specific geographical or cultural references – is indistinguishable from that of US poets immediately to the south.

The impression given to the rest of the English-speaking world by recent poetry from Britain is very much coloured by its conservative and unadventurous 'establishment' publishers. Many large British publishers, indeed, no longer care to continue bearing the financial loss that poetry usually incurs; those that still do publish poets limit themselves to 'safe' names. It is inconceivable that a radical departure from present tastes in Britain could ever come via such publishers. In other words, as in the time of the young Wordsworth nearly two centuries ago, what is being published today in Britain is what *was* poetry yesterday. (By contrast, mainstream publishers in Australia, Canada and the US seem more willing to take a gamble on something new.) So the rest of the world hears only of already established British poets, those whose most adventurous work is safely in the past. Of course, most English-speakers are aware of such 'British' poets as T. S. Eliot (a native of St Louis, Missouri), W. H. Auden (who lived many years on the East Coast of America), Thom Gunn (who now lives in California), Ted Hughes (who was married to the American poet Sylvia Plath), and so on. In any case, we can only pay attention to so many poets at once, and in general people of one country or region will naturally put their own poets first.

Britain has gone from being the only source of English poetry to being just one of many English-speaking countries where poets write today. In former Commonwealth countries such as Australia, Canada and New Zealand, attention has shifted away from the British and towards the work of US poets. This is hardly surprising, seeing that the population of the United States outweighs the combined total of the rest of the English-speaking world. The perception of US poetry in these countries, as well as in Britain, however, is to a large degree also set by British publishers. Most poetry readers outside the US know of Robert Bly, Robert Creeley, Robert Duncan, Robert Frost, Robert Lowell, and so on, simply because these are the poets earmarked by British publishers as 'significant'. Many hundreds of equally gifted poets are never heard beyond the borders of their own regions of the US.

So we all have a somewhat incomplete picture of the true state of things in the world of English poetry. It's the same in all matters of national identity – we tend to develop a media-conditioned picture of Yanks as gun-toting, bomb-dropping imperialists, of Brits as bowler-wearing tea-drinking strikemongers, of Australians as sunburnt surf-riding jackeroos. In the same way we form a false 'national' picture of the poets and poetry of each of these societies.

In real life, each of these countries is made up of a number of regions, with one of these regions predominating and projecting a national image. In the US this is New York/East Coast, just as in Britain it is London, in Canada Toronto, and in Australia Sydney/Melbourne. It's not surprising that each of these predominating regions is based on a megalopolis. The audience for new poetry is small and specialist, and the city may be the only realistic place for a poet to go looking for one. Moreover, most publishers are located in a large city. The subject matter of much poetry may be rural and scenic, but its creators are apt to live in high-density housing. Moreover, the city is where upper-class taste (something very much linked with the general development of a cultural awareness of poetry as an art-form) originates.

Geophysical and sociopolitical pressures can determine what will be considered a successful or significant poem. Audiences in the American Midwest enjoy a poetry which East Coast intellectuals would call sentimental or 'corny'; the concerns of the typical Midwesterner are more bound up with industry, agriculture and unemployment than they are with the subjugation of Latin American peasants to US economic and political interests, a subject more to the fore on the East Coast. The same could be said of the different regions of the other English-speaking countries of the world: certain matters will be considered important and fitting for poetry, others will not. This aspect of poetry too is continually changing, as poets continue to be as unpredictable and inventive as ever.

Contrary to popular myth, there has never been a society which did not have room for its poets. This is why, in a country such as the US, you will find as many tastes for poetry as there are discernibly different cultures within that country. On the other hand, many poets grow to perceive themselves as social eccentrics, and will leave the milieu from which they sprang to live among strangers, a few carefully selected friends (mainly other poets and artists) and, of course, 'the public' without which the poet is nothing.

A poet usually 'makes it' by first of all having a poem accepted for publication in some kind of magazine or newspaper. Payment, if any, will be extremely small. After a time, and probably after one or two major successes (a reading on a radio or television network, publication in a national magazine or newspaper), the poet will approach a publisher with a 'collection' of poems – usually about thirty. The publisher's decision (assuming the firm is ready to carry the financial loss that books of poetry usually incur) will be based largely on the length and impressiveness of the poet's earlier publications list. Occasionally some kind of testimonial from an established poet or literary critic may be used as additional persuasion, though this will not cut any ice with the reader, of course. An even more dubious public reaction is possible if the collection includes a dedication to an established poet – it is generally felt that this is akin to special pleading: 'The famed poet Bloggs takes notice of me, so should you.' (Actually, this is a very old, though generally ineffective, attention-seeking device, used by poets for centuries.)

Some cultures have such a stereotypical image of what a poet should be, do, and look like, that it is easy for poets to grow into this image. I recall an Australian poet who for years reinforced the social perception of the poet as word-magician by dressing as a conjurer (top hat, black cape, gloves, cane, and so forth) not only at his readings, but habitually in public. More commonly, poets are perceived as being emotionally unstable, fickle lovers, somewhat effeminate or else excessively macho, duplicitous (everyone knows about 'poetic licence'), and 'different' from society in general. This is a social concept in part based on individual experience but more extensively created from the stereotypes of social myth and the 'lives of the great poets' approach of teachers and literary commentators.

We need to be careful, whether we are reading or reciting a poem, or listening to it, not to allow the biographical details of the poet's life to obscure our enjoyment of the poem – which should, after all, be our chief interest. Some writers – Shelley and Poe are examples – are 'famous poets' more because of their lives than their works. It is easier, if you are a teacher, a literary editor, a chat-show producer, to dwell on details of the poet's life – especially if the poet conforms to stereotype and has led a colourful one – than it is to listen to the poem. Yet what is the point of even the most colourful biographical details if the poet's works offer little or nothing?

When I think of the role of the poet in society, I conjure up an image of a crowded marketplace. There are rows of stalls, with people selling fruits and vegetables, pots and pans, trinkets and toys. Here and there are public entertainers. An old man plays a flute: occasionally someone throws a coin or a bit of bread into his collection basket. Two girls do acrobatic stunts: the crowd smiles and claps appreciatively after each one. There is someone else working on a mural, laying on great slabs of colour.

Then, in the midst of this mêlée, we find someone who is doing nothing more than playing with words – the words of our own language, but sounding different somehow. Their flow sets up a strong rhythmic awareness in the minds of all who hear them. Although we may not understand all the meaning of the words, we are attracted by the sound they make, and what they suggest. But some stay only for a moment or two and then pass on to other attractions. Occasionally the word-man may try to attract more listeners by raising his voice, by standing up, waving his arms, and even dancing to the rhythms of his speech. Most of the time, though, he sits without moving, almost as though listening with everyone else to the emerging patterns of speech and sound.

It's not hard to see why some people are attracted. Adults who respond to poetry have usually retained a very strong but open-minded awareness of the nature of these pleasures from childhood. And it's not hard to understand why others turn away – they have other, more tangible, things to divert themselves with; and poetry is, after all, only a game.

Poets often talk of inspiration, and of the phenomenon of a poem 'writing itself', of a flow of words appearing from nowhere, and leading to an end which the poet could not have dreamed of. Perhaps no excitement offered by poetry can be greater than that of its seemingly spontaneous creation. But we are all conditioned to the idea of similar possibilities – religious revelation or falling in love – through what we have observed in others. Some poets have recorded what they heard or saw in divine visions; many others have celebrated their experience of nature or love in poetry inspired by external objects – the landscape, the beloved, the vision of Heaven or Hell. Most of these have been conventional subjects for poetry of all languages as far back as we can go. I do not question in any way the reality of the experience of poetic inspiration – I myself have experienced it more than once, and could not possibly do so. But it *is* very largely made possible through common social and cultural preconceptions, which are part of the world the poet grows up in. What would life be without the possibility of such magical experiences, and the poems or other works of art (as we call them) which proceed from them?

I have tried in this book to avoid assigning any particular sexual identity to 'the poet' whenever I have had to speak of the creator of the poem. Nevertheless, the general perception in most English cultures is that major poets are likely to be men. Why is this so? Probably because of the attitude we bring to most poetry, that it must be 'serious'. (A poet of either sex who makes us laugh is usually thought to be of secondary importance only, though occasional light or comic poems from usually serious poets – such as T. S. Eliot's *Old Possum's Book of Practical Cats* – are permissible, even often received with gratitude. We feel a kind of relief that the poet is able to descend from Parnassus and laugh with the rest of us.) It follows that the poet's role, then, must also be taken seriously as a life's vocation – and traditionally in male-dominated society the more glamorous social roles have been reserved for men, with women generally being left to cope with the child-raising and housekeeping chores. This picture is changing, though, and so is the traditional view of poetry as an exclusively male production.

Some poets hold that the function of women in the writing of poetry is to inspire, to act as a muse and bring forth the poem in the mind of the poet, who is thus a mere agent for its appearance on paper. (Robert Graves's *The White Goddess* is one of many expressions of this view.) In fact, society's conception of a woman poet is similar to its perception of a woman engineer, preacher, farmer or politician. A woman encounters much the same obstacles in being accepted as a serious poet as she does in attempting to break into any traditionally male role.

A poem requires two parties to work: a reader and a listener. In the earliest days of English poetry, the poet was the reader, reciting the poem to a tangible audience. Over ten centuries, the positions have become diametrically opposite: the poet today is usually no more than the distant creator of a poem, while reader and listener tend to be one and the same person. This means that every potential reader of a poem should know something about how to read it as the poet heard it at the time of its creation, if the poem is to have any chance of success.

There is no great mystery about how to read a poem successfully, though it is a matter on which tastes vary considerably, as they do in all matters of the performing arts. First of all, you should be sure of how each word sounds. In the case of a modern English poem this is not too difficult, but poetry of earlier periods calls for more work. (See Appendix B for guidance on the pronunciation of Old and Middle English.) It will also help your appreciation of the poem if you first of all clarify, by exaggerating if need be, its rhythmic and phonemic patterns. Further than that, just be sure that you read the poem in a quiet place. Nothing is so destructive to the sound of poetry as background music – it will completely disrupt the rhythmic and phonemic patterns of the poem. Above all, try to approach each word as though it were a new creation.

How you read a poem to yourself is one thing, but how you read, or recite, a poem to a group of people is quite another. I have heard a number of vehemently expressed opinions on this subject, from those who say the creator of a poem is the best person to read it, to those who say the creator should step aside and let the poem speak for itself. Some prefer the individual and quirky tones of the poet's voice, which becomes a major part of their experience of that poem, while others would choose the professional tones of a trained actor or radio announcer. Some poets, such as Dylan Thomas, are renowned as fine reciters of their own works, packing their performances with dramatic tones and mellifluous enunciation. Others, such as Robert Graves, sound reluctant to add any extra emotion to the actual words and speech-sounds of the poem, delivering their recitations in neutral tones, virtually devoid of any flexional music. Different poets, like wines of different degrees of dryness or sweetness, are for different performances. What is right for one occasion may seem quite wrong for another.

There is no one correct way to read a poem. Do remember, however, that certain sound effects in a particular poem (such as rhythms, sound patterns, ironic tones, pauses) which may seem quite obvious to you, especially if you know the poem, may need a good deal more emphasis if they are to come through to a larger audience. Timing is absolutely central to the communication of these effects. (This is one of the mysteries of every performing art, which has to be laboriously discovered by most performers.) Some of them may need a great deal of emphasis, even exaggeration, if they are to come over effectively. At the same time, one has to be careful not to go too far. Over-exaggeration of *every* pattern and nuance in the poem is the most common fault of the professional actor–reader, and can be even more off-putting than the dry performances of poets such as Graves. It is particularly irritating to have to suffer the performance of an actor 'emoting', rather than reciting, a poem.

The most important thing for a reader who wants to develop a good ear is to give full and undivided attention to the poem. The more you can free your mind from other considerations and make it fully receptive to the poem, the more rewarding you will find the experience. It also follows that you must be relaxed. The poem is a thing of emotion: it will be impossible for you to sense this emotion if your own heart is gripped with overriding feelings. Hear the poem, listen to it alone until it rings in your mind.

Every bright child enjoys word-games, and playing with the sounds of speech in simple ways. Later, nursery rhymes attract the child's ear, and become the grounding for all rhythmic, phonemic, and structural creativity found in more sophisticated English poetry. Much of this development is reinforced by the company of other children, both at school and in play. One learns to react to simple jokes, riddles and even obvious puns by observing how others react to them. Appreciation of the humour of a pun in England, for example, is conventionally shown by groaning, not by laughter: this is a culturally reinforced reaction to a specific type of word-play.

At the same time as these early word-games are learned, the child absorbs a great deal of other information about language and how to use it to communicate effectively. As certain levels of competence are reached, so the language-games that appeal become ever more complex. Ultimately, the child encounters the most complex and 'adult' word-game of all: the poem.

At this point something seems to go wrong in the process. It is hard to put a finger on exactly what, but I have a few ideas. Here is one: the child's first word-games occur either in a family setting, or in some kind of association with siblings and friends. No duress is involved; in fact, it is the desire of children to learn and repeat these early word-games that makes them our strongest living oral tradition.* On the other hand, unless the child comes from an unusually literary background, the exposure to more sophisticated poetry will be something that takes place in school, authoritatively handed down by a teacher, something that has to be studied and learned.

Each child will have a different reaction to a poem. Yet none will be able to react to these sounds socially, simply because at no point are children encouraged to work this out on their own among their peers. Why? Because much poetry is too difficult, too complex. If everyday adult language is a complex and demanding medium for the child to master, adult poetry is a hundred, a thousand, times more so. The teacher has to elucidate, to explain what to listen for, to guide the reading, to enthuse over the various effects of poetry, so the students will be able to pass a final 'examination' in the 'subject'. But, inevitably, for most this marks the end of any interest in poetry.

This context for poetry is totally artificial, and far removed from that of children's first word-games. Apart from the great demands of technical knowledge presented by much poetry, the whole experience of it is made individual and private. Of course, students are physically gathered together in the room where poetry is 'taught', but their reaction to it is not a social one. The main object of attention, the poem, remains external to their own experience; there is little attempt to make them aware of the social effects of a particular poem, or of poetry in general. At the end of the process, a student may be able to talk about various technical aspects of poetry,

---

* See the Opies' book on *The Lore and Language of Schoolchildren* for a full treatment of this.

the kind of thing covered in this book, but will still have little idea of what poetry can actually *do*.

The experience of poetry has been spoiled for many of us by the force-feeding approach of teachers and academics. A friend recently told me of having to study the whole of Milton's *Paradise Lost* for her final secondary-school examinations ('A' levels) in England some years ago. The motive for setting such a long and demanding poem seems to have been that a maximum of 'great works' should be 'taught' to students as early on as possible, before they opted out of the educational system. The possibility that the experience would turn her, and probably most of the others in her class, against all poetry for ever after was apparently not even considered.

A poem such as *Paradise Lost* has an enormous reputation among scholars and teachers, but we should be careful to understand why this is. First of all, it is of epic length, so there is endless material for discussion – not only material having to do directly with the poetry, but background material as well – religious, historical, biographical, classical, propagandist, and so on. Moreover, its very length is often assumed to be additional reason to revere it – as though size in itself were an indication of quality.

The problem is even greater when Shakespeare is studied in school. The difficulties of language in his works are far beyond the capability of even gifted school students, perhaps beyond most university graduates. Ideally, one would study Shakespeare only after becoming competent to appreciate and understand what is going on in simpler poetry written closer to our own day. The countering argument, of course, is that for most people this day may never come, and it is better to have *some* Milton and Shakespeare, no matter how imperfect the experience. Unfortunately, the end result is likely to be a lifelong aversion not only to Milton and Shakespeare, but to all poetry.

Milton is an interesting case of a poet who wrote to be heard. Because *Paradise Lost* is so long, the temptation is to approach it as a kind of novel or verse drama, to be continually asking oneself, as one might in reading a news story: 'What's going to happen next?' and 'What is Milton trying to say?' Little attention is ever given to the sound of his blank verse, its careful syntactic organization, the way in which its five-stress lines are constructed (using enjambment and similar devices) to sound metrically satisfying.

My own experience of *Paradise Lost*, as a first-year undergraduate in Canada, was not quite as unfortunate as that of my friend in England. To some degree this was because I soon realized that the poem was impossible to concentrate upon for more than a page at a time if I only read it silently. The only way I was able to develop any appreciation of it, however fragmentary, was to read the whole thing aloud to myself, which I did (over a period of three days). The end result, apart from some hoarseness, was an increased respect for Milton's awareness and use of sound as the basis of poetry.

We have already seen that the composition and expectations of audiences in earlier periods of English poetry were quite different from those of today. Audience reaction must have been immediate and often sharp. We can imagine Chaucer's audience laughing at his many comic punches, growing serious at the philosophical and moral parts, and applauding enthusiastically at the end of his tales and other poetic works. Although the advent of print brought some change, poetry remained a public medium, even in its most private and intimate manifestations, well into the nineteenth century. Most members of a poet's audience could be assumed to have a good ear, to be able to pick up any technical effects appreciatively, to understand most extra-textual references, and to be aware of what was new and praiseworthy or problematical in what the poet was doing. Newcomers to the audience (young people, for instance) would gradually absorb all this knowledge through observation and imitation.

A modern analogy which occurs to me is with the spectators at a Spanish bullfight. If you ever attend a corrida without any awareness of the conventions involved, you may be puzzled to discover that the death of the bull is not generally perceived as the point of the event. Furthermore, the behaviour of the spectators is hard to understand – the bull makes a pass at the matador, and the crowd sits in stony silence, or perhaps even boos. The bull makes another similar-looking pass, and the ring erupts with a chorus of appreciative *olés*. It is only by repeated observation that one learns what to look for, what it is that pleases the crowd, and what it is that displeases them. Eventually one becomes an aficionado.

Some people argue that poetry is in a bad state today because its appeal is very largely to an extremely small group – an audience of intellectuals, of people who love dictionaries and the ring of well-chosen words, of people who enjoy pushing their own exploration of language to the limits. But the audience for the most ambitious and demanding poetry has always been small. For every Anglo-Saxon who gave appreciative ear to a poem such as *Beowulf* there must have been a thousand who never got much past simple jingles. Every age has its popular and its élitist poetry. Some popular pieces may have elements of sophistication in them – we can see this in some of the carols, the traditional ballads and, later, the lyrics of such poets as Robert Burns, Alfred Tennyson, Christina Rossetti, Dylan Thomas, Leonard Cohen and John Lennon, to mention a few. But élitist poetry is usually the ultimate word-game, the most concentrated experience – and, in the context of a book such as this one, the most rewarding to focus on, offering more in less space than any other form of language. For this reason, it's often the most difficult to penetrate.

Perhaps you feel disappointed because I have spent so much time on the technical aspects of poetry in this book, and so little on its magical effects. The magic of poetry is something bestowed on it by the reader or listener; it cannot possibly exist independently in the spoken or printed words of the poem. This magic is similar to the magic of falling in love: external elements combine to bring about a magical experience in one's own mind. We call it magical simply because we cannot account for it in any rational way.

You may search far and wide for the poem or poems which sound 'right' to you and cause this kind of magical effect. At times, it seems hard enough just to find an enjoyable poem. In the anthology section I have tried to offer enough variety for you to have a good chance of finding something appealing. And the text of this book may help you to become more aware of the many effects different poems may contain, so that the whole experience may be more rewarding. This may ultimately help you to develop your appreciation for poetry in general.

But, even without this book, if you read enough poetry, every so often you are bound to come upon one particular poem that will, at first hearing, seem absolutely 'right', one that will hit your consciousness hard – even though you don't give a moment's thought to *how* it does what it did. In this way you bestow a kind of magic on the language of the poem, making it live in your mind as distinct from the wash of other poems and other kinds of language which, by comparison, seem to recede into a grey background.

Such magic is more common in other social contexts. The magical experience of people falling in love suggests to the other members of their society that such an experience *is* possible; moreover, it demonstrates the kind of response it may bring about. But it's not as easy to demonstrate the magic of a poem. No matter how much you may rave or otherwise try to communicate the magic of a poem that has affected you, most people who listen to it with you afterwards will still only hear it as the sum of its parts – not as the far greater thing it has become for you. At least your enthusiastic reaction will help to reinforce a general awareness that such a reaction to poetry *is* possible, and create in others the desire to find such a poem, one which will become a permanent part of their consciousness.

# 8  A Final Analysis

> You can tear a poem apart to see what makes it technically tick,
> and say to yourself, when the words are laid out before you, the
> vowels, the consonants, the rhymes and rhythms, 'Yes, this is it.
> This is why the poem moves me so. It is because of the crafts-
> manship.' But you're back again where you began. You're back
> with the mystery of having been moved by words.

> The idea [of a literary work] is not contained in any however
> successfully-chosen excerpts, but is expressed in its entire artistic
> structure. The scholar who does not understand this and who
> seeks the idea in isolated citations resembles a person who,
> having learned that a house has a plan, starts to break down the
> walls in search of the place where this plan is immured. The plan
> is not to be found hidden away in a wall, but is realised in the
> proportions of the entire building. The plan is the architect's idea;
> the structure of the building is its realisation. The content of ideas
> of a work is its structure. — Yury Lotman

Before we pull together all the different things we have so far talked
about in this book, to see how they may be applied to our experience
of a single poem, I want to spend a moment on some new approaches
to poetry which have greatly expanded our awareness of the many
different features of English poetry and how they work.

There is virtually no recorded writing *about* poetry in English
from before Caxton's time. Since the sixteenth century, however,
many writers have attempted to analyse and account for the
different artistic effects of poetry. Some, particularly in the sixteenth and seventeenth centuries, have been quite objective, almost
scientific in their approach. Others, such as those of the nineteenth
century, have used a more intuitive, 'literary' approach, in which
their main intent seems to have been to whip the reader into a state
of enthusiasm through sympathetic reaction.

The early years of the twentieth century saw a turning against this, with the ostensibly more objective 'practical criticism' of I. A. Richards and others. But a more methodical approach to the effects of poetry has come in the past thirty years or so, with the application of linguistics to literary studies. Much of this work is far too technical for me to be able to discuss it adequately in a book as brief as this one. Indeed, the opacity of some of these linguistic studies, especially considering that they attempt to illuminate works of literature, has led to hostility from many traditional literary critics. But one matter on which practically all modern linguists and critics agree is that the language of poetry does not have the same effect on the listener as everyday language does. This is mainly because of the way poetic language continually draws attention to *itself*, not just to the semantic meaning of its words – which may, in a good many poems, be of minor importance.

An American linguist, Samuel Levin, has argued that the main distinguishing feature of poetic language is what he calls 'coupling'. He subdivides coupling into two varieties: *syntagmatic* (having to do with sequential relationships), and *paradigmatic* (having to do with the whole range of choices available at any point in a sequence). As an example, let's take a simple sentence:

John painted the house.

The relationship between these words is a syntagmatic one. A rearrangement such as

John the house painted.

would reflect a different syntagmatic relationship, one not usually considered 'normal' in English. (You can see that in a discussion of English speech-order, 'syntagmatic' and 'syntactic' have more or less equivalent meanings.)

If we take our original sentence again, and reflect on all the different words in English that could be used in place of the first one, 'John', we would have a long (though finite) list, including 'Mary', 'Tom', 'The father', 'A worker', and so forth, called a *paradigm*. A paradigm, then, consists of all possible variants of a certain invariant type. In this case, the invariant type is 'Active animate singular subject'. The paradigm for the second position in the sentence, 'Past tense active verb', would also be extremely long, and would consist of such variants as 'washed', 'covered', 'hit', and so forth. The third paradigm, 'Article or possessive adjective', would be somewhat shorter, consisting of 'a', 'an', 'one', 'my', and so on, while the fourth, 'Inanimate object of subject's action', would be extremely lengthy, with variants such as 'barn', 'garage', 'table', and so forth.

One feature of poetic language is that the word chosen by the poet to fill a given syntagmatic slot may be quite unexpected. Dylan Thomas's phrase 'a grief ago' is notable because 'grief' is used as though it were a member of the 'Fixed period of time' paradigm, which in everyday English it is not. The usual members of this paradigm are words like 'day', 'month', 'year'. Thomas has stretched the paradigm to include this rather unusual variant.

Levin suggests that couplings in poetry may be either syntagmatic or paradigmatic in effect: the phenomenon depends on what he calls 'naturally equivalent forms' – that is, elements of speech closely related in sound, or sense, or both. Rhyme and other phonemic patterns serve to create this kind of relationship in sound, while words of nearly identical or totally opposite meanings (that is, synonyms or antonyms) have a similar kind of relationship, this time a semantic one. A pair of words such as 'denies/satisfies' is a good example of a semantic coupling, one of opposites (antonyms).

A peculiar quality of such couplings is that equivalence of sense can highlight possible ways in which the sounds also might be considered as equivalent. In the 'denies/satisfies' example, we note the /ɒiz/ ending of each – though in 'denies' this is the stressed syllable, and in 'satisfies' it is unstressed – so it is not, strictly speaking, a rhyme. A similar effect occurs in a phrase like, 'Get my nephew and call my niece', where the semantic equivalence of the two pairs, 'get/call' and 'nephew/niece' (together with the alliteration of 'nephew/niece'), has the effect of causing us to dwell on the phonemic similarities of their opening consonants (both are produced by the back of the tongue hitting the soft palate) rather than on their differences (/g/ is voiced, but /k/ is not).

The same thing happens on the semantic level. In the phrase, 'He painted the house and whitewashed the garage', the fact that 'house' and 'garage' are placed in a similar semantic relationship to 'painted' and 'whitewashed' leads us to emphasize their paradigmatic sense equivalence (both are wooden buildings) rather than their difference (one houses people, the other cars). *

Levin argues that this kind of 'coupling' is what makes a poem unique and memorable. Of course, too much of it can make a poem banal, as can too much of any patterning. But good poets avoid this danger by using words which are equivalent in sense but not exactly in sound, or vice versa – or, if the words are equivalent in both sound and sense, by making sure they are rhythmically different (as with 'denies/satisfies'), or that they are not in parallel syntactical positions.

Many other linguists have turned their attention to the language of poetry in the past three decades or so. One of the more recent is Yury Lotman, who was mentioned in Chapter 7. Lotman's chief work to date, *Analysis of the Poetic Text*, makes the point that the language of poetry is above all *iconic*: it symbolizes *itself*, rather than some external reality. In order to isolate and understand how this works, we first of all have to decide which aspects of our language convey meaning, or are 'functional'.

A simple example will illustrate what is functional and what is not. In English speech, each person has a slightly different way of pronouncing words, as unique as that individual's fingerprints. A careful phonetic transcription of these speech sounds will show such differences in full detail. In spite of this, all English speakers derive meaning from these individual sounds by treating them as generalized abstractions, *phonemes*. To take an extreme example, a very young child, when pronouncing 'carrot' or 'flower', may actually say [kræ.rət] or [fwæ.wə]; nevertheless, others will still react to them as /kæ.rət/ or /flæ.wər/. Phonemes are generalized invariants, based on the numberless phonetic variants which we hear around us every day. Whatever meaning we may draw from someone else's speech is based mainly on our understanding of phonemic invariants, rather than on the infinite number of phonetic variants which we may be actually hearing.

The language of poetry differs from everyday language in that individual variants may be taken as functional in themselves,

* See Levin, p. 35. The examples are his.

without having to be 'translated' into some invariant form first. Thus, if the words 'crarrot' and 'fwower' appeared in a piece of writing, they could convey the information 'child talking' in addition to the phonemically derived 'carrot' and 'flower' meanings. It would be a mistake if the reader dismissed them as meaningless, or as mere typographical slips.

In the same way, departures from conventional grammar, which in other kinds of language would probably just be 'corrected' (that is, converted into grammatical invariants) by the reader or hearer, could very well have additional meaning of their own in a poem. Take the opening stanza of no. 72:

> I'm  scared a lonely. Never see my son,
>          easy be not to see anyone,
>          combers out to sea
>          know they're goin somewhere but not me.
>          Got a little poison, got a little gun,
> I'm  scared a lonely.

Although our initial reaction to the opening line may be to 'correct' it to 'I'm scared and lonely', its sound may just as well recall 'I'm scared of lonely' (that is, of being lonely). Moreover, the departure from convention itself conveys extra information: the informality of the speaker's diction, the lack of precision in both enunciation and vocabulary which underlies the content of the words and, above all, the ambiguity of the two possible interpretations of 'a' in the first and sixth lines. The result, characteristic not only of poetry but of all art, is to prevent the reader or listener from treating this as a conventional matter.

The language of poetry is far more than the neutral bearer of meaning: it makes itself an aspect of meaning. It follows, as we have already seen, that a poem has an extremely high information content – not just the semantic information of the separate words, but everything contributing to the impact of the poem. It also explains why predictable poetry fails: it does not carry sufficient information to keep audience attention fully engaged.

Lotman presents an illuminating notion of prose literature as 'minus poetry'. He points out, first of all, that prose literature does not develop in a given language until the conventions of poetry are already firmly established. This is because the language of poetry must in its origins be as different as possible from everyday language. Only when the idea of 'poetic convention' is culturally established can poets develop new poetry which plays down some of these differences, or prose, which keeps some of the literary conventions of poetry (plot, characterization, and so on), but discards its emphasis on sound and performance. Once the conventions of poetry have been firmly established, then, writers may develop other forms of creative writing which are closer to everyday speech.

In all forms of creative endeavour, the discerning perceiver must be aware of what is missing, as well as what is present. This is why in poetry simplicity is paradoxically more complex than complexity; it depends on the full development of complexity before it can come into existence and be perceived not only as simple but also as poetic.* Extreme simplicity is also more difficult to investigate (as with the lyric), because there are fewer positive features to talk about. This is why some of the greatest poems in English are the least easy to teach.

The idea of resemblance is central to poetic effect. Resemblances may be ones of parallelism (near-identity) – for example, the semantic parallel of 'hot' and 'torrid', the rhythmic parallel of 'calendar' and 'pineapple', or the phonemic parallel of 'cold' and 'bold'. On the other hand, we may also find resemblances of opposition or antithesis – for example, the semantic opposition of 'hot' and 'cold', the rhythmical opposition of 'seventy' and 'seventeen', and the phonemic opposition of 'senate' and 'tennis'.

The idea of parallelism as incomplete recurrence is important. There are very few words in English that have a perfect synonym: for example, 'cold', 'icy', 'frigid' and 'freezing' are semantic parallels which are roughly synonymous, but each one has connotations which the others lack. Even a case of exact repetition, as in the opening phrases of the lines

'O where ha you been, Lord Randal, my son?
And where ha you been, my handsome young man?'

(no. 14)

---

* 'Artistic simplicity is more complex than artistic complexity, for it arises as the simplification of the latter, and against its background.' Lotman, *Analysis of the Poetic Text*, p. 25.

is not, strictly speaking, complete recurrence: the repetition has an echoic effect which is not present in the first appearance. The echo adds to the overall semantic content of the second line.

In the same way, we may see rhythm as made up of a number of variants which work together to create our sense of the encompassing invariant – metre. But our perception of metre must not become automatic – there is no surer way to put an audience to sleep than by allowing this to happen. This is why skilled poets continually disrupt regular rhythmical patterns.

The metre and the meaning of a poem are not independent of each other: they both arise from the language used. We should try to be aware of how the two interact, and how the poem may counteract recurrence in one with variation in the other. This effect is particularly noticeable in the usual inverse relationship between rhythm and rhyme: in a strictly rhymed poem the rhythm will probably be extremely variable; but in a strongly rhythmic poem the poet will often minimize the effect of rhyme (where it is present) by using enjambed lines and other such devices.

In any poem, some of these effects will be of great importance, others will not. For example, rhyme will probably have little obvious effect in a poem in blank verse. You should be purposeful and selective in considering which effects really contribute to the success of a poem, and which do not. Some effects may change the way other aspects of the poem are perceived. For example, if you analyse the phonemic patterning of a poem, you may discover that certain sounds, by the end of the poem, have taken on meanings of their own. These meanings work only within the context of that particular poem, of course, and are comparable to the effect of phonolexis, mentioned in Chapter 3. You may also discover an inverse relationship between phonemic patterning and syntax: in a poem where sound patterns are an important effect, conventional word order will probably be disregarded to some extent. Formality and richness in one tends to be counterbalanced by informality and simplicity in the other.

The shorter a message, the more important every word becomes. The restricted context of the world of the poem may dictate quite new meanings for conventional words. So the meanings of the words of a poem, particularly a short one, may be quite different from those we would find in a dictionary, which limits itself to everyday usage. Furthermore, as we have already seen, all information in a poem must be interpreted as bearing meaning. In an everyday context, if we overheard an isolated statement such as, 'He is tired of that place', we would say that 'He' and 'that' are devoid of meaning: we have to know the identities of 'He' and 'that place' before they convey anything specific. In a poem, however, the same remark must be treated as meaningful, even if specific assignments of meaning are never made:

> He is tired of that place. His life
> has  sunk into tangles of spice; his wife,
>  he  says, has dreams of empty shells
> and  knows not what they mean . . .

If we made a glossary of these lines, it would have to include such entries as:

> He – a married male expressing dissatisfaction with present
>     situation,
> That place – the present situation of He,

and so forth.

Poetry often uses lexically empty words in this way. A frequent mistake of literary critics is to assume that such usages may be interpreted as though they were ordinary language. The matter of personal pronouns is a frequent pitfall. In a poem beginning,

> I will arise and go now, and go to Innisfree,
>
> (no. 54)

the reader may be tempted to try to speculate who the 'I' of the poem actually is. But 'I' cannot have any meaning beyond that stated in the poem. To assume 'I = William Butler Yeats' makes no more sense than assuming 'I ≠ William Butler Yeats': both are quite irrelevant and have no basis in the context of the poem. 'I' in a poem can only relate to other words of that poem. Nevertheless, it is not uncommon to read or hear critics who say that the 'I' in a certain poem *is* 'the poet' (or 'William Wordsworth', or whoever) *because* the poem is known to be based on autobiographical fact. This unwarranted assumption is extremely persistent, even in the work of such a 'linguistic' critic as Geoffrey Leech, most of which is above reproach.

After considering the primary effects of the poem, its rhythm and metre, its sound patterns, its organization and use of words, we may move on to look at its larger units – its line, combinations of lines, and stanza, where these are present. What is of particular interest is to see how these may reinforce, or counteract, the poem's primary effects. For example, is the stanza form of the poem something separate from its syntax (as in the second part of no. 72)? Or do the stanzas of the poem conform to its syntactical patterns (as in no. 67)? Finally we may consider the structural organization of the separate features of the poem. Do they function in harmony, or in opposition; as a whole, or as discrete elements? And does the composition as a whole answer conventional and cultural expectations (as in a reverdie, such as no. 4), or negate them? How do the language and other effects of the poem compare to others of the same period – to what came before and what followed? The answers to such questions may reveal much about the overall effect of the poem.

Let's look at a short poem to put this all into practice. I have chosen one of my own, part of a longer work, *Will's Dream*. My reason for choosing this poem instead of one from the anthology is that I would like to leave those for you to examine on your own. Moreover, this particular poem is not primarily a semantic 'message', even though all its words have literal meanings. But first, read it aloud a couple of times.

> The  rich red coral torn from Mary's
>           brain (Will misses the signs)
>           leeches the sky, fingers the plate
>           yearning for acid, then dies.
>
>           Chords she struck always move from
>           home with a start on pitch
>           falling to the sea, and end
>           flat in a packet of yeast.

Will paces a square round the rooms
of  friends in the world's corners.
      Sides don't add up, always goodbye
is a  dash for the two last trains

where the  kick of finally making
    the con · nection is so great
        we  only realise stations later
            all we are kissing is air.

Let's first look at the poem's patterns of rhythm and metre, as these are probably its most significant effects. We'll use the dot notation developed in Chapter 2:

| | | | |
|---|---|---|---|
| The rich red | coral | torn from | Mary's |
| ●○ | ●○ | ●○ | ●○ |
| brain (Will | misses the | signs) | |
| ●○ | ●○○ | ● | * |
| leeches the | sky, | fingers the | plate |
| ●○○ | ● | ●○○ | ● |
| yearning for | acid, then | dies. | |
| ●○○ | ●○○ | ● | * |
| | | | |
| Chords she | struck | always | move from |
| ●○ | ● | ●○ | ●○ |
| home with a | start on | pitch | |
| ●○○ | ●○ | ● | * |
| falling | to the | sea, and | end |
| ●○ | ●○ | ●○ | ● |
| flat in a | packet of | yeast. | |
| ●○○ | ●○○ | ● | * |
| | | | |
| Will | paces a | square round the | rooms |
| ● | ●○○ | ●○○ | ●/○ |
| of friends in the | world's | corners. | |
| ●○○ | ● | ●○ | * |
| Sides don't add | up, | always good- | bye |
| ●○○ | ● | ●○○ | ●/○○ |
| is a dash for the | two last | trains | |
| ●○○ | ●○ | ● | */○○ |
| | | | |
| where the kick of | finally | making | |
| ●○ | ●○○ | ●○ | */○○ |
| the con·nection | is so | great | |
| ●○ | ●○ | ● | */○ |
| we only | realise | stations | later |
| ●○ | ●○ | ●○ | ●○ |
| all we are | kissing is | air. | |
| ●○○ | ●○○ | ● | * |

The poem uses a very common kind of quatrain, one with four-stress lines. The second and fourth lines consistently end with a silent stress, often associated with some punctuational pause, and indicated in this notation by the asterisks. This is, you will remember, the conventional metre of the popular ballad and of a great deal of narrative and lyric poetry in English, so these are associated 'cultural' meanings for a reader already familiar with these traditional genres. How the content of this particular poem reinforces or clashes with the 'meaning' of this metre will be examined in a moment.

Look at the rhythms first. As we have seen, the standard measure in English poetry is the duplet, and the first line of the poem suggests that at least in this regard the poem may be quite conventional: all four measures are duplets. The second line, too, opens with a duplet. However, at this point regularity is disrupted: not another duplet occurs in the remaining measures of the stanza. The rest are all either triplets or singlets. What is the effect of this negation of the rhythmical expectations set up by the first line?

The table takes a closer look at the way these three different rhythms are deployed in the poem.

| stanza | singlets | duplets | triplets |
| --- | --- | --- | --- |
| 1st | 6 | 5 | 5 |
| 2nd | 6 | 6 | 3 |
| 3rd | 5 | 3 | 8 |
| 4th | 3 | 9 | 4 |
| all | 20 | 23 | 20 |

The breakdown shows that the number of singlets and triplets in the poem is exactly the same. Duplets outnumber them, but not by much.* Many of the lines seesaw between singlet and triplet rhythms:

* I take a silent stress as rhythmically equivalent to a sounded one. As was explained in Chapter 2, any weak syllables which open a line are included in the last measure of the preceding line. So the measure formed by the silent stress which closes the third stanza and the two weak syllables which open the fourth stanza (' – / where the') is a triplet. In other words, ●○○ and ∗/○○ are equivalent.

| leeches the | sky, | fingers the | plate |
|---|---|---|---|
| ●○○ | ● | ●○○ | ● |

and

| flat in a | packet of | yeast. | |
|---|---|---|---|
| ●○○ | ●○○ | ● | * |

and

| Sides don't add | up, | always good- | bye |
|---|---|---|---|
| ●○○ | ● | ●○○ | ●/○○ |

This oscillation between triplet and singlet rhythms maintains the impression of duplets as the metrical invariant norm, against which the other two rhythms are variants, especially as the number of triplets and the number of singlets in the poem is exactly the same.

So the poem opens with lines in which rhythm, phonemic patterning and syntax all coincide. Then, beginning in the third stanza and reaching a peak in the fourth stanza, come lines where the last measure runs on to the next line, reinforced with frequent enjambment. Even the final measure of stanza three is enjambed. (The absence of any punctuation at the end of the concluding line of this stanza makes this clear.) Rhythm also dramatizes the semantic content of these lines when the speeded-up delivery of frequent triplets parallels such a statement as:

| | Sides don't add | up, | always good- | bye |
|---|---|---|---|---|
| | ●○○ | ● | ●○○ | ●/○○ |
| is a | dash for the | two last | trains | |
| | ●○○ | ●○ | ● | *○○ |

The first and second stanzas of the poem are metrically the most regular. In the third stanza, more enjambed lines are used and this continues through the first two lines of the fourth stanza. Only in the last two lines of the poem – metrically very similar to the opening two lines – do we sense anything like a return to regularity.

Another pattern in the poem is set up by the relative strengths of enjambed and run-on lines in each stanza. There is clearly a marked syntactical pause at the end of the first stanza (shown by the full stop). I'll use a number 1 to show that in such a line any feeling of running-on is at a minimum. The pause at the end of the second line, though clearly perceptible because of the silent stress of the last measure, is not as great: we may denote this with a 2. The first and third lines are more clearly run-on – particularly the first, which ends with a possessive noun – 'Mary's', which obviously requires an object, 'brain', to open the following line. This is the most strongly enjambed line in the stanza, so we'll give this a 4, and the remaining line, the third, a 3. The run-on strength pattern of the lines of this stanza, then, is 4231. Now, if you look at the remaining stanzas of the poem, you will find that the same 4231 pattern occurs in all but the third stanza (which I read as 2143). In other words, a pattern of relative run-on strengths is set up in the first stanza which is then repeated throughout the poem, except in stanza three.

Now, I am not supposing for a moment that any reader or listener, however diligent and keen, could pick up, from merely hearing this poem, everything I have just presented here. Nevertheless, the effects are *there* in the poem, and it would be wrong to suppose that they do not contribute to the total effect, even if the listener is not consciously aware of them. Many of them depend on the widespread cultural preconception of duplet rhythms as a metrical norm in English poetry.

Let's leave the rhythm and metre of the poem now – just remembering that in a number of ways the third stanza has already been marked as 'different' from the other stanzas of the poem – and turn our attention to its patterns of sound. What I would like to do first is lay out the stressed syllables of the poem, in the order in which they appear, using the phonemic symbols which are explained in Appendix A. (I'm including all consonant sounds here, even when these sounds may actually be merely adjacent to the stressed syllable and not, strictly speaking, part of it.) You will find it helps to read out each line of the poem, exaggerating the pronunciation of the stressed syllables.

| The rich red | coral | torn from | Mary's |
|---|---|---|---|
| /rɪtʃ/ | /kor/ | /torn/ | /mɛr/ |
| brain (Will | misses the | signs) | |
| /brɛin/ | /mɪs/ | /sainz/ | * |
| leeches the | sky, fingers the | plate | |
| /litʃ/ | /skai//fɪŋ/ | /plɛit/ | |

yearning for    acid, then      dies.
/jɜrn/            /æs/           /daiz/  *

Chords she    struck always     move from
/kordz/        /strʌk//ɒl/     /muv/

home with a    start on      pitch
/hoʊm/        /start/       /pɪtʃ/  *

falling    to the    sea, and    end
/fɒl/     /tu/      /si/        /ɛnd/

flat in a    packet of    yeast.
/flæt/     /pæk/      /jist/  *

Will paces a    square round the    rooms
/wɪl//pɛis/    /skwɛr/           /rumz/

of friends in the    world's corners.
/frɛndz/        /wɜrldz//korn/  *

Sides don't add    up, always goodbye
/saidz/        /ʌp//ɒl/      /bai/

is a dash for the    two last    trains
/dæʃ/          /tu/       /trɛinz/  *

where the kick of    finally    making
/kɪk/           /fain/   /mɛik/  *

the con·nection   is so    great
/nɛk/        /ɪz/   /grɛit/  *

we only realise    stations    later
/oʊn//ri/       /stɛiʃ/   /lɛit/

all we are    kissing is    air.
/ɒl/       /kɪs/      /ɛr/  *

Now, with a little paperwork, we may better isolate the dominant sound patterns of the poem. For example, if we look at the dominant consonant sounds in these stressed syllables, we find three sounds standing out: /t/, /s/, and /r/, together with combinations beginning with these sounds, such as /tr/ and /tʃ/, /st/ and /sk/, and /rn/ and /rdz/. Each of the three groups is roughly equal in size (in fact, there are 14 occurrences of the /t/ group and 13 of each of the other two), but they are not evenly distributed throughout the poem. The /r/ sound, for instance, does not occur on its own at all in stanza two, though it is there in the combinations /rdz/ and /rt/. The /t/ and /s/ sounds, on the other hand, occur regularly throughout the poem. Other consonantal sounds appear less frequently, but still play their part in the overall effect. The /k/ sound, for example, occurs 10 times in the whole poem, but fully half of these occurrences are in the fourth stanza.

The sounds /t/ and /s/ are unvoiced, of course. Their voiced equivalents, /d/ and /z/, appear far less frequently – /d/ three times, and /z/ only once, in the last stanza, and in a position ('is so') where it would be pronounced more like /s/ anyway. The voiced equivalent of /k/, which is /g/, is entirely absent, except in the combination /gr/ in stanza four. The same is true of the less frequently used consonants: the unvoiced consonants /f/ and /p/ are used five times each, but their voiced counterparts, /v/ and /b/, only twice and once, respectively. The unvoiced /ʃ/ occurs twice on its own, but its voiced counterpart /ʒ/ is not found at all. Unvoiced consonants clearly dominate the poem. (It might also be worth noting that along with /ʒ/, the consonant sounds /ð/ and /θ/ are entirely absent, and that /h/ occurs only once.)

In the same way, certain stressed vowels and diphthongs (vowel combinations) dominate the phonic patterning of the poem. Leading in frequency is the vowel /ɪ/ and the diphthong /ɛi/, each used eight times. Next come /ai/ and /ɛ/, each of which occurs six times. Following these, tied for third place, are /o/, /ɑ/, /u/, /i/, and /æ/.

Some distinct patterns begin to emerge if we consider how these vowel sounds are distributed throughout the poem. The sound /ɪ/, for example, occurs eight times in the poem as a whole, but three of these appearances are in the first stanza and three in the final stanza. The effect, then, is that of concluding the poem with a return to a vowel sound not placed in the foreground since the beginning. The sound /ɛi/ occurs twice in the first stanza, and only once in the second; however, we find two further appearances in the third stanza, and four in the final one. Here, then, is the effect of a sound only mildly highlighted at the beginning being used increasingly as the poem concludes.

Other vowel sounds, such as /o/ and /æ/, are used frequently early in the poem, and not at all in the conclusion, while still others, such as /ɒ/ and /u/, do not appear at all in the first stanza. Even these differ in effect, as /ɒ/ continues to be used throughout the poem after its first appearance in stanza two, whereas /u/ is used only in the two middle stanzas, and is entirely absent from the conclusion. We could make graphs for each of these sounds to show that while the lines for some sounds rise as the poem proceeds, those for others fall or remain level. The simultaneous waxing, waning, and constancy of the different vowels is another distinctive effect of the poem.

What about phonemic patterning? Traditional patterns such as rhyme and alliteration are obviously not much used. You might notice, however, that the phrase 'Chords she struck' (line 5) uses a kind of reverse consonance: /kordz/ and /strʌk/, except that the ending of the first, /rdz/, is voiced, while the opening of the second, /str/, is not. There is also a clear link between the sounds of 'coral' and 'chords'. You will probably also have picked up the partial rhyme of such combinations as 'coral' and 'torn' (line 1), the assonance of 'signs' and 'dies', which appear in conventional rhyme positions (lines 2 and 4); as well as those of 'flat' and 'packet' (line 8); 'sides' and 'goodbye' (line 11); 'making' and 'great'; and 'stations' and 'later' (lines 13, 14 and 15). Less obvious, but still part of the total effect, are the partial consonances of 'torn' and 'Mary's' (line 1); and 'kick', 'making', and 'connection' (lines 13 and 14).

Overall, we can see a fairly clear progression in the degree of sound patterning in the poem. Certain sounds enunciated in the opening stanza are then used in different patterns as the poem proceeds. If we count up the different phonemes, both consonantal and vocalic, used in the stressed syllables of each stanza, we arrive at the totals shown in the table. The greatest number of different sounds occurs in the two middle stanzas, and the least in the final stanza, probably what we should expect of a satisfying conclusion.

| stanza | *different vowels/diphthongs* | *different consonants* |
|---|---|---|
| 1st | 8 | 17 |
| 2nd | 10 | 18 |
| 3rd | 10 | 19 |
| 4th | 7 | 12 |

As with the consonants, we should consider which vowels are not used at all. Missing from the whole poem are the /ʊ/ sound ('put'), and the diphthong /oi/ and /aʊ/ sounds ('boy' and 'down' respectively). Of more interest is the fact that the stressed vocalics which appear the least frequently – /ɜ/, /ʌ/, /a/, and /oʊ/ – always occur with the most common consonants: /ɜ/ with /r/, /ʌ/ in /strʌk/ and /ʌp/, /a/ in /start/, and /oʊ/ in /hoʊm/ (a partial exception, as this is the only appearance of /h/ in the poem) and /oʊn·li/. In this way they fit harmoniously into the sound structure of the poem.

We may also link some of these vocalic and consonantal sound patterns to the semantic meaning of the poem. For example, /r/ is very clearly associated at the outset with Mary, while /s/ and /z/ become linked with Will, though as the poem progresses and the characters interact, these phonemes are more generally used. This might, in turn, lead to some phonolexical association – 'liquid' resonants suggesting Mary as opposed to 'hissing' fricatives suggesting Will. I leave it to you to look for other examples of this in the poem.

Please do not think that it is necessary always to be this aware of the separate sounds of a poem. Normally, I would not dream of dissecting a poem I happened to be reading this minutely. But one *may* analyse a poem in this way to try to understand why it brings (or does not bring) pleasure or artistic satisfaction to the listener. Life is too short for such analyses to be carried out on every poem that one may encounter; and of course, they do not, in themselves, *necessarily* add to one's appreciation of the poem. But they may supply some objective evidence to justify an intuitive reaction to it.

Now, I do not for a moment believe that poets need be consciously aware of all such effects as they work on a poem. They are conscious, always, only of what sounds *right*. Of course, if a poet chooses to use a rhyme-scheme in the poem, attention will have to be given to getting just the right stressed syllables at the end of each line. But within the line, and through the poem generally, such patterns are usually developed more or less unconsciously. In the case of the poem above, I did the analysis on the poem many years after it was published. Another point: the author of a poem is no more qualified to discuss the way in which it works than anyone else – the act of analysis demands a frame of mind which many poets would find antithetical to the act of creation.

Let's consider the poem's grammar and vocabulary. Remember

'coral' and 'brain' inverts that of the zoological 'brain coral'. (The same effect is employed in no. 76; 'Dying | Is an art', a rearrangement of the cliché 'a dying art'.) 'Round' also couples with 'plate' (line 3), even though here one is an adverb and the other a noun.

Most of these equivalences, or couplings, are dual ones. The poem also contains four subject couplings: 'Mary('s)' with 'Will', 'Mary('s)' with 'she', 'Mary('s)' and 'Will' with 'two last trains' (by implication) – and 'two last trains' with 'we' (also by implication), which occurs twice. The dualistic nature of these couplings is reinforced by other more obvious pairs already mentioned – 'sky' and 'sea', 'square' and 'round', 'coral' and 'brain', 'leeches' and 'fingers', to mention a few.

If we look at the distribution of grammatical 'parts of speech', we can see something else going on. The first stanza contains 6 nouns, the second 7, and the third 9 – but the last stanza has only 3: 'kick', 'connection' and 'air'. If we narrow this list down to visible or tangible nouns, the effect is even more striking: 6, 4, and 5 in the first three stanzas, none at all in the last. (Remember, 'stations' is being used adverbially, to modify 'realise'.) The effect of the poem is to carry the reader from a tactile concrete world to one of pure emotion.

The grammar and syntax of the poem are quite conventional, but work in a kind of counterpoint to its metrical and phonemic patterns. You can see quite easily that the first stanza forms a complete sentence, as does the second. The third stanza, on the other hand, has one sentence which ends in mid-stanza, and another which is enjambed to the fourth stanza, continuing to the end of the poem. Each of the first three sentences is a simple active statement, each with a subject ('coral', 'chords', 'Will') and associated active verbs ('leeches', 'fingers', 'dies'; 'move', 'end'; 'paces'). The syntax is quite conventional, though the import of the words may not make literal sense: 'coral' can't literally 'leech the sky' nor 'chords' 'end | flat in a packet of yeast'. On the other hand, 'Will paces a square round the rooms | of friends in the world's corners' does make some literal sense.

The final sentence, however, is more complicated. The meaning of the statement, 'Sides don't add up', is ambiguous: it could mean that the list of the words used in a given poem is the entire vocabulary of the universe of that poem. If we make a list of the animate subjects of the poem, for example, it is limited to 'Mary' (which occurs in the possessive case only), 'Will' (which is repeated), 'she' (which presumably refers to 'Mary') and 'we' (which also occurs twice, but whose relationship to the other subjects of the poem is never made explicit). The list of animate subjects will also have to stretch to include the 'coral' which 'leeches the sky, fingers the plate . . . then dies', as well as the 'chords' which 'always move from | home . . . and end | flat in a packet of yeast.' In the paradigm 'Animate subjects', then, the poem includes one word, 'coral', which we do not usually perceive as animate, and another, 'chords', which is in conventional usage not animate at all. Similarly, the poem's 'Active verbs' paradigm includes not only such conventional items as 'misses' and 'dies', but also words more commonly found as nouns: 'leeches', 'fingers' and 'end'.

We may look for equivalences, or what Levin calls 'couplings', in these and other paradigms implicit in the poem, remembering that they may work through parallelism or opposition – of sound, or of sense, or of both simultaneously. The two verbs, 'leeches' and 'fingers', also have, as nouns, similar qualities of size, shape and movement – they are cylindrical, animate, a few inches long, filled with blood, tactile, questing, and so forth. Moreover, they are both rhythmic duplets. Among the poem's nouns, 'sky' and 'sea'; 'coral' and 'brain'; 'home' and 'start'; 'pitch' (in the sense used by brewers) and 'yeast'; 'packet of yeast', 'square', and 'corners'; 'rooms' and 'corners'; 'sides' and 'corners'; 'trains' and 'connection'; and 'sky' and 'air' are lexical parallels. In the 'Adverbs' paradigm we find on case of repetition, 'always', and one of contrast, 'flat' and 'roun (both normally adjectives).

We may also uncover semantic parallels between members different grammatical paradigms – such as 'trains', a noun, a 'stations', which functions as part of an adverbial phrase, 'stati later'. The verb 'misses' and the adjective 'yearning' form ano similar pair. Perhaps the strongest example of this yokin dissimilar grammatical units is the juxtaposition of the 'square' with the preposition 'round'. This effectively inverts a mon oxymoron ('round square') just as the order of the cou literally that 'sides' do not find the sum of numbers. It's more likely that we should derive its meaning from the idiomatic expression, 'It doesn't add up', meaning, 'It doesn't make sense' – in this case, 'The whole thing doesn't make sense.' The opening sentence of this, the third stanza, contrasts with all that has preceded. It is not an active sentence like the others, but purely descriptive, the kind of thing that could be conveyed by a short sentence such as, 'It is senseless', in which the only meaningful word is the adjective 'senseless'. The same holds true for the rest of the sentence, which could be condensed to 'goodbye is a dash', or simply 'goodbye = dash'. In this way the last sentence, made up of what amounts to two adjectival statements, is in distinct contrast to the 'subject/active verb' sentences which come before.

We have not yet considered cultural overtones – the fact, for example, that the ear of an experienced reader of Engish literature might link the 'coral' of the opening line with the 'coral' of Shakespeare's song 'Full fadom five' (no. 19), and might recall its frequent /ɛi/ assonances ('made', 'fade', 'change', 'strange') through the frequent repetitions of the same diphthong in this poem. The stanza form, the poem's narrative beginning, and the absence of the pronouns 'I' and 'you' as subjects might suggest to such a reader that the poem is modelled after traditional popular forms such as the ballad and the lyric, while the shift to the pronoun 'we' recalls earlier communal genres such as the carol. Here, by contrast, its use is essentially private, a 'we' limited to two.

One effect Lotman mentions which has frequently been discussed by other critics and by poets is that of 'the alien word' – a word (or any semantic element, for that matter) which appears in some way unusual or out of conventional context. This is a sequential effect: some kind of context has to be created first. For example, the opening, 'The rich red coral . . .', is a series of words which is not in itself unusual (though we might not perhaps expect the name of a colour to follow the adjective 'rich'). 'Torn' is more of a surprise, perhaps: though it could evoke a literal image of coral being 'torn' from the sea-bed. However, it is probable that nothing in our earlier linguistic or cultural experience will have prepared us for the words 'from Mary's | brain' – particularly 'brain'. The only conventional link between 'brain' and 'coral' is the one already mentioned, an inversion of 'brain coral'. So 'brain' is the most clearly alien word in this stretch of the poem. It has the effect of de-automatizing the listener's perception of all the language in this stanza, of communicating the basic message of all poetry: whatever this is, it is not simply meaning.

Other alien words in the poem are not as obvious, but their effect is quite perceptible none the less. 'Chords she struck always move' is interesting in that the tense of the second verb is present, not past, as we would expect ('Chords she struck always *moved*' would make more conventional sense). But we are able to make literal sense out of this one: the chords go on moving. 'Move' could also be interpreted in the sense of 'cause an emotional experience' – except that the next words, 'from home', besides suggesting the 'home key' of a piece of music, recall another conventional sense of 'move': 'to pack one's belongings and leave a dwelling-place'. The 'chords' may not be literal, therefore – perhaps they are drawn from the conventional expression, 'strike a responsive chord'. However, line six returns to terminology associated with music, 'start on pitch | falling . . .' But 'falling' in music (to a lower note, or pitch) is only figurative, not the same as the act of 'falling to the sea'. 'And end | flat in a packet of yeast' defies conventional explanation: 'packet of yeast' is the most alien phrase in the whole stanza. We accommodate it by perceiving the assonantal link of 'packet' and 'flat', the semantic coupling of 'yeast' and 'pitch' ('to pitch yeast', it has been pointed out, is a brewing term), and the opposing connotative overtones of 'yeast' (bubbly, zesty, lively), and 'flat'.

In contrast to the first two stanzas, the third stanza makes a good deal of literal sense, until the expression, 'always goodbye | is a dash for the two last trains'. This is easily interpreted figuratively as: 'the act of leavetaking is always associated with rushing to catch the two last trains.' (Why *two* last trains? Presumably two parties, departing for different destinations, are involved: this is reinforced by 'Mary' and 'Will' earlier in the poem, and by the two appearances of 'we' which follow.)

The alien word of the last stanza is perhaps not as easy to perceive, and it requires some interpretation of what has preceded: that 'the kick' (that is, the intense physical and emotional pleasure) of 'making the connection' (on one level, catching the trains; on another, concerned with any physical connection which may have existed between 'Mary' and 'Will' in their leavetaking) 'is so great' that 'we' (to whom does this refer? – no assignment of meaning is specifically made) 'only realise stations later' (that is, after the separating trains have already been under way for some time), 'all we are kissing is air'. The surprise in this line is the present continuative 'are kissing', when '*were* kissing', at the earlier time of 'goodbye', would be more likely. The 'kissing' continues even after the separation, though what 'we are kissing' turns out to be no more than 'air'. The implication may be that the act carried on to this length has become empty of meaning. There are other possibilities, however. 'Are kissing' may be used in a generalized sense: 'all we are kissing whenever we say goodbye is air.' A further ambiguity is carried by 'we', which could refer to the two parties collectively, or simply to the narrator of the poem, as an editorial 'we'.

Many critics have commented on the use of *deictic* words in poetry. Deictic words 'point' or particularize something. In 'The rich red coral', 'The' is deictic: particular coral is referred to. 'Mary's', 'Will', and 'we' also function deictically: they particularize the action, tell us that these and no others are the specific subjects of the action of the poem. The 'the' of 'the sky' is not really deictic: there is only one sky. But the 'the' of 'the plate' is: it suggests that some particular plate is intended. In ordinary language this deictic sense would be unacceptable unless the speaker or writer made quite clear just *which* plate was being referred to. There is no such specifying here: we may assume 'Will's plate', or 'Mary's plate', or 'our plate', or even 'the narrator's plate' – but the only logically acceptable interpretation is 'the plate in this poem'.

Let's now try to bring together the different strands of investigation we have been pursuing to see if they can be drawn into one coherent and progressive pattern. In many levels of the poem, particularly those of rhythm, phonemic patterning, and sentence structure or syntax, we have seen that the third stanza is the 'alien' element of the whole poem. The first stanza sets up expectations on all these levels which are reinforced by what happens in the second stanza. The third stanza is a departure from these expectations, but the final stanza is a return to them, in some cases even a redoubling of them.

I said at the outset that the paraphrasable meaning of a poem may be only a small aspect of its total effect, and I chose this poem to analyse because I believe it well demonstrates this. Nevertheless, it may be useful to attempt a paraphrase, if only to clarify the relationships between the words.* Here is one possible inter-pretation.

'The 'rich red coral torn from Mary's | brain' moves like a leech against the sky, appearing to 'finger' a certain 'plate' in a desire for 'acid', before dying. The implication may be that some aspect of Mary's intellect has been forcibly removed, and is here, on 'the plate', observed dying an agonized death. Attention then turns to 'chords she [presumably Mary] struck', and how these chords, phonemically linked to the opening 'coral', continue to move in a downward progression 'to the sea' – in other words, back to the origins of the 'coral' – 'and end' (again, die). The 'packet of yeast' has no clear meaning, but it suggests the potential energy and suspended animation of dried yeast, which needs only warm sweet (as opposed to cold salt) water to return to life. 'Flat' suggests 'without life', as well as 'two-dimensional' (like the 'packet'); it also has a musical link to the downward-moving 'chords'.

The rest of the poem presents a more concrete scene: first, we see Will, who 'paces' round the rooms of friends in different far-flung parts of the world. We are not told why he does this – possibly anxiety, impatience, boredom or worry. Whatever the case, 'paces' conveys that he is not at peace with himself. 'Sides don't add up' might mean that the opposing parties (Will and Mary, perhaps) either do not interrelate, or do not make sense. The first of these two possible interpretations is reinforced by what follows in the poem; an act of farewell is described as being a 'dash' for two trains which bear the parties apart from each other. The manner of their leave-taking is like 'kissing . . . air' – in other words, there is no physical (or perhaps even emotional) connection.

The dominant emotion of the poem is one of sadness, of mourn-ing for a richly creative spirit now absent (Mary), and for the inadequacy of human relationships. Its somewhat pessimistic and cynical tone is balanced by the aesthetic effects of the other aspects

* Geoffrey Leech's advice is salutary: 'Do not be afraid of paraphrase as a means of getting at *part* of the significance of a poem.' *A Linguistic Guide to English Poetry*, p. 221.

of the poem at which we have already looked – rhythm and metre, phonemic patterning, syntax and grammar, and all the different kinds of parallelism or coupling which occur. All combine in the reader's or listener's ear, resulting in a unique and highly complex experience.

None of a poem's effects functions in isolation. Each one works against a backdrop set up not only by the poem itself, but by all the literary and artistic conventions of our culture. The relationship of our analysis of it to the poem itself is like the relationship of a laboratory dissection of living tissue to life itself. The total of all the separate parts can in no way add up to the functioning whole. Above all, an analysis such as this cannot communicate the magic of a poem to someone else: it is the act of analysis that may be revealing. Reading someone else's analysis will communicate very little. The exercise I have just concluded is to be taken as an example of how to proceed, not as a demonstration of the effects of the poem, which will have to stand on its own merits.

If you have read many other books about poetry, you will know that the majority of them pay a good deal of attention to matters which have not really occupied me greatly in this book – symbolism, development of plot and character, the use of allegory and myth, and so forth. These are common to all types of literature. My interest here has been to look at what is unique and most apt to be misunderstood in poetry as distinct from other literary genres. The other matters are of great importance too, but there is no lack of good information about them. Likewise, you will find many more 'user-friendly' books about poetry than this one, ones that in the end do little more than present a number of the author's favourite poems for your enjoyment. This is fine if you already like poetry, but it's not much help if you don't. I want this book to do more than that.

# A Chronological
# Anthology of English Poetry
# from the Tenth to the
# Twentieth Century

## Introduction

The purpose of this anthology is not only to illustrate points I have made in the main body of the book but, more important, to offer a selection of English poetry of most periods, types and forms. The unorthodox placing of the lines is fully explained in Chapter 2; here I will just point out that the opening stresses of the lines are aligned in a vertical stress-column. In

### Loveliest of trees

Loveliest of trees, the cherry now
Is  hung with bloom along the bough,

'Love-' is the first stressed syllable in the first line, and 'hung' the first stressed syllable in the second line. This lay-out, I hope, will have two effects: first, guiding you quickly to the opening stress of each line (after which the remaining stresses will usually follow more easily); second, reinforcing the fact that a poem is not just a piece of print, but must be *heard* if it is to work.

At various points along the way you may disagree with my reading, and feel that a different syllable should receive the first stress of the line. The ambiguous rhythms of some lines are part of their effect. In the end, there is no 'correct' reading, other than the one which gives maximum satisfaction to each reader. All I have tried to do is present stress-patterns which seem to me to work; in most cases these will be found to coincide with the rhythms of ordinary speech. Wherever possible, from the time of Yeats onward, I have based my reading on a specific recorded performance by the poet. Of course, even the poet is not the final judge of how the rhythms of a line may be best realized. In the end, only you can decide.

# Contents

63. e.e. cummings: chanson innocente (1930)
64. William Carlos Williams: Smell (1935)
65. Ogden Nash: Everybody Makes Poets (1938)
66. Stevie Smith: To the tune of the Coventry Carol (19—)
67. Louis MacNeice: Prognosis (1939)
68. Robert Graves: Warning to Children (1941)
69. L. A. MacKay: from *The Ill-Tempered Lover* (1948)
70. A. D. Hope: The Death of the Bird (1948)
71. Dylan Thomas: Do not go gentle into that good night (1951)
72. John Berryman: from *The Dream Songs* (1955)
73. Langston Hughes: Daybreak in Alabama (1957)
74. Robert Lowell: Grandparents (1959)
75. James K. Baxter: Election 1960 (1961)
76. Sylvia Plath: Lady Lazarus (1962)
77. William Stafford: Introduction to Literature (1970)
78. Philip Davies Roberts: The Years (1975)
79. Louis Zukofsky: Julia's Wild (19—)
80. Robert Mazzocco: All Night (1978)
81. Sherod Santos: Married Love (1985)

1. *from* **Beowulf**                                    late 10th century

> Hwæt! we Gar-Dena in            geardagum,
> Hey! We of the spear-Danes in   yore days
>
> theodcyninga       thrym gefrunon,
> the kings' glory   power have asked to hear,
>
> hu tha æthelingas     ellen fremedon!
> how the princelings   deeds performed!
>
> Oft Scyld Scefing   sceathena threatum,
> Oft Scyld Scefing   of the enemies from the throng,
>
> monegum mægthum   meodosetla ofteah,
> many tribes'          mead-seats took off,
>
> egsode eorlas,   syththan ærest wearth
> scared earls,    after (he) first was
>
> feasceaft funden;   he thæs frofre gebad,
> abandoned found;   he for that consolation saw,
>
> weox under wolcnum   weorthmyndum thah,
> waxed under welkin   in glory throve,
>
> oth thæt him æghwylc     ymbsittendra
> until that to him every one   of the by-dwellers
>
> ofer hronrade         hyran scolde,
> over the whales' road   obey had to,
>
> gomban gyldan;   thæt wæs god cyning! . . .
> tribute yield;   that was a good king! . . .
>
>                         (lines 1–11)
>
>                     Forth near æt stop,
>                     Forth nearer he stepped,
>
> nam that mid handa   higethihtigne
> seized then with hand   the strong-hearted
>
> rinc on ræste,         ræhte ongean
> warrior on the bed,   reached toward (Beowulf)

feond mid folme;     he onfeng hrathe
the fiend with hand;    he (Beowulf) received (him) at once

inwit-thancum     ond with earm gesæt.
with hostile intent    and with (leaning against his) arm sat up.

Sona thæt onfunde,    fyrena hyrde,
Soon he realized,     the master of crimes,

thæt he ne mette     middangeardes,
that he had not met,   in this world,

eorthan sceata      on elran men
these earth's regions,  in any man

mundgripe maran,    he on mode wearth
more of a handgrip,   he in heart became

forht on ferthe,   no thy ær fram meahte.
afraid in spirit,    he could not go any sooner.

Hyge wæs him hinfus,         wolde on heolster fleon,
His mind was keen to get away,   he wished to fly into the dark

secan deofla gedræg;        ne wæs his drohtoth thær
to seek out the devils' swarm;   his plight there was not

swylce he on ealderdagum   ær gemette . . .
such as he in all his days    before had met . . .

                        (lines 745–57)

Listen! We've always wanted to hear about the glories of the Spear-Dane kings in days of yore, and how the princes did great deeds. Often Shyld Shefing captured the mead-halls of troops of enemies, of many peoples. He made their noblemen quake with fear – he who was first found destitute (he was consoled for that, waxed great under the heavens and throve in honour) – until each one of his neighbours from over the whale's road had to obey him and to yield tribute to him. He was a great king! . . .

Forward and nearer he stepped, and then seized the strong-hearted warrior on the bed; the fiend reached towards him. Beowulf received him at once with hostile intent and, supporting himself on his arm, sat up. Soon he realized, the master of crimes, that he had not met, in all the regions of the world, anyone with such a strong grip. Deep in his heart his courage failed, and he couldn't get away soon enough. He was anxious to get away, he wanted to flee into the dark to find the swarm of devils. His plight was not like anything he had ever encountered before.

– Anonymous

2.                     **Sumer is icumen in**         early 13th century

> Sumer is icumen in!
> Lhudë sing, cuccu!
> Groweth sed and bloweth med
> And springth the wudë nu –
> Sing, cuccu!
>
> Awë bleteth after lomb,
> Louth after calvë cu,
> Bulluc sterteth, buckë verteth,
> Murie sing, cuccu!
> Sing, cuccu!
>
> Cuccu, cuccu,
> Well singës thu, cuccu –
> Ne swik thu naver nu!

Spring has arrived! Sing loud, cuckoo! Seed grows, meadow flowers, and now the wood springs (with leaves). Sing, cuckoo! The ewe bleats after the lamb, the cow lows after the calf, the bullock starts, the buck farts – sing merry, cuckoo! Cuckoo, cuckoo, you sing well, cuckoo – now don't you ever stop!

– Anonymous

3.     *from* **Sir Orfeo**                           *c.*1310

In the castel the steward sat attë mete,
    And mani lording was bi him sete.
        Ther were trompours and tabourers,
        Harpours felë, and crouders.
        Miche melody thai makëd alle,
And Or·feo sat stillë in the halle,
    And herkneth. When thai ben al stille,
     He toke his harp and tempred schille,
    The blisse fulest notes he harpëd there
That ever ani man yherd with ere;
        Ich man likëd wele his gle.
    The steward biheld and gan yse,
    And knewe the harp als blive.
        'Menstrel,' he seyd, 'so mot thou thrive,
 Where hadestow this harp, and hou?
     Y pray that thou me tellë now.'
        'Lord,' quath he, 'in uncouthe thede,
        Thurch a wildernes as Y yede,
        Ther Y foundë in a dale
With ly·ouns a man to-torn smale,
    And wolves him frete with teth so scharp.
     Bi him Y fond this ich harp;
        Wele ten yere it is ygo.'

                              (lines 519–41)

In the castle the steward sat to eat, and many a noble was seated by him.
There were trumpeters and drummers, many harpers, and fiddlers. They all
made much melody, and Orpheus sat still in the hall and listened. When
they were all still he took his harp and tuned it brightly. There he harped
the most joyful notes that any man has ever heard; each man liked his
entertainment well. The steward saw this and immediately knew (recognized) the harp. 'Minstrel,' he said, 'good health to you! Where did you get
this harp, and how? I beg you, tell me now.' 'My lord,' he answered, 'in an
unknown land, as I went through a wilderness, I found in a dale a man torn
up into little pieces by lions, and eaten by wolves with teeth so sharp. Next
to him I found this same harp. That was a full ten years ago.'

                                                    – Anonymous

4.                     **Lenten ys come with love to toune**     *c.*1325

             Lenten ys come with love to toune,
with blosmen and with briddës roune
that al this blissë bryngeth;
    dayes-eyes in this dales,
    notes suete of nyhtegales,
    uch foul song singeth.
The threstelcoc him threteth oo;
a · way is huerë wynter woo,
when wodërovë springeth.
This foulës singeth ferly fele,
ant wlyteth on huere wynnë wele,
that al the wodë ryngeth.

Lenten-tide (spring) is come lovingly to the world, with the blossoms and bird-song that bring all this joy; daisies in these dales, sweet notes of nightingales, each bird sings a song. The song-thrush bickers continually; gone is their winter woe when the woodruff grows. A great number of these birds sing and warble in their wealth of joys, so that all the forest rings.

                                     – Anonymous

5.                     *from* **Piers Plowman**                *c.*1377

    'By · hote God,' quod Hunger, 'hennes ne wil I
        wende
Til I have dyned bi this day and ydronke bothe.'
'I have no peny,' quod Peres, 'poletes for to bigge,
Ne neyther gees ne grys, but two grene cheses,
A few cruddes and creem, and an haver-cake,
And two loves of benes and bran ybake for my fauntis;
And yet I sey, by my soule, I have no salt bacoun
Ne no kokeney, bi Cryst, coloppes for to maken.
Ac I have percil, and porettes, and many
        koleplantes,
And eke a cow and a kalf, and a cart-mare
To drawe afelde my donge the while the
        drought lasteth.

And bi this lyflode we mot lyve til Lammasse tyme;
And bi that I hope to have hervest in my croft,
And thanne may I dighte thi dyner as me dere liketh.'
Alle the pore peple tho pesecoddes fetten,
    Benes and baken apples thei broughte in
     her lappes,
    Chibolles and chervelles and ripe
     chiries manye,
  And profred Peres this present to plese
    with Hunger . . .

        (B. VI. 280–97)

'I vow to God,' said Hunger, 'I will not go from here till I have both dined and drunk this day.' 'I have no penny,' said Piers, 'to beg pullets with, nor geese nor pigs either, but (only) two fresh cheeses, a few curds and cream, and an oat-cake, and two loaves of beans and bran baked for my children; and yet I say, by my soul, I have no salt bacon nor any onions, by Christ, to prepare steaks with. But I have parsley, and shallots, and many cabbages, and also a cow and a calf, and a cart-mare to draw my manure into the field while the drought lasts. And with these few things we must live till Lammas-tide; and with that I hope to have harvest in my fields, and then may I spread a feast for you as I'd dearly like.' All the poor people fetched their peasecods, beans and baked apples they brought in their laps, spring onions and chervils and many ripe cherries, and proffered Piers this present to satisfy Hunger.

        – William Langland


6.    *from* Sir Gawain and the Green Knight c.1375–1400

Thenn Arthour before the high dece that aventure
    byholdez,
And rekenly hym reverenced, for rad was he never,
And sayde, 'Wyghe, welcum iwys to this place.
The hede of this ostel, Arthour I hat.
    Light luflych adoun and lenge, I the praye,
And quat-so thy wylle is we schal wyt after.'
'Nay, as help me,' quod the hathel, 'he that on hyghe
    syttes,

> To  wone any quyle in this won, hit watz not myn
>       ernde . . .
>      Ye may be seker bi this braunch that I bere
>       here
> That I  passe as in pes, and no plyght seche;
> For had I  founded in fere in feghtyng wyse,
> I have a  hauberghe at home and a helmë bothe,
>      A  schelde and a scharp spere, schinande bryght,
> Ande other  weppenes to welde, I wene wel, als;
> But for I  wolde no were, my wedez ar softer.
>      Bot if thou be so bold as alle burnez tellen,
> Thou wyl  grant me godly the gomen that I ask
>      bi  ryght.'
>
>      Arthour con onsware,
>      And  sayd, 'Sir cortays knyght,
>      If  thou crave batayl bare,
>      Here  faylez thou not to fyght . . .'

(lines 250–78)

Then Arthur before the high dais beholds that adventurer, and greeted him courteously, for he was never afraid, and said, 'Sir, welcome indeed to this place. The head of this house, Arthur I am called. Kindly dismount and stay (with us) I pray thee, and whatever thy wish is we shall learn afterwards.' 'Nay, so help me,' said the man, 'He who sits on high (God), to dwell any while in this dwelling was not my errand . . . You may be sure by this (holly) branch that I bear here that I pass in peace and seek no peril; for had I come dressed in warlike fashion, I have a hauberk at home and a helmet both, a shield and a sharp spear, shining bright, and other weapons to wield, I also well believe; but because I wish no war my clothing is softer. However, if you are as bold as all men tell, you will graciously grant me the sport that I ask by right.' Arthur answered, and said, 'Sir, noble knight, if you crave bare battle you won't fail to (find a) fight here.'

– Anonymous

7.          *from* **The Parlement of Foules**          1375–85

Nowe welcome, Somor, with sonnë softe
 That hast these wintres wedres overeshake
 And drevine away the langë nightës blake.
Saint Valentine, that ert full hye alofte,
Thus singen smal fowlës for thy sake.

Nowe welcome, Somor, with sonnë softe
 That hast these wintres wedres overeshake.

     Wele han they causë for to gladen ofte,
Sethe ech of hem recoverede hathe his make:
 Full blisseful mowe they ben when they wake.

Nowe welcome, Somor, with sonnë softe
 That hast these wintres wedres overeshake,
 And drevine away the langë nightës blake.

                              (lines 680–92)

Now welcome, Spring, with soft sunshine that has shaken away these
winter storms, and driven away the long black nights. Saint Valentine, who
art full high aloft, small birds sing thus for thy sake . . . Well have they
cause to be glad often, since each of them has recovered his mate: they may
(well) be very joyful while they are awake . . .

                              – Geoffrey Chaucer

8.          *from* **The Canterbury Tales**          1386–1400

     Whan that Aprill with his shoures soote          sweet showers
 The droughte of March hath percëd to the roote,          pierced
 And bathëd every veyne in swich licour          vine
  Of which vertu engendred is the flour;          flower
Whan Zephirus eek with his sweetë breeth          also, breath
  In · spired hath in every holt and heeth          wood, heath
 The tendre croppes, and the yongë sonne
Hath in the Ram his halvë cours yronne,          (Aries), run
And smalë foweles maken melodye,          birds
That slepen al the nyght with open ye          eye
 (So priketh hem nature in hir corages);          them, their hearts

Thanne longen folk to goon on pilgrimages,                    go
  And palmeres for to seken straungë strondes,      pilgrims, shores
   To fernë halwes, kowthe in sondry londes;      far shrines, known
  And specially from every shirës ende
   Of Engelond to Caunterbury they wende,
  The hooly blisful martir for to seke,                    (Thomas à Becket)
 That hem hath holpen whan that they were          them, helped,
      seke.                                                 sick
   Bi·fil that in that seson on a day,               it happened, one day
   In Southwerk at the Tabard as I lay                     (an inn)
      Redy to wenden on my pilgrymage                      wend
   To Caunterbury with ful devout corage,                 feeling
   At nyght was come into that hostelrye
  Wel nyne and twenty in a compaignye,
   Of sondry folk, by aventure yfalle     various, gathered by chance
   In felaweshipe, and pilgrimes were they alle,
 That toward Caunterbury wolden ryde.                      wished to
  The chambres and the stables weren wyde,        rooms, were ample
  And wel we weren esëd attë beste.          were treated to the best
  And shortly, whan the sonnë was to reste,               went
   So hadde I spoken with hem everichon             them everyone
 That I was of hir felaweshipe anon,                      at this time
  And madë forward erly for to ryse,                       plans
   To take oure wey ther as I yow devyse . . .      describe to you

                                               (lines 1–34)
                                             – Geoffrey Chaucer


9.        **I synge of a myden**                  early 15th century

   I synge of a myden that is makëles,
      Kyng of alle kynges to here sone che ches.

  He cam also stylle ther his moder was
  As dew in Aprylle that fallyt on the gras.

  He cam also stylle to his moderes bowr
  As dew in Aprille that fallyt on the flour.

He cam also stylle there his moder lay
As dew in Aprille that fallyt on the spray.

Moder and mayden was never non but che –
Wel may swych a lady godës moder be.

I sing of a maiden that is matchless, she chose the king of all kings as her
son. He came as still to where his mother was as dew in April that falls on
the grass. He came as still to his mother's bower as dew in April that falls on
the flower. He came as still to where his mother lay as dew in April that falls
on the spray. No one but her was ever both a mother and a maiden (virgin) –
well may such a lady be God's mother.

– Anonymous

10.      **Of My Lady**                         early 15th century

Of my lady well me rejoise I may!
Hir golden forheed is full narw and small;
Hir browes been lik to dim, reed coral;
And as the jeet hir yën glistren ay.                    jet, eyes

Hir bowgy cheekës been as softe as clay,         bulgy
With largë jowës and substancial;                       jaws
Hir nose a pentice is that it ne shal              penthouse
Reine in hir mouth though she uprightës lay.     upwards

Hir mouth is nothing scant with lippës gray;       large
Hir chin unnethë may be seen at al;              scarcely
Hir comly body shape as a footbal,                   lovely
And she singeth full like a papëjay.                 parrot

– Thomas Hoccleve

11.      **Bring Us in Good Ale**               later 15th century

*Burden:* Bring us in good ale, and bring us in good ale,
Fore our blessed Lady sak, bring us in good          sake
ale.

Bring us in no browne bred, fore that is mad
of brane;                                             bran

Nor bring us in no whit bred, fore therin is no
  game:
But bring us in good ale.

Bring us in no befe, for ther is many bones;
But bring us in good ale, for that goth downe at
  ones,                                                      once
And bring us in good ale.

Bring us in no bacon, for that is passing             rather
  fat:
But bring us in good ale, and give us inought of      enough
  that,
And bring us in good ale.

Bring us in no mutton, for that is ofte lene;
Nor bring us in no tripes, for they be seldom clene:
But bring us in good ale.

Bring us in no egges, for ther ar many shelles;
But bring us in good ale, and give us nothing elles,
And bring us in good ale.

Bring us in no butter, for therin ar many
  heres;                                                     hairs
Nor bring us in no pigges flesh, for that will mak
  us bores:
But bring us in good ale.

Bring us in no podinges, for therin is all gotes      goats'
  blod;
Nor bring us in no venison, for that is not for our
  good:
But bring us in good ale.

Bring us in no capon's flesh, for that is ofte
  der;
Nor bring us in no dokes flesh for they slobber in
  the mer:
But bring us in good ale.

– Anonymous

12.    **The Corpus Christi Carol**    early 16th century

    Lul · ly, lulley, lully, lulley,
    The fawcon hath born my mak away.    falcon, mate

    He bare him up, he bare him down,
    He bare him into an orchard brown.

    In that orchard ther was an hall
    That was hangëd with purpill and pall.    rich purple cloth

    And in that hall ther was a bed:
    It was hangëd with gold so red.

    And in that bed ther lythe a knight,
    His woundës bleding day and night.

By that bedës side ther kneleth a may,    maiden
    And she wepeth both night and day.

    And by that bedes side ther stondeth a ston,
    'Corpus Christi' wreten theron.    'The Body of Christ'

                               – Anonymous

13.    *from* **The Tunnynge of Elynour Rummyng**    c.1508

    Tell you I chyll,    will
    If that ye wyll
    A whyle be styll,
    Of a comely gyll    woman
    That dwelt on a hyll:
    But she is not gryll,    fierce
    For she is somwhat sage
    And well worne in age;
    For her vysage    visage
    It would aswage    quell
    A mannes courage.
    Her lothely lere    loathsome complexion
    Is nothynge clere,    not at all
    But ugly of chere,    appearance

Droupy and drowsy,
Scurvy and lowsy;
Her face all bowsy,
Comely crynklyd,                                    beautifully crinkled
Woundersly wrynkled,
Like a rost pygges eare,                            roast
Brystled wyth here.                                 hair
Her lewde lyppes twayne,                            two ugly lips
They slaver, men sayne,                             say
Like a ropy rayne,                                  heavy rain
A gummy glayre:                                     glare
She is ugly fayre;                                  extremely ugly
Her nose somdele hoked,                             somewhat hooked
And camously croked,                                turned up
Never stoppynge,
But ever droppynge;                                 dripping
Her skynne lose and slacke,
Grained lyke a sacke;                               rough
With a croked backe . . .

(lines 1–33)
– John Skelton

14.                     **Lord Randal**                    16th century

'O where ha you been, Lord Randal, my son?
And where ha you been, my handsome young man?'
'I ha been at the greenwood; Mother, mak my bed soon,
For I'm wearied wi hunting, and fain wad lie down.'

'And wha met you there, Lord Randal, my son?
And wha met you there, my handsome young man?'
'Oh, I met wi my true-love; Mother, mak my bed soon,
For I'm wearied wi huntin, and fain wad lie down.'

'And what did she give you, Lord Randal, my son?
And what did she give you, my handsome young man?'
'Eels fried in a pan; Mother, mak my bed soon,
For I'm wearied wi huntin, and fain wad lie down.'

'And wha gat your leavins, Lord Randal, my son?
And wha gat your leavins, my handsome young man?'
'My hawks and my hounds; Mother, mak my bed soon,
For I'm wearied wi hunting, and fain wad lie down.'

'And what becam of them, Lord Randal, my son,
And what becam of them, my handsome young man?'
'They stretched their legs out and died; Mother, mak
my bed soon,
For I'm wearied wi huntin, and fain wad lie down.'

'O, I fear you are poisoned, Lord Randal, my son!
I fear you are poisoned, my handsome young man!'
'O yes, I am poisoned; Mother, mak my bed soon,
For I'm sick at the heart, and I fain wad lie down.'

'What d'ye leave to your mother, Lord Randal, my son?
What d'ye leave to your mother, my handsome young man?'
'Four and twenty milk kye; Mother, mak my bed soon,    cows
For I'm sick at the heart, and I fain wad lie down.'

'What d'ye leave to your sister, Lord Randal, my son?
What d'ye leave to your sister, my handsome young man?'
'My gold and my silver; Mother, mak my bed soon,
For I'm sick at the heart, and I fain wad lie down.'

'What d'ye leave to your brother, Lord Randal, my son?
What d'ye leave to your brother, my handsome young man?'
'My houses and my lands; Mother, mak my bed soon,
For I'm sick at the heart, and I fain wad lie down.'

'What d'ye leave to your true-love, Lord Randal, my son?
What d'ye leave to your true-love, my handsome young
man?'
'I leave her hell and fire; Mother, mak my bed
soon,
For I'm sick at the heart, and I fain wad lie down.'

                                         – Anonymous

15.     **They Fle from Me**                                    1530–40

They fle from me, that sometyme did me seke
With naked fotë, stalking in my chambr.                         foot
  I have seen them, gentill, tame, and meke,
That now are wyld, and do not remembr
That sometyme they put theimself in daunger
  To take bred at my hand; and nowe they raunge,          roam
  Besely seking with a continuell                        busily seeking
    chaunge.

  Thanckëd be fortune it hath ben othrewise
  Twenty tymës better; but ons in speciall,               once
In thyn arraye, after a pleasaunt gyse,                         thin, diversion
When her losë gown from her shoulders did fall,                loose
And she me caught in her armës long and small,                 slender
  And therewith all swetely did me kysse
And softely saide, Dere hert, howe like you this?

It was no dreammë: I lay brodë waking.                          fully awake
But all is tornëd, thorough my gentilnes,                      turned, through
  Into a straungë faeshion of forsaking;
And I have leve to goo, of her goodenes;                        go, thanks to
And she also to use new fangilnes;                             practise fickleness
But syns that I so kyndëly am servëd,                          generously
  I wold fain knowë what she hath                         would like to
    deservëd.

                    – Thomas Wyatt


16.     *from* **The Faerie Queene**                            1589

A gentle Knight was pricking on the plaine,                     riding
Y·cladd in mightie armes and silver shielde,                   clad
Where·in old dints of deepe wounds did remaine,
The cruel markes of many a bloudy fielde;
Yet armes till that time did he never wield:
His angry steede did chide his foming bitt,
As much disdayning to the curbe to yield:

Full  jolie knight he seemd, and faire did sitt,                       handsome
  As  one for knightly giusts and fierce encounters              jousts
      fitt.

And  on his brest a bloudie crosse he bore,
The  deare remembrance of his dying Lord,
  For  whose sweete sake that glorious badge he wore,
And  dead as living ever him ador'd:
    U · pon his shield the like was also scor'd.
  For  soveraine hope, which in his helpe he had:
Right  faithfull true he was in deede and word,
  But  of his cheere did seeme too solemne sad;              appearance
  Yet  nothing did he dread, but ever was ydrad . . .          dreaded

(lines 1–18)
– Edmund Spenser

17.     *Song from* **Summers Last Will and Testament**   1600

    A · dieu, farewell earths blisse,
      This world uncertaine is,
      Fond are lifes lustfull joyes,                       foolish
      Death proves them all but toyes,
      None from his darts can flye;
      I am sick, I must dye:
      Lord, have mercy on us.

      Rich men, trust not in wealth,
      Gold cannot buy you health;
      Phisick himselfe must fade.                       Medicine
      All things to end are made,
  The  plague full swift goes bye;
      I am sick, I must dye:
      Lord, have mercy on us.

      Beauty is but a flowre
  Which  wrinckles will devoure,
      Brightnesse falls from the ayre,
      Queenes have died yong and faire,
      Dust hath closde Helens eye.

I am sick, I must dye:
Lord, have mercy on us.

Strength stoopes unto the grave,
Worms feed on Hector brave,
Swords may not fight with fate,
Earth still holds ope her gate.          open
Come, come, the bells do crye.
I am sick, I must dye:
Lord, have mercy on us.

Wit with his wantonnesse
Tasteth deaths bitternesse:
Hells executioner
Hath no ears for to heare
What vaine art can reply.
I am sick, I must dye:
Lord, have mercy on us.

Haste therefore eche degree          all social levels
To welcome destiny:
Heaven is our heritage,
Earth but a players stage,
Mount wee unto the sky.
I am sick, I must dye:
Lord, have mercy on us.

– Thomas Nash


18.          *from* **Hamlet**          1600–1601

(*Hor:*)     Two nights together, had these Gentlemen
(Mar·cellus and Bernardo) on their Watch
In the  dead wast and middle of the night          waste
Beene  thus encountered. A figure like your Father,
Arm'd at all points exactly, *Cap a pe*,          from head to foot
Ap·peares before them, and with sollemne march
Goes  slow and stately: By them thrice he walkt,
By  their opprest and feare-surprized eyes,

    With · in his Truncheons length; whilst they bestil'd
        Almost to Jelly with the Act of feare,
  Stand dumbe and speake not to him. This to me
    In dreadfull secrecie impart they did,
    And I with them the third Night kept the Watch,
  Where · as they had deliver'd both in time,
        Forme of the thing; each word made true and
            good,
    The Apparition comes. I knew your Father:
  These hands are not more like.
(*Ham:*)                          But where was this?
(*Mar:*) My Lord, upon the platforme where we watcht.
(*Ham:*)    Did you not speake to it?
(*Hor:*)                    My Lord, I did;
    But answere made it none: yet once me thought
    It lifted up it head, and did addresse
    It selfe to motion, like as it would speake:
    But even then, the Morning Cocke crew lowd;
    And at the sound it shrunke in hast away . . .       haste

                         (Act I, Scene ii)
                       – William Shakespeare


19.          *Song from* **The Tempest**         *c.*1610

    Full fadom five thy Father lies,
        Of his bones are Corrall made:
        Those are pearles that were his eies,
        Nothing of him that doth fade
        But doth suffer a Sea-change
        Into something rich, and strange:
        Sea-Nimphs hourly ring his knell.
  *Chorus:* Ding dong, ding dong.
        Harke now, I heare them, ding-dong bell.

                       – William Shakespeare

20. **Sonnet**                                                    *c.*1610

Like as the waves make towards the pibled shore,          pebbled
So do our minuites hasten to their end;
Each changing place with that which goes before,
In sequent toile all forwards do contend.                  struggle
Na·tivity, once in the maine of light,                    broad expanse
Crawles to maturity, wherewith being crown'd,
Crooked eclipses gainst his glory fight,
And time that gave doth now his gift confound.
Time doth transfixe the florish set on youth               bloom
And delves the paralels in beauties brow,            ploughs the furrows
Feedes on the rarities of natures truth,
And nothing stands but for his sieth to mow.               scythe
And yet to times in hope my verse shall stand,         in future times
Praising thy worth, dispight his cruell hand.             despite

– William Shakespeare

21.      **Hymne to Cynthia**                                  1616

Queene and Huntresse, chaste and faire,
Now the Sunne is laid to sleepe,
Seated in thy silver chaire,
State in wonted manner keepe:
Hesperus intreats thy light,
Goddesse, excellently bright.

Earth, let not thy envious shade
Dare it selfe to interpose;
Cynthias shining orbe was made
Heaven to cleere when day did close:
Blesse us then with wishëd sight,
Goddesse, excellently bright.

Lay thy bow of pearle apart,
And thy cristall shining quiver;
Give unto the flying hart
Space to breathe, how short soever:

Thou that mak'st a day of night,
Goddesse, excellently bright.

– Ben Jonson

22.    *from* **Christmas**                                    c.1630

The shepherds sing; and shall I silent be?
My God, no hymne for thee?
My soul's a shepherd too; a flock it feeds
 Of thoughts, and words, and deeds.
The pasture is thy word: the streams thy grace
 En · riching all the place.
   Shepherd and flock shall sing, and all my powers
Out · sing the day-light houres.
Then we will chide the sunne for letting night
   Take up his place and right:
We sing one common Lord; wherefore he should
Him · self the candle hold.
   I will go searching, till I finde a sunne
Shall stay, till we have done;
 A willing shiner, that shall shine as gladly
 As frost-nipt sunnes look sadly.
Then we will sing, and shine all our own day,
And one another pay:
His beams shall cheer my breast, and both so twine
Till ev'n his beams sing, and my musick shine.

(lines 15–34)

– George Herbert

23.    **The Good-morrow**                                    1633

I wonder by my troth, what thou, and I
   Did, till we lov'd? were we not wean'd till then?
But sucked on countrey pleasures, childishly?
 Or snorted we in the seaven sleepers den?

T'was  so; But this, all pleasures fancies bee.
    If  any beauty I did see,
Which  I desir'd, and got, t'was but a dreame of thee.

  And  now good morrow to our waking soules,
Which  watch not one another out of feare;
   For  love, all love of other sights controules,
  And  makes one little roome, an every where.
   Let  sea-discoverers to new worlds have gone,      be gone
   Let  Maps to other, worlds on worlds have showne,
   Let  us possesse one world, each hath one, and is one.

   My  face in thine eye, thine in mine appeares,
  And  true plaine hearts doe in the faces rest,
       Where can we finde two better hemispheares
With · out sharpe North, without declining West?
What  ever dyes, was not mixt equally;
    If  our two loves be one, or, thou and I
Love  so alike, that none doe slacken, none can die.

                     – John Donne

24.     *from* **Holy Sonnets**        1633

At the  round earths imagin'd corners, blow
 Your  trumpets, Angells, and arise, arise
From  death, you numberlesse infinities
   Of  soules, and to your scattred bodies goe,
      All whom the flood did, and fire shall o'erthrow,
      All whom warre, death, age, agües, tyrannies,
  De · spaire, law, chance, hath slaine, and you whose eyes
      Shall behold God, and never tast deaths woe.    taste

  But  let them sleepe, Lord, and mee mourne a space,   time
 For,  if above all these, my sinnes abound,
 'Tis  late to ask abundance of thy grace
When  wee are there; here on this lowly ground
      Teach me how to repent; for that's as good
   As  if thou'hadst seal'd my pardon, with thy blood.

                     – John Donne

25.               **Song**                                    *c.*1640

          Goe lovely Rose,
   Tell her that wastes her time and me,
  That now she knowes,
When I resemble her to thee,
  How sweet and fair she seems to be.

   Tell her that's young,
  And shuns to have her Graces spy'd,
  That hadst thou sprung
   In Desarts, where no men abide,
Thou must have uncommended dy'd.

      Small is the worth
   Of beauty from the light retir'd;
      Bid her come forth,
      Suffer her selfe to be desir'd,
  And not blush so to be admir'd.

Then die, that she
  The common fate of all things rare
May read in thee:
How small a part of time they share
      That are so wondrous sweet and faire.

                  – Edmund Waller

26.    **When I Consider How My Light Is Spent**          1655

When I consider how my light is spent
  Ere half my days, in this dark world and wide,          before
And that one Talent which is death to hide,
   Lodg'd with me useless (though my Soul more bent
  To serve therewith my Maker, and present
  My true account, lest he returning chide),
Doth God exact day-labour, light denied?
   I fondly ask. But Patience, to prevent          foolishly
  That murmur, soon replies: God doth not need
    Either man's work or his own gifts; who best

Bear his mild yoak, they serve him best. His State
Is  kingly. Thousands at his bidding speed
And  post o'er Land and Ocean without rest:
They  also serve who only stand and waite.

                                                 – John Milton

27.       *from* **Paradise Lost**                                  1667

Of  Man's First Disobedience, and the Fruit
Of  that Forbidden Tree, whose mortal tast
Brought  Death into the World, and all our woe,
With  loss of Eden, till one greater Man
Re · store us, and regain the blissful Seat,
    Sing, Heav'nly Muse, that, on the secret top
Of  Oreb, or of Sinai, didst inspire
That  Shepherd, who first taught the chosen Seed,
    In the Beginning how the Heav'ns and Earth
    Rose out of Chaos: or, if Sion Hill
De · light thee more, and Siloa's Brook that flow'd
    Fast by the Oracle of God: I thence
In · voke thy aid to my advent'rous Song,
That  with no middle flight intends to soar
A · bove th'Aonian Mount, while it pursues
    Things unattempted yet in Prose or Rhime.
And  chiefly Thou O Spirit, that dost prefer
Be · fore all Temples th'upright heart and pure,
In · struct me, for Thou know'st; Thou from the first
Wast  present, and with mighty wings outspread
    Dove-like satst brooding on the vast abyss
And  mad'st it pregnant: What in me is dark
Il · lumin; what is low raise and support;
    That to the highth of this great Argument        height
I  may assert Eternal Providence,
And  justifie the wayes of God to men . . .

                                   (lines 1–26)
                                 – John Milton

28.                    **To His Coy Mistress**                    1672

     Had we but World enough, and Time,
  This coyness Lady were no crime.
     We would sit down, and think which way
   To walk, and pass our long Loves Day.
     Thou by the *Indian Ganges* side
Should'st Rubies find: I by the Tide
   Of *Humber* would complain. I would
     Love you ten years before the Flood:
  And you should if you please refuse
     Till the Conversion of the *Jews*.
   My vegetable Love should grow
     Vaster than Empires, and more slow.
   An hundred years should go to praise
 Thine Eyes, and on thy Forehead Gaze.
  Two hundred to adore each Breast:
  But thirty thousand to the rest.
   An Age at least to every part,
And the last Age should show your Heart.
  For Lady you deserve this State;
  Nor would I love at lower rate.

     But at my back I alwaies hear
 Times wingèd Charriot hurrying near:
  And yonder all before us lye
     Desarts of vast Eternity.
   Thy Beauty shall no more be found;
     Nor, in thy marble Vault, shall sound
   My ecchoing Song: then Worms shall try
  That long preserv'd Virginity:
  And your quaint Honour turn to dust;
  And into ashes all my Lust.
  The Grave's a fine and private place,
  But none I think do there embrace.

  Now therefore, while the youthful hew
     Sits on thy skin like morning dew,
  And while thy willing Soul transpires

At every pore with instant Fires,
Now let us sport us while we may;
And now, like am'rous birds of prey,
    Rather at once our Time devour,
Than languish in his slow-chapt pow'r.
    Let us roll all our Strength, and all
Our sweetness, up into one Ball:
And tear our Pleasures with rough strife,
    Thorough the Iron gates of Life.
    Thus, though we cannot make our Sun
Stand still, yet we will make him run.

– Andrew Marvell

29.       *Song from* **Marriage à la Mode**      1672

Why should a foolish Marriage Vow,
Which long ago was made,
Ob·lige us to each other now,
When passion is decay'd?
We lov'd, and we lov'd, as long as we cou'd,
Till our love was lov'd out in us both;
But our Marriage is dead when the Pleasure is fled:
'Twas Pleasure first made it an Oath.

If I have Pleasures for a Friend,
And farther love in store,
What wrong has he whose joys did end,
And who cou'd give no more?
'Tis a madness that he should be jealous of me,
Or that I shou'd bar him of another:
For all we can gain is to give our selves pain,
When neither can hinder the other.

– John Dryden

30.           *from* **An Essay on Man**                    1733

        Know then thy-self, presume not God to scan;
   The proper study of mankind is Man.
        Plac'd on this Isthmus of a middle state,
     A Being darkly wise, and rudely great;
 With too much knowledge for the Sceptic side,
 With too much weakness for a Stoic's pride,
    He hangs between; in doubt to act, or rest,
    In doubt to deem himself a God, or Beast,
    In doubt his mind or body to prefer,
        Born but to die, and reas'ning but to err;
     A·like in ignorance, his Reason such,
        Whether he thinks too little, or too much:
        Chaos of Thought and Passion, all confus'd;
        Still by himself abus'd, or dis-abus'd;
  Cre·ated halt to rise, and half to fall;
 Great Lord of all things, yet a Prey to all;
  Sole Judge of Truth, in endless Error hurl'd;
  The Glory, Jest, and Riddle of the world! . . .

                                        (II. 1–18)
                                   – Alexander Pope


31. *from* **Jubilate Agno**                    1759–63

For I will consider my Cat Jeoffry.
For he is the servant of the Living God duly and daily.
For at the first glance of the glory of God in the East
        he worships in his way.
For is this done by wreathing his body seven times round
        with elegant quickness.
For then he leaps up to catch the musk, which is the
        blessing of God upon his prayer.
For he rolls upon prank to work it in.
For having done duty and received blessing he begins to
        consider himself.
For this he performs in ten degrees.

For  first he looks upon his fore-paws to see if they are
     clean.
For  secondly he kicks up behind to clear away there.
For  thirdly he works it upon stretch with the fore paws
     extended.
For  fourthly he sharpens his paws by wood.
For  fifthly he washes himself.
For  sixthly he rolls upon wash.
For  seventhly he fleas himself, that he may not be
     interrupted upon the beat.
For  eighthly he rubs himself against a post.
For  ninthly he looks up for his instructions.
For  tenthly he goes in quest of food.
For  having consider'd God and himself he will consider his
     neighbour.
For  if he meets another cat he will kiss her in kindness.
For  when he takes his prey he plays with it to give it a
     chance.
For  one mouse in seven escapes by his dallying.
For  when his day's work is done his business more
     properly begins.
For  he keeps the Lord's watch in the night against the
     adversary.
For  he counteracts the powers of darkness by his
     electrical skin & glaring eyes.
For  he counteracts the Devil, who is death, by brisking
     about the life.
For  in his morning orisons he loves the sun and the sun
     loves him.
For  he is of the tribe of Tiger . . .

(B. 695–722)
– Christopher Smart

32.                    **A Red, Red Rose**                    1796

   O My Luve's like a red, red rose,
  That's newly sprung in June;
   O My Luve's like the melodie
  That's sweetly played in tune.

   As fair art thou, my bonnie lass,
   So deep in luve am I;
  And I will luve thee still, my dear,
   Till a' the seas gang dry.

   Till a' the seas gang dry, my dear,
  And the rocks melt wi' the sun:
   O I will love thee still, my dear,
  While the sands o' life shall run.

   And fare thee weel, my only luve,
   And fare thee weel awhile!
   And I will come again, my luve,
  Though it were ten thousand mile.

        – Robert Burns


33.                    **Kubla Khan**                    1797–8

  In Xanadu did Kubla Khan
   A stately pleasure dome decree:
 Where Alph, the sacred river, ran
 Through caverns measureless to man
   Down to a sunless sea.
  So twice five miles of fertile ground
  With walls and towers were girdled round:
  And there were gardens bright with sinuous rills,
 Where blossomed many an incense-bearing tree;
  And here were forests ancient as the hills,
  En · folding sunny spots of greenery.

  But oh! that deep romantic chasm which slanted
   Down the green hill athwart a cedarn cover!

A savage place! as holy and enchanted
As e'er beneath a waning moon was haunted
By woman wailing for her demon-lover!
And from this chasm, with ceaseless turmoil seething,
As if this earth in fast thick pants were breathing,
A mighty fountain momently was forced:
A·mid whose swift half-intermitted burst
Huge fragments vaulted like rebounding hail,
Or chaffy grain beneath the thresher's flail:
And 'mid these dancing rocks at once and ever
It flung up momently the sacred river.
Five miles meandering with a mazy motion
Through wood and dale the sacred river ran,
Then reached the caverns measureless to man,
And sank in tumult to a lifeless ocean:
And 'mid this tumult Kubla heard from far
An·cestral voices prophesying war!
The shadow of the dome of pleasure
    Floated midway on the waves;
    Where was heard the mingled measure
    From the fountain and the caves.
It was a miracle of rare device,
A sunny pleasure dome with caves of ice!

A damsel with a dulcimer
In a vision once I saw:
It was an Abyssinian maid,
And on her dulcimer she played,
    Singing of Mount Abora.
Could I revive within me
    Her symphony and song,
    To such a deep delight 'twould win me,
    That with music loud and long,
    I would build that dome in air,
That sunny dome! those caves of ice!
And all who heard should see them there,
And all should cry, Beware! Beware!
His flashing eyes, his floating hair!

Weave a circle round him thrice,
And close your eyes with holy dread,
For he on honey-dew hath fed,
And drunk the milk of Paradise.

– Samuel Taylor Coleridge

34. *from the first version of* **The Prelude**     1798–9

And in the frosty season, when the sun
Was set, and visible for many a mile
The cottage windows through the twilight blaz'd,
  I heeded not the summons: – clear and loud
The village clock toll'd six; I wheel'd about
  Proud and exulting, like an untired horse
That cares not for its home. All shod with steel
We hiss'd along the polished ice in games
Con·federate, imitative of the chace        hunt
And woodland pleasures, the resounding horn,
The Pack loud bellowing, and the hunted hare.
  So through the darkness and the cold we flew,
And not a voice was idle; with the din,
  Meanwhile, the precipices rang aloud;
The leafless trees and every icy crag
  Tinkled like iron; while the distant hills
  Into the tumult sent an alien sound
 Of melancholy, not unnoticed, while the stars,
  Eastward, were sparkling clear, and in the west
The orange sky of evening died away.

Not seldom from the uproar I retired
  Into a silent bay, or sportively
Glanced sideway, leaving the tumultuous throng,
  To cut across the shadow of a star
That gleam'd upon the ice: and oftentimes
When we had given our bodies to the wind,
And all the shadowy banks, on either side,
Came sweeping through the darkness, spinning still

> The rapid line of motion; then at once
> Have I, reclining back upon my heels,
> Stopp'd short – yet still the solitary Cliffs
> Wheeled by me, even as if the earth had roll'd
> With visible motion her diurnal round;
> Be·hind me did they stretch in solemn train
>     Feebler and feebler, and I stood and watch'd
> Till all was tranquil as a summer sea . . .

(lines 150–85)
– William Wordsworth

35.        **London**           1794

> I wander thro' each charter'd street,
> Near where the charter'd Thames does flow,
> And mark in every face I meet
>     Marks of weakness, marks of woe.
>
> In every cry of every Man,
> In every Infant's cry of fear,
> In every voice, in every ban,
> The mind-forg'd manacles I hear.
>
>     How the chimney-sweeper's cry
>     Every black'ning church appals;
>     And the hapless soldier's sigh
>     Runs in blood down palace walls.
>
> But most thro' midnight streets I hear
>     How the youthful harlot's curse
>     Blasts the new-born infant's tear,
> And blights with plagues the marriage hearse.

– William Blake

36.                    *from* **Milton**                    1804

And  did those feet in ancient time
        Walk upon England's mountains green?
And  was the holy Lamb of God
    On  England's pleasant pastures seen?

And  did the Countenance Divine
Shine  forth upon our clouded hills?
And  was Jerusalem builded here
    A · mong these dark Satanic Mills?

        Bring me my bow of burning gold!
        Bring me my arrows of desire!
        Bring me my spear! O clouds, unfold!
        Bring me my chariot of fire!

    I  will not cease from mental fight,
Nor  shall my sword sleep in my hand,
Till  we have built Jerusalem
    In  England's green and pleasant land.

*Would to God that all the Lord's people were Prophets.*
                                Numbers xi.29
                                – William Blake


37.              **So We'll Go No More A-roving**              1817

So we'll  go no more a-roving
        So  late into the night,
Though the  heart be still as loving,
    And the  moon be still as bright.

    For the  sword outwears its sheath,
    And the  soul wears out the breast,
    And the  heart must pause to breathe,
        And  love itself have rest.

Though the  night was made for loving,
    And the  day returns too soon,

> Yet we'll  go no more a-roving
> By the  light of the moon.

– Lord Byron

38.       *from* **Don Juan**                     1818–23

> But   Adeline was not indifferent: for
>       (*Now* for a commonplace!) beneath the snow,
>       As a volcano holds the lava more
> With · in – *et caetera*. Shall I go on? – No!
>    I   hate to hunt down a tired metaphor,
>   So   let the often-used volcano go.
> Poor   thing! How frequently, by me and others,
>    It   hath been stirred up till its smoke quite smothers!

> I'll   have another figure in a trice: –
> What   say you to a bottle of champagne?
>        Frozen into a very vinous ice,
> Which   leaves few drops of that immortal rain,
>        Yet in the very centre, past all price,
>    A · bout a liquid glassful will remain;
>  And   this is stronger than the strongest grape
> Could   e'er express in its expanded shape:

> 'Tis the   whole spirit brought to a quintessence;
>   And   thus the chilliest aspects may concentre
>     A   hidden nectar under a cold presence.
>   And   such are many – though I only meant her
>  From   whom I now deduce these moral lessons,
>    On   which the Muse has always sought to enter.
> And your   cold people are beyond all price,
>  When   once you have broken their confounded ice . . .

(Canto 13, stanzas 36–8)
– Lord Byron

39.     **To Sleep**                                          1819

   O  soft embalmer of the still midnight,
       Shutting, with careful fingers and benign,
Our  gloom-pleas'd eyes, embower'd from the light,
En · shaded in forgetfulness divine;
   O  soothest Sleep! if so it please thee, close,
   In  midst of this thine hymn, my willing eyes,
   Or  wait the amen, ere thy poppy throws
   A · round my bed its lulling charities;
Then  save me, or the passëd day will shine
  U · pon my pillow, breeding many woes;
       Save me from curious conscience, that still lords
  Its  strength for darkness, burrowing like a mole;
       Turn the key deftly in the oilëd wards,
And  seal the hushëd Casket of my Soul.

                             – John Keats


40.                **To Jane**                                1822

      The  keen stars were twinkling
  And the  fair moon was rising among them,
     Dear  Jane.
  The gui · tar was tinkling
  But the  notes were not sweet 'till you sung them
       A · gain. –
    As the  moon's soft splendour
  O'er the  faint cold starlight of Heaven
       Is  thrown –
  So your  voice most tender
    To the  strings without soul had then given
     Its  own.

      The  stars will awaken,
Though the  moon sleep a full hour later,
      To · night;
      No  leaf will be shaken
While the  dews of your melody scatter

> De·light.
> Though the sound overpowers
> Sing a·gain, with your dear voice revealing
> A tone
> Of some world far from ours,
> Where music and moonlight and feeling
> Are one.

— Percy Bysshe Shelley

41.         **Song**                    1842–64

I peeled bits of straw and I got switches too
From the gray peeling willow as idlers do,
And I switched at the flies as I sat all alone
Till my flesh, blood, and marrow was turned to dry bone.
My illness was love, though I knew not the smart,
But the beauty of love was the blood of my heart.
Crowded places, I shunned them as noises too rude
And fled to the silence of sweet solitude,
Where the flower in green darkness buds, blossoms, and fades,
Un·seen of all shepherds and flower-loving maids —
The hermit bees find them but once and away;
There I'll bury alive and in silence decay.

I looked on the eyes of fair woman too long,
Till silence and shame stole the use of my tongue:
When I turned to speak to her I'd nothing to say,
So I turned myself round and she wandered away.
When she got too far off, why, I'd something to tell,
So I sent sighs behind her and walked to my cell.
Willow switches I broke and peeled bits of straws,
Ever lonely in crowds, in nature's own laws —
My ball-room the pasture, my music the bees,
My drink was the fountain, my church the tall trees.
Who ever would love or be tied to a wife
When it makes a man mad all the days of his life?

— John Clare

42.                **Memorabilia**                          1851

     Ah, did you once see Shelley plain,
    And did he stop and speak to you
    And did you speak to him again?
   How strange it seems and new!

    But you were living before that,
   And also you are living after;
And the memory I started at —
   My starting moves your laughter.

     I crossed a moor, with a name of its own
  And a certain use in the world no doubt,
  Yet a hand's-breadth of it shines alone
'Mid the blank miles round about:

   For there I picked up on the heather
  And there I put inside my breast
    A molted feather, an eagle-feather!
  Well, I forget the rest.

                   – Robert Browning

43.                **Dover Beach**                          1851

The sea is calm tonight.
The tide is full, the moon lies fair
  U·pon the straits; on the French coast the light
  Gleams and is gone; the cliffs of England stand,
  Glimmering and vast, out in the tranquil bay.
  Come to the window, sweet is the night-air!
  Only, from the long line of spray
Where the sea meets the moon-blanched land,
  Listen! you hear the grating roar
  Of pebbles which the waves draw back, and fling,
  At their return, up the high strand,
  Be·gin and cease, and then again begin,
With tremulous cadence slow, and bring
The e·ternal note of sadness in.

Sophocles long ago
Heard it on the Aegean, and it brought
Into his mind the turbid ebb and flow
Of human misery; we
Find also in the sound a thought,
Hearing it by this distant northern sea.

The Sea of Faith
Was once, too, at the full, and round earth's shore
Lay like the folds of a bright girdle furled.
But now I only hear
Its melancholy, long withdrawing roar,
Re·treating, to the breath
Of the night-wind, down the vast edges drear
And naked shingles of the world.

Ah, love, let us be true
To one another! for the world, which seems
To lie before us like a land of dreams,
So various, so beautiful, so new,
Hath really neither joy, nor love, nor light,
Nor certitude, nor peace, nor help for pain;
And we are here as on a darkling plain
Swept with confused alarms of struggle and fight,
Where ignorant armies clash by night.

– Matthew Arnold

44.       **The Eagle: A Fragment**               1851

He clasps the crag with crooked hands;
Close to the sun in lonely lands,
Ring'd with the azure world, he stands.

The wrinkled sea beneath him crawls:
He watches from his mountain walls,
And like a thunderbolt he falls.

– Alfred, Lord Tennyson

45.        **Darest thou now O soul**                    1855

Darest thou now O soul,
Walk out with me toward the unknown region,
Where neither ground is for the feet nor any path to
        follow?

No map there, nor guide,
Nor voice sounding, nor touch of human hand,
Nor face with blooming flesh, nor lips, nor eyes, are
        in that land.

I know it not O soul,
Nor dost thou, all is a blank before us,
All waits undream'd of in that region, that
        inaccessible land.

Till when the ties loosen,
All but the ties eternal, Time and Space,
Nor darkness, gravitation, sense, nor any bounds
        bounding us.

Then we burst forth, we float,
In Time and Space O soul, prepared for them,
Equal, equipt at last (O joy! O fruit of all!)
        them to fulfil O soul.

                                        – Walt Whitman


46.              **Jabberwocky**                          1855

'Twas  brillig, and the slithy toves
  Did  gyre and gimble in the wabe;
  All  mimsy were the borogoves,
And the  mome raths outgrabe.

  'Be · ware the Jabberwock, my son!
  The  jaws that bite, the claws that catch!
  Be · ware the Jujub bird, and shun
  The  frumious Bandersnatch!'

He took his vorpal sword in hand;
Long time the manxome foe he sought –
So rested he by the Tumtum tree,
And stood awhile in thought.

And, as in uffish thought he stood,
The Jabberwock, with eyes of flame,
Came whiffling through the tulgey wood,
And burbled as it came!

One, two! One, two! And through and through
The vorpal blade went snicker-snack!
He left it dead, and with its head
He went galumphing back.

'And hast thou slain the Jabberwock?
Come to my arms, my beamish boy!
O frabjous day! Callooh! Callay!'
He chortled in his joy.

'Twas brillig, and the slithy toves
Did gyre and gimble in the wabe;
All mimsy were the borogoves,
And the mome raths outgrabe.

– Lewis Carroll


47.     **Uphill**                                    1858

Does the road wind uphill all the way?
Yes, to the very end.
Will the day's journey take the whole long day?
From morn to night, my friend.

But is there for the night a resting place?
A roof for when the slow dark hours begin.
May not the darkness hide it from my face?
You cannot miss that inn.

Shall I meet other wayfarers at night?
Those who have gone before.
Then must I knock, or call when just in sight?
They will not keep you standing at that door.

Shall I find comfort, travel-sore and weak?
Of  labour you shall find the sum.
Will there be beds for me and all who seek?
Yea,  beds for all who come.

– Christina Rossetti


48.    **My Orcha'd in Linden Lea***                                    1859

'Ith · in the woodlands, flow'ry gleäded,                     within, gladed
By the woak tree's mossy moot,                        oak, moat
The sheenèn grass-bleädes, timber-sheäded            shining
Now do quiver under voot;                                    foot
An' birds do whissle auver head,                             over
An' water's bubblèn in its bed;
An' there vor me the apple tree
Do leän down low in Linden Lea.                              lean

When leaves that leätely wer a-springèn
Now do feäde 'ithin the copse,                              fade
An' painted birds do hush their singèn
Up upon the timber's tops;
An' brown-leav'd fruit's a-turnèn red,
In cloudless zunsheen, auver head,                       sunshine
Wi' fruit vor me, the apple tree
Do leän down low in Linden Lea.

Let other vo'k meäke money vaster              folk, make, faster
In the air o' dark-room'd towns,
I don't dread a peevish meäster;            fear, bad-tempered
Though noo man do heed my frowns,
I be free to goo abrode,
Or teäke my hwomeward road                              take
To where, vor me, the apple tree
Do leän down low in Linden Lea.

– William Barnes

* The diacritical marks in this poem are Barnes's own, intended to convey the sound of rural
Dorset English.

49.                    **Because I Could Not Stop for Death**              1863

       Be · cause I could not stop for Death,
       He kindly stopped for me;
      The carriage held but just ourselves
     And Immortality.

      We slowly drove, he knew no haste,
     And I had put away
      My labor, and my leisure too,
     For his civility.

      We passed the school where children played,
    Their lessons scarcely done;
      We passed the fields of grazing grain
      We passed the setting sun.

      We paused before a house that seemed
      A swelling on the ground;
      The roof was scarcely visible,
      The cornice but a mound.

    Since then 'tis centuries; but each
    Feels shorter than the day
       I first surmised the horses' heads
    Were toward eternity.

                          – Emily Dickinson

50.                         **A Nightmare**                          1870

When you're lying awake with a dismal headache, and repose
             is taboo'd by anxiety,
    I con · ceive you may use any language you choose to
             indulge in without impropriety;
  For your brain is on fire – the bedclothes conspire of
             usual slumber to plunder you
  First your counterpane goes and uncovers your toes, and
             your sheet slips demurely from under you;
  Then the blanketing tickles – you feel like mixed
             pickles, so terribly sharp is the pricking,

And you're hot, and you're cross, and you tumble and toss
    till there's nothing 'twixt you and the
    ticking.
Then the bedclothes all creep to the ground in a heap,
    and you pick 'em all up in a tangle;
Next your pillow resigns and politely declines to remain
    at its usual angle!
Well, you get some repose in the form of a doze, with hot
    eyeballs and head ever aching,
But your slumbering teems with such horrible dreams that
    you'd very much better be waking;
For you dream you are crossing the Channel, and tossing
    about in a steamer from Harwich,
Which is something between a large bathing machine and a
    very small second-class carriage;
And you're giving a treat (penny ice and cold meat) to a
    party of friends and relations –
They're a ravenous horde – and they all came on board at
    Sloane Square and South Kensington Stations.
And bound on that journey you find your attorney
    (who started that morning from Devon);
He's a bit undersized, and you don't feel surprised
    when he tells you he's only eleven.
Well, you're driving like mad with this singular lad (by the
    bye the ship's now a four-wheeler),
And you're playing round games, and he calls you bad names
    when you tell him that 'ties pay the dealer';
But this you can't stand, so you throw up your hand,
    and you find you're as cold as an icicle,
In your shirt and your socks (the black silk with gold
    clocks), crossing Salisbury Plain on a
    bicycle:
And he and the crew are on bicycles too – which
    they've somehow or other invested in –
And he's telling the tars all the particulars of a
    company he's interested in –
It's a scheme of devices, to get at low prices, all
    goods from cough mixtures to cables

        (Which  tickled the sailors) by treating retailers as
                though they were all ve*get*ables –
        You  get a good spadesman to plant a small tradesman
               (first take off his boots with a boot-tree),
     And his  legs will take root, and his fingers will shoot,
               and they'll blossom and bud like a
               fruit-tree –
  From the  greengrocer tree you get grapes and green pea,
               cauliflower, pineapple, and cranberries,
 While the  pastry-cook plant cherry-brandy will grant –
               apple puffs, and three-corners, and
               banberries –
      The  shares are a penny, and ever so many are taken
               by Rothschild and Baring,
      And  just as a few are allotted to you, you awake
               with a shudder despairing –
   You're a  regular wreck, with a crick in your neck, and
               no wonder you snore, for your head's on the
               floor, and you've needles and pins from
               your soles to your shins, and your flesh is
               a-creep, for your left leg's asleep, and
               you've cramp in your toes, and a fly on your
               nose, and some fluff in your lung, and a
               feverish tongue, and a thirst that's intense,
               and a general sense that you haven't been
               sleeping in clover;
  But the  darkness has passed, and it's daylight at last,
               and the night has been long – ditto, ditto
               my song – and thank goodness they're both
               of them over!

                               – W. S. Gilbert

51.       **The Windhover: To Christ Our Lord*** 1877

        I caught this morning morning's minion, king-
dom of daylight's dauphin, dapple-dawn-drawn Falcon, in
        his riding
Of the rolling level underneath him steady air, and
        striding
        High there, how he rung upon the rein of a
        wimpling wing
In his ecstasy! then off, off forth on swing,
  As a skate's heel sweeps smooth on a bow-bend: the hurl
        and gliding
  Re·buffed the big wind. My heart in hiding
        Stirred for a bird, – the achieve of, the mastery
        of the thing!

Brute beauty and valour and act, oh, air, pride, plume
        here
        Buckle! AND the fire that breaks from thee then,
        a billion
        Times told lovelier, more dangerous, O my
        chevalier!

  No wonder of it: shéer plód makes plough down sillion
        Shine, and blue-bleak embers, ah my dear,
        Fall, gall themselves, and gash gold-vermilion.

                          – G. M. Hopkins


52.       **Spring and Fall: to a young child*** 1880

        Márgarét, áre you gríeving
        Over Goldengrove unleaving?
        Leáves, líke the things of man, you
        With your fresh thoughts care for, can you?
        Áh! ás the heart grows older
        It will come to such sights colder

* The accent marks in nos. 51 and 52 are those of the poet.

By and by, nor spare a sigh
Though worlds of wanwood leafmeal lie;
And yet you wíll weep and know why.
Now no matter, child, the name:
Sórrow's spríngs áre the same.
Nor mouth had, no, nor mind, expressed
What heart heard of, ghost guessed:
It ís the blight man was born for,
It is Margaret you mourn for.

– G. M. Hopkins

53.     **Crossing the Bar**     1889

Sunset and evening star,
And one clear call for me!
And may there be no moaning of the bar,
When I put out to sea,

But such a tide as moving seems asleep,
Too full for sound and foam,
When that which drew from out the boundless deep
Turns again home.

Twilight and evening bell,
And after that the dark!
And may there be no sadness of farewell,
When I embark;

For tho' from out our bourne of Time and Place
The flood may bear me far,
I hope to see my Pilot face to face
When I have crossed the bar.

– Alfred, Lord Tennyson

54.     **The Lake Isle of Innisfree**                              1890

        I will arise and go now, and go to Innisfree,
    And a small cabin build there, of clay and wattles made:
    Nine bean-rows will I have there, a hive for the honeybee,
    And live alone in the bee-loud glade.

    And I shall have some peace there, for peace comes
                dropping slow,
            Dropping from the veils of the morning to where the
                cricket sings;
    There midnight's all a glimmer, and noon a purple glow,
    And evening full of the linnet's wings.

        I will arise and go now, for always night and day
      I hear lake water lapping with low sounds by the
                shore;
    While I stand on the roadway, or on the pavements gray,
      I hear it in the deep heart's core.

                                                – W. B. Yeats


55.                 **Loveliest of trees**                          1896

            Loveliest of trees, the cherry now
        Is hung with bloom along the bough,
        And stands about the woodland ride
            Wearing  white for Eastertide.

        Now, of my threescore years and ten,
            Twenty will not come again,
        And take from seventy springs a score,
            It only leaves me fifty more.

        And since to look at things in bloom
            Fifty springs are little room,
          A · bout the woodlands I will go
        To  see the cherry hung with snow.

                                            – A. E. Housman

56.                    **The Love Song of J. Alfred Prufrock**        1910–11

S'io credessi che mia risposta fosse
a persona che mai tornasse al mondo,
questa fiamma staria senza più scosse.
Ma per ciò che giammai
non tornò vivo alcun, s'i'odo il vero,
senza tema d'infamia ti rispondo. *

Let us go then, you and I,
When the evening is spread out against the sky
Like a patient etherised upon a table;
Let us go, through certain half-deserted streets,
The muttering retreats
Of restless nights in one-night cheap hotels
And sawdust restaurants with oyster-shells:
Streets that follow like a tedious argument
Of in·sidious intent
To lead you to an overwhelming question . . .
Oh, do not ask, 'What is it?'
Let us go and make our visit.

In the room the women come and go
Talking of Michelangelo.

The yellow fog that rubs its back upon the
window-panes,
The yellow smoke that rubs its muzzle on the
window-panes
Licked its tongue into the corners of the evening,
Lingered upon the pools that stand in drains,
Let fall upon its back the soot that falls from
chimneys,
Slipped by the terrace, made a sudden leap,
And seeing that it was a soft October night,
Curled once about the house, and fell asleep.

And in·deed there will be time
For the yellow smoke that slides along the street,
Rubbing its back upon the window-panes;

* For a translation of this epigraph, see note on page 125.

There will be time, there will be time
To pre·pare a face to meet the faces that you meet;
There will be time to murder and create,
And time for all the works and days of hands
That lift and drop a question on your plate;
Time for you and time for me,
And time yet for a hundred indecisions,
And for a hundred visions and revisions,
Be·fore the taking of a toast and tea.

In the room the women come and go
Talking of Michelangelo.

And indeed there will be time
To wonder, 'Do I dare?' and, 'Do I dare?'
Time to turn back and descend the stair,
With a bald spot in the middle of my hair –
(They will say: 'How his hair is growing thin!')
My morning coat, my collar mounting firmly to the
chin,
My necktie rich and modest, but asserted by a simple
pin –
(They will say: 'But how his arms and legs are
thin!')
Do I dare
Dis·turb the universe?
In a minute there is time
For de·cisions and revisions which a minute will reverse.

For I have known them all already, known them all: –
Have known the evenings, mornings, afternoons,
I have measured out my life with coffee spoons;
I know the voices dying with a dying fall
Be·neath the music from a farther room.
So how should I presume?

And I have known the eyes already, known them all –
The eyes that fix you in a formulated phrase,
And when I am formulated, sprawling on a pin,
When I am pinned and wriggling on the wall,

    Then  how should I begin
        To  spit out all the butt-ends of my days and ways?
    And  how should I presume?

    And  I have known the arms already, known them all —
        Arms that are braceleted and white and bare
        (But in the lamplight, downed with light brown
            hair!)
        Is it perfume from a dress
    That  makes me so digress?
        Arms that lie along a table, or wrap about a
            shawl.
    And  should I then presume?
    And  how should I begin?

       .     .     .     .     .

    Shall I  say, I have gone at dusk through narrow streets
    And  watched the smoke that rises from the pipes
    Of  lonely men in shirt-sleeves, leaning out of
        windows? . . .
        I should have been a pair of ragged claws
        Scuttling across the floors of silent seas.

       .     .     .     .     .

        And the afternoon, the evening, sleeps so
            peacefully!
        Smoothed by long fingers,
      A · sleep . . . tired . . . or it malingers,
        Stretched on the floor, here beside you and me.
        Should I, after tea and cakes and ices,
  Have the  strength to force the moment to its crisis?
        But though I have wept and fasted, wept and
            prayed,
        Though I have seen my head (grown slightly bald)
            brought in upon a platter,
        I am no prophet — and here's no great matter;
  I have  seen the moment of my greatness flicker,
  And I have  seen the eternal Footman hold my coat, and snicker,

And, in short, I was afraid.

And would it have been worth it, after all,
   After the cups, the marmalade, the tea,
A · mong the porcelain, among some talk of you and me,
   Would it have been worth while,
To have bitten off the matter with a smile,
To have squeezed the universe into a ball
   To roll it toward some overwhelming question,
   To say: 'I am Lazarus, come from the dead,
Come back to tell you all, I shall tell you all' –
   If one, settling a pillow by her head,
Should say: 'That is not what I meant at all,
   That is not it, at all.'

And would it have been worth it, after all,
   Would it have been worth while,
   After the sunsets and the dooryards and the
      sprinkled streets,
   After the novels, after the teacups, after the
      skirts that trail along the floor –
And this, and so much more? –
   It is impossible to say just what I mean!
But as if a magic lantern threw the nerves in patterns
      on a screen:
   Would it have been worth while
If one, settling a pillow or throwing off a shawl,
And turning toward the window, should say:
   'That is not it at all,
That is not what I meant, at all.'

      .         .         .         .         .

   No! I am not Prince Hamlet, nor was meant to be;
   Am an attendant lord, one that will do
To swell a progress, start a scene or two,
Ad · vise the prince; no doubt, an easy tool,
Defe · rential, glad to be of use,
   Politic, cautious, and meticulous;

Full of high sentence, but a bit obtuse;
At times, indeed, almost ridiculous –
Almost, at times, the Fool.

I grow old . . . I grow old . . .
I shall wear the bottoms of my trousers rolled.

Shall I part my hair behind? Do I dare to eat a peach?
I shall wear white flannel trousers, and walk upon the
beach.
I have heard the mermaids singing, each to each.

I do not think that they will sing to me.

I have seen them riding seaward on the waves
Combing the white hair of the waves blown back
When the wind blows the water white and black.

We have lingered in the chambers of the sea
By sea-girls wreathed with seaweed red and brown
Till human voices wake us, and we drown.

– T. S. Eliot


57.                    **The Oxen**                    1915

Christmas Eve, and twelve of the clock.
'Now they are all on their knees,'
An elder said as we sat in a flock
By the embers in hearthside ease.

We pictured the meek mild creatures where
They dwelt in their strawy pen,
Nor did it occur to one of us there
To doubt they were kneeling then.

So fair a fancy few would weave
In these years! Yet, I feel,
If someone said on Christmas Eve,
'Come; see the oxen kneel

'In the lonely barton by yonder coomb          farmyard, valley
Our childhood used to know,'

I should go with him in the gloom,
Hoping it might be so.

— Thomas Hardy

58.            **Ancient Music**                        1916

Winter is icummen in,
Lhude sing Goddamm,
Raineth drop and staineth slop,
And how the wind doth ramm!
Sing: Goddamm.
Skiddeth bus and sloppeth us,
An ague hath my ham.
Freezeth river, turneth liver,
Damn you, sing: Goddamm.
God·damm, Goddamm, 'tis why I am, Goddamm,
So 'gainst the winter's balm.
Sing goddamm, damm, sing Goddamm,
Sing goddamm, sing goddamm, DAMM.

— Ezra Pound

59.        **Thirteen Ways of Looking at a Blackbird**   1917

I

A·mong twenty snowy mountains,
The only moving thing
Was the eye of the blackbird.

II

I was of three minds,
Like a tree
In which there are three blackbirds.

III

The blackbird whirled in the autumn winds.
It was a small part of the pantomime.

IV

A man and a woman
Are one.
A man and a woman and a blackbird
Are one.

V

I do not know which to prefer,
The beauty of inflections
Or the beauty of innuendoes,
The blackbird whistling
Or just after.

VI

Icicles filled the long window
With bar · baric glass.
The shadow of the blackbird
Crossed it, to and fro.
The mood
Traced in the shadow
An indecipherable cause.

VII

O thin men of Haddam,
Why do you imagine golden birds?
Do you not see how the blackbird
Walks around the feet
Of the women about you?

VIII

I know noble accents
And lucid, inescapable rhythms;
But I know, too,
That the blackbird is involved
In what I know.

IX

When the blackbird flew out of sight,
It marked the edge
Of one of many circles.

### X

At the  sight of blackbirds
    Flying in a green light,
    Even the bawds of euphony
Would  cry out sharply.

### XI

  He  rode over Connecticut
In a  glass coach.
    Once, a fear pierced him,
    In that he mistook
The  shadow of his equipage
For  blackbirds.

### XII

The  river is moving.
The  blackbird must be flying.

### XIII

It was  evening all afternoon.
It was  snowing
    And it was going to snow.
The  blackbird sat
In the  cedar-limbs.

– Wallace Stevens

60.      **Futility**            1918

    Move him into the sun –
    Gently its touch awoke him once,
At  home, whispering of fields unsown.
    Always it woke him, even in France,
Un · til this morning and this snow.
If  anything might rouse him now
The  kind old sun will know.

    Think how it wakes the seeds –
    Woke, once, the clay of a cold star.
Are  limbs, so dear-achieved, are sides

Full - nerved – still warm – too hard to stir?
    Was it for this the clay grew tall?
– O  what made fatuous sunbeams toil
To  break earth's sleep at all?

                               – Wilfred Owen

61         **After Apple-Picking**         1923

My  long two-pointed ladder's sticking through a
          tree
Toward  heaven still,
And  there's a barrel that I didn't fill
Be · side it, and there may be two or three
    Apples I didn't pick upon some bough.
But  I am done with apple-picking now.
    Essence of winter sleep is on the night,
The  scent of apples: I am drowsing off.
  I  cannot rub the strangeness from my sight
  I  got from looking through a pane of glass
  I  skimmed this morning from the drinking trough
And  held against the world of hoary grass.
  It  melted, and I let it fall and break
But  I was well
Up · on my way to sleep before it fell,
And  I could tell
What  form my dreaming was about to take.
    Magnified apples appear and disappear,
    Stem end and blossom end,
And  every fleck of russet showing clear.
My  instep arch not only keeps the ache,
  It  keeps the pressure of a ladder-round.
  I  feel the ladder sway as the boughs bend.
And  I keep hearing from the cellar bin
The  rumbling sound
Of  load on load of apples coming in.
For  I have had too much
Of  apple-picking: I am overtired

Of the great harvest I myself desired.
There were ten thousand thousand fruit to touch,
     Cherish in hand, lift down, and not let fall.
     For all
   That struck the earth,
     No matter if not bruised or spiked with stubble,
  Went surely to the cider-apple heap
  As of no worth.
        One can see what will trouble
   This sleep of mine, whatever sleep it is.
Were he not gone,
   The woodchuck could say whether it's like his
  Long sleep, as I describe its coming on,
   Or just some human sleep.

                                        – Robert Frost


62.     **Ars Poetica**                        1926

    A poem should be palpable and mute
 As a globed fruit,
      Dumb
   As old medallions to the thumb,

      Silent as the sleeve-worn stone
   Of casement ledges where the moss has grown –

    A poem should be wordless
 As the flight of birds.

                              *

    A poem should be motionless in time
 As the moon climbs,

        Leaving, as the moon releases
        Twig by twig the night-entangled trees,

        Leaving, as the moon behind the winter leaves,
        Memory by memory the mind –

    A poem should be motionless in time
 As the moon climbs.

                              *

237

    A poem should be equal to:  
Not true.  
For all the history of grief  
An empty doorway and a maple leaf.  
For love  
The leaning grasses and two lights above the sea –  
    A poem should not mean  
But be.

– Archibald MacLeish

63.            **chanson innocente**            1930

in Just-  
    spring    when the world is mud-  
    luscious the little  
    lame balloonman

    whistles    far    and wee

and eddieandbill come  
    running from marbles and  
    piracies and it's  
    spring

when the world is puddle-wonderful

the queer  
    old balloonman whistles  
    far    and    wee  
and bettyandisbel come dancing

from hop-scotch and jump-rope and

it's  
    spring  
and  
the

    goat-footed

bal·loonMan    whistles
       far
and
       wee

               – e. e. cummings

64.      **Smell**                    1935

Oh  strong ridged and deeply hollowed
     nose of mine! what will you not be smelling?
What  tactless asses we are, you and I, boney nose,
     always indiscriminate, always unashamed,
and  now it is the souring flowers of the bedraggled
     poplars: a festering pulp on the wet earth
be·neath them. With what deep thirst
we  quicken our desires
to that  rank odor of a passing springtime!
     Can you not be decent? Can you not reserve your
        ardors
for  something less unlovely? What girl will care
for  us, do you think, if we continue in these ways?
     Must you taste everything? Must you know
        everything?
     Must you have a part in everything?

              – William Carlos Williams

65.      **Everybody Makes Poets**        1938

     Poets aren't very useful,
Be·cause they aren't very consumeful or very
        produceful.
     Even poets of great promise
     Don't contribute much to trade and commerce,
To  which, indeed, even poets of great achievement
     Are a positive bereavement,

Be · cause they aren't very sensible,
Be · cause they think buying and selling are cheap
        and lousy and reprehensible,
And this is a topic about which poets are people
        to whom you cannot tell anything,
Be · cause they are people who cannot afford to buy
        anything and are seldom glib enough to sell
        anything,
So there is some excuse for the way they feel,
Be · cause they have seen lots of sunsets but no big
        deals so it follows naturally that they
        consider a sunset more important than a
        big deal.
    Some poets are bitter,
But they are preferable to the poets who are all of
        a twitter,
But even the poets who are all of a twitter are as
        dependable as Rotary
Com · pared to what each of them has around him which
        is a rapturous coterie,
Be · cause every poet is threatened constantly by one
        disaster,
Which is that a lot of otherwise thwarted male and
        female ladies will go around calling him
        Master,
And then there is nothing to do but surrender,
And then it is good-bye old poetry, hello old
        theosophy and gender,
And yet on the other hand if a poet isn't fed by a
        lot of male and female ladies who are
        affected,
Why un · til long after he is dead or gets the Pulitzer
        Prize, why he is neglected.
But the worst thing that can happen to a poet
Is to be ashamed of poetry as poetry so that he
        excuses himself for writing it by writing
        it sociologically in terms of Moscow or
        Detroet,

Which is  something I regret,
  Be · cause it is like a preacher taking a couple of
      highballs and telling a dirty story just to
      prove that he is a hail fellow well met,
So  my advice to mothers is if you are the mother of
      a poet don't gamble on the chance that
      future generations may crown him.
  Follow your original impulse and drown him.

                         – Ogden Nash

66.             **To the Tune of the Coventry Carol**    19—

  The  really right
  And  yet not quite
    In  love is wholly evil
  And  every heart
  That  loves in part
    Is  mortgaged to the devil.

    I  loved or thought
    I  loved in sort
  Was  this to love akin
    To  take the best
  And  leave the rest
  And  let the devil in?

    O  lovers true
  And  others too
Whose  best is only better
  Take  my advice
  Shun  compromise
  For · get him and forget her.

                         – Stevie Smith

67.                    **Prognosis**                    1939

Good · bye, Winter,
  The days are getting longer,
  The tea-leaf in the teacup
  Is herald of a stranger.

      Will he bring me business
  Or will he bring me gladness
  Or will he come for cure
      Of his own sickness?

      With a pedlar's burden
      Walking up the garden
      Will he come to beg
  Or will he come to bargain?

      Will he come to pester,
  To cringe or to bluster,
  A promise in his palm
  Or a gun in his holster?

      Will his name be John
  Or will his name be Jonah
      Crying to repent
  On the Island of Iona?

      Will his name be Jason
      Looking for a seaman
      Or a mad crusader
  With · out rhyme or reason?

      What will be his message –
      War or work or marriage?
      News as new as dawn
      Or an old adage?

      Will he give a champion
      Answer to my question
  Or will his words be dark
      And his ways evasion?

> Will his name be Love
> And all his talk be crazy?
> Or will his name be Death
> And his message easy?

– Louis MacNeice

68.  **Warning to Children**  1941

Children, if you dare to think
Of the greatness, rareness, muchness,
Fewness of this precious only
Endless world in which you say
You live, you think of things like this:
Blocks of slate enclosing dappled
Green and red, enclosing tawny
Yellow nets, enclosing white
And black acres of dominoes,
Where a neat brown paper parcel
Tempts you to untie the string.
In the parcel a small island,
On the island a large tree,
On the tree a husky fruit.
Strip the husk and pare the rind off:
In the centre you will see
Blocks of slate enclosed by dappled
Red and green, enclosed by tawny
Yellow nets, enclosed by white
And black acres of dominoes,
Where the same brown paper parcel –
Children, leave the string alone!
For who dares undo the parcel
Finds himself at once inside it,
On the island, in the fruit,
Blocks of slate about his head,
Finds himself enclosed by dappled
Red and green, enclosed by yellow
Tawny nets, enclosed by black

<pre>
        And   white acres of dominoes,
   With the   same brown paper parcel
             Still unopened on his knee.
             And, if he then should dare to think
             Of the fewness, muchness, rareness,
             Greatness of this endless only
             Precious world in which he says
        He   lives – he then unties the string.
</pre>

– Robert Graves

69.          *from* **The Ill-Tempered Lover**                    1948

I

<pre>
        I   wish my tongue were a quiver the size of a
               huge cask
            Packed and crammed with long black venomous
               rankling darts.
      I'd   fling you more full of them, and joy in the
               task,
    Than   ever Sebastian was, or Caesar, with
               thirty-three swords in his heart.

      I'd   make a porcupine out of you, or a pin-cushion,
               say;
      The   shafts should stand so thick you'd look like a
               headless hen
    Hung   up by the heels, with the long bare red neck
               stretching, curving, and dripping away
 From the   soiled floppy ball of ruffled feathers standing
               on end.

You should   bristle like those cylindrical brushes they use
               to scrub out bottles,
     Not   even to reach the kindly earth with the soles
               of your prickled feet.
     And   I would stand by and watch you wriggle and
               writhe, gurgling through the barbs in your
               throttle
</pre>

Like a  woolly caterpillar pinned on its back – man,
    that would be sweet!

II

From  love of you such strength did flow,
   I  was a god to drink of it;
And  now, by God, I hate you so
   It  makes me weak to think of it.

– L. A. MacKay

70.      **The Death of the Bird**      1948

For  every bird there is this last migration:
Once  more the cooling year kindles her heart;
With a  warm passage to the summer station
Love  pricks the course in lights across the chart.

    Year after year a speck on the map, divided
By a  whole hemisphere, summons her to come;
    Season after season, sure and safely guided,
    Going away she is also coming home.

And  being home, memory becomes a passion
With  which she feeds her brood and straws her nest,
A · ware of ghosts that haunt the heart's possession
And  exiled love mourning within the breast.

The  sands are green with a mirage of valleys;
The  palm-tree casts a shadow not its own;
    Down the long architrave of temple or palace
    Blows a cool air from moorland scarps of stone.

And  day by day the whisper of love grows stronger;
That  delicate voice, more urgent with despair,
    Custom and fear constraining her no longer,
    Drives her at last on the waste leagues of air.

A  vanishing speck in those inane dominions,
    Single and frail, uncertain of her place,
A · lone in the bright host of her companions,
    Lost in the blue unfriendliness of space,

She   feels it close now, the appointed season:
The   invisible thread is broken as she flies;
    Suddenly, without warning, without reason,
The   guiding spark of instinct winks and dies.

    Try as she will, the trackless world delivers
No   way, the wilderness of light no sign,
The   immense and complex map of hills and rivers
    Mocks her small wisdom with its vast design.

And   darkness rises from the eastern valleys,
And the   winds buffet her with their hungry breath,
And the   great earth, with neither grief nor malice,
Re · ceives the tiny burden of her death.

                             – A. D. Hope


71.　　　　**Do not go gentle into that good night**　　　　1951

Do   not go gentle into that good night,
Old   age should burn and rave at close of day;
Rage,   rage against the dying of the light.

Though   wise men at their end know dark is right,
Be · cause their words had forked no lightning they
Do   not go gentle into that good night.

  Good men, the last wave by, crying how bright
Their   frail deeds might have danced in a green bay,
Rage,   rage against the dying of the light.

  Wild men who caught and sang the sun in flight,
And   learn, too late, they grieved it on its way,
Do   not go gentle into that good night.

  Grave men, near death, who see with blinding sight
  Blind eyes could blaze like meteors and be gay,
Rage,   rage against the dying of the light.

And   you, my father, there on the sad height,
Curse,   bless me now with your fierce tears, I pray.

Do  not go gentle into that good night.
Rage,  rage against the dying of the light.

— Dylan Thomas

72.            *from* **The Dream Songs**              1955

### 40

I'm  scared a lonely. Never see my son,
     easy be not to see anyone,
     combers out to sea
     know they're goin somewhere but not me.
     Got a little poison, got a little gun,
I'm  scared a lonely.

I'm  scared a only one thing, which is me,
from  othering I don't take nothin, see,
 for  any hound dog's sake.
But  this is where I livin, where I rake
 my  leaves and cop my promise, this' where we
     cry oursel's awake.

     Wishin was dyin but I gotta make
  it  all this way to that bed on these feet
where  peoples said to meet.
     Maybe but even if I see my son
for·ever never, get back on the take,
     free, black & forty-one.

### 45

He  stared at ruin. Ruin stared straight back.
He  thought they was old friends. He felt on the stair
where her  papa found them bare
     they became familiar. When the papers were lost
     rich with pals' secrets, he thought he had the
               knack
 of  ruin. Their paths crossed

and  once they crossed in jail; they crossed in bed;
and  over an unsigned letter their eyes met,

```
       and  in an Asian city
        di · rectionless & lurchy at two & three,
         or  trembling to a telephone's fresh threat,
  and when  some wired his head

         to  reach a wrong opinion, 'Epileptic.'
    But he  noted now that: they were not old friends.
       He  did not know this one.
             This one was a stranger, come to make amends
        for  all the imposters, and to make it stick.
             Henry nodded, un-.
```

          – John Berryman

73.    **Daybreak in Alabama**     1957

```
   When  I get to be a composer
          I'm gonna write me some music about
          Daybreak in Alabama
     And  I'm gonna put the purtiest songs in it
          Rising out of the ground like a swamp mist
     And  falling out of heaven like soft dew.
          I'm gonna put some tall tall trees in it
 And the  scent of pine needles
 And the  smell of red clay after rain
     And  long red necks
     And  poppy colored faces
     And  big brown arms
 And the  field daisy eyes
      Of  black and white black white black people
     And  I'm gonna put white hands
     And  black hands and brown and yellow hands
     And  red clay earth hands in it
          Touching everybody with kind fingers
     And  touching each other natural as dew
 In that  dawn of music when I
          Get to be a composer
```

And  write about daybreak
In  Alabama.

– Langston Hughes

74.        **Grandparents**                                1959

They're altogether otherworldly now,
 those adults champing for their ritual Friday spin
    to pharmacist and five-and-ten in Brockton.
       Back in my throw-away and shaggy span
    of adolescence, Grandpa still waves his stick
       like a policeman;
       Grandmother, like a Mohammedan, still wears her
           thick˙
       lavender mourning and touring veil,
   the Pierce Arrow clears its throat in a horse-stall.
Then the dry road dust rises to whiten
  the fa · tigued elm leaves –
   the nineteenth century, tired of children, is gone.
They're all gone into a world of light; the farm's my own.

   The farm's my own!
       Back there alone,
     I keep indoors, and spoil another season.
     I hear the rattley little country gramophone
        racking its five foot horn:
   'O Summer Time!'
       Even at noon here the formidable
       *Ancien Régime* still keeps nature at a distance.
           Five
       green shaded light bulbs spider the
           billiards-table,
     no field is greener than its cloth,
  where Grandpa, dipping sugar for us both,
   once spilled his demitasse.
   His favorite ball, the number three,
  still hides the coffee stain.

          Never again
   to  walk there, chalk our cues,
   in · sist on shooting for us both.
          Grandpa! Have me, hold me, cherish me!
          Tears smut my fingers. There
          half my life-lease later,
    I  hold an *Illustrated London News*,
  dis · loyal still,
    I  doodle handlebar
mus · taches on the last Russian Czar.

– Robert Lowell

75.      **Election 1960**             1961

          Hot sun. Lizards frolic
          Fly-catching on the black ash
That was  green rubbish. Tiny dragons
   They  dodge among the burnt brown stems
     As  if the earth belonged to them
  with · out condition. In the polling booths
      A  democratic people have elected
  King  Log, King Stork, King Log, King Stork again.
    Be · cause I like a wide and silent pond
          I voted Log. That party was defeated.
   Now  frogs will dive and scuttle to avoid
  That  poking idiot bill, the iron gullet:
    De · linquent frogs! Stork is an active King,
     A  bird of principle, benevolent,
  And  Log is Log, an old time-serving post
          Hacked from a totara when the land was young.

– James K. Baxter

76.       **Lady Lazarus**                    1962

I have  done it again.
        One year in every ten
    I   manage it –

    A   sort of walking miracle, my skin
        Bright as a Nazi lampshade,
   My   right foot

    A   paperweight,
   My   face a featureless, fine
        Jew linen.

        Peel off the napkin
        O my enemy.
        Do I terrify? –

        Yes, yes Herr Professor,
        It is I.
  Can   you deny

  The   nose, the eye pits, the full set of teeth?
  The   sour breath
  Will  vanish in a day.

        Soon, soon the flesh
  The   grave cave ate will be
   At   home on me

  And   I a smiling woman.
        I am only thirty.
  And   like the cat I have nine times to die.

        This is Number Three.
        What a trash
 To an · nihilate each decade.

What a  million filaments.
  The   peanut-crunching crowd
        Shoves in to see

Them un · wrap me hand and foot –
  The   big strip tease.
        Gentlemen, ladies

These are my hands, my knees.
I may be skin and bone,
I may be Japanese,

Neverthe·less I am the same identical woman.
The first time it happened I was ten.
It was an accident.

The second time I meant
To last it out and not come back at all.
I rocked shut

As a seashell.
They had to call and call
And pick the worms off me like sticky pearls.

Dying
Is an art, like everything else.
I do it exceptionally well.

I do it so it feels like hell.
I do it so it feels real.
I guess you could say I've a call.

It's easy enough to do it in a cell.
It's easy enough to do it and stay put.
It's the theatrical

Comeback in broad day
To the same place, the same face, the same brute
A·mused shout:

'A miracle!'
That knocks me out.
There is a charge

For the eyeing of my scars, there is a charge
For the hearing of my heart —
It really goes.

And there is a charge, a very large charge
For a word or a touch
Or a bit of blood

Or a piece of my hair or my clothes.

So, so, Herr Doktor.
So, Herr Enemy.

I am your opus,
I am your valuable,
The pure gold baby

That melts to a shriek.
I turn and burn.
Do not think I underestimate your great concern.

Ash, ash —
You poke and stir.
Flesh, bone, there is nothing there —

A cake of soap,
A wedding ring,
A gold filling.

Herr God, Herr Lucifer
Be·ware
Be·ware.

Out of the ash
I rise with my red hair
And I eat men like air.

— Sylvia Plath

77.     **Introduction to Literature**                    1970

Look: no one ever promised for sure
that we would sing. We have decided
to moan. In a strange dance that
we don't understand till we do it, we
have to carry on.

Just as in sleep you have to dream
the ex·act dream to round out your life,
so we have to live that dream into stories
and hold them close at you, close at the
edge we share, to be right.

We  find it an awful thing to meet people,
    serious or not, who have turned into vacant
ef · fective people, so far lost that they
    won't believe their own feelings
e · nough to follow them out.

The au · thentic is a line from one thing
    a · long to the next; it interests us.
    Strangely, it relates to what works,
but is  not quite the same. It never
    swerves for revenge,

Or  profit, or fame: it holds
to · gether something more than the world,
this  line. And we are your wavery
    efforts at following it. Are you coming?
    Good: Now it is time.

                              – William Stafford


78.                    **The Years**                  1975

The  door is low. Stoop down
    deep. Count the darkening
    lines of vintages.

We  tell off the years
with  open enchantment –
'sixty  - two, 'sixty-three – some

    even from those times,
    now great past recognition,
in · capable of change.

Some  thin years too:
we're  not short of those here,
it's  hard country.

A  few contain some promise,
but  most are slugged out
for the  odd sad friend.

Next door, the kitchen
where Sunday after noon
we dream up new sensations:

bullsblood, beeswax, benny –
they never go down well,
stun the tongue.

Per · haps the palate dulls.
Maybe one expects too many
instant ageless knockouts.

While we're still in the game
but seem to get down fewer
lines each year

a · round the back
terraces of iron vines
hearts laid grey and bare

knot and die
in sullen rage
to tell the real story.

– Philip Davies Roberts

79.     **Julia's Wild**                                    19—

Come shadow, come, and take this shadow up,
Come shadow shadow, come and take this up,
Come, shadow, come, and take this shadow up,
Come, come shadow, and take this shadow up,
Come, come and shadow, take this shadow up,
Come, up, come shadow and take this shadow,
And up, come, take shadow, come this shadow,
And up, come, come shadow, take this shadow,
And come shadow, come up, take this shadow,
Come up, come shadow this, and take shadow,
Up, shadow this, come and take shadow, come
Shadow this, take and come up shadow, come
Take and come, shadow, come up, shadow this,

Up, come and take shadow, come this shadow,
Come up, take shadow, and come this shadow,
Come and take shadow, come up this shadow,
Shadow, shadow come, come and take this up,
Come, shadow, take, and come this shadow, up,
Come shadow, come, and take this shadow up,
Come, shadow, come, and take this shadow up.

— Louis Zukofsky

80.     **All Night**                                    1978

All night
I  drift apart all night
In  these bad times bad hours all night I look at
            what's to come

All night
The  faces suddenly gone the sicknesses drifting past
            all night
The  smiles of the lost adrift in the faceless dark

All night
Nothing to save them nothing left with which to
            save myself all night
I  move toward the same path they travel as we drift
            apart

All night
Not in light but the deepest flight and mystery
            all night
The  maps accumulate not to be sorted or known but
            suffered without release

All night
We dis · cover in night all the traps that seem to fit
            in which all night
Our  past lives fill the future in which the only
            traps are what we've been

All night
The  sparrows at rest in the trees and the fingers
      that close the book all night
Our · selves and others caught on ice floes moving
      through the dark

All night
Where  we go the day cares not the day awaits its new
      beginnings all night
The  day prepares its survivors feast those who'll
      synchronize their watches with the sun

All night
But the  night is different the night harbors the desolate
      all night
The  angels at their portholes the gates in the moon
      that open or shut

All night
In ex · tremity the night offers its one balm having gone
      so far go one step further all night
As in an instant at the sea's edge the madman
      leaps and the shapes of night relent

All night
Yet  there are those other faces other voices that all
      night
Rise about us like white poppies as in a fever we
      drift in and out of the dark

All night
And  if through love they'll enter through the deepest
      betrayal they'll leave yet all night
They re · turn we hear them at our pillows all night the
      voices that whisper

All night
Of the  dark that is the last chance and all the chances
      missed all night
The  voices that say *forgive the unforgivable and you*
      *will heal else nothing lives*

          All night
     In  these bad times bad hours as we drift through our
               sicknesses as all night
     The  fevers rise about us and sleepless once more all
               night we dream our passage through the dark

                                              – Robert Mazzocco


81.          **Married Love**                              1985

As they  sat and talked beneath the boundary trees
              In the abandoned park, neither one mentioning
              Her husband or his wife, it seemed as though
     Their  summer shadows had detached themselves
              In the confusion of those thousand leaves: but
                   no more
   Than  they could call those shadows back from the air
  Could  they ignore the lives they had undone,
    And  would undo once more, that afternoon,
      Be · fore giving in to what they knew, had always known . . .
    And  yet, in turning away, what they would say was not
              That thing, but something else, that mild excuse
   That  lovers use of how things might have been
    Had  they met somewhere else, or in some better time,
  Were  they less like themselves than what they are.

                                              – Sherod Santos

# Appendix A
## Phonemic Alphabet

*Take care of the Sense and the Sounds will take care of themselves*
*— Lewis Carroll*

Many alphabets and systems have been devised to represent the different sounds of English since Christian missionaries introduced their Roman alphabet from the fifth century. They used combinations of Roman letters, such as 'th', 'sh' and 'gh', to do duty for English speech-sounds which do not exist in the Latinate languages. This kind of compromise has been a feature of most 'phonetic' alphabets since then; most dictionaries today use various kinds of phonetic symbol which are based on the Roman alphabet and which can be printed without recourse to 'special sorts'.

The problem with the various dictionary systems is that they are not standard. Each publisher has a different system, so a casual reader can never hope to become familiar with all of them. For that reason I have used the only internationally recognized system, the International Phonetic Alphabet, as the basis of the phonemic transcriptions in this book. The disadvantage of using the IPA for transcribing English sounds is that it involves learning fourteen new, non-Roman, symbols. The much larger advantage is that these symbols are standard, and are part of a larger alphabet which includes all known human speech sounds.

In Chapter 8 I discuss the difference between phonetics and phonemics. Phonetics refers to a detailed transcription of the speech-sounds of a particular individual: phonemics refers only to those sounds which have meaning for an entire speech community – for example, that of English. Phonetics is a particular and concrete realization of speech: phonemics is a general and abstract account of the meaningful sounds of language. A trained phonetician should be able to transcribe the speech-sounds of any individual without any understanding whatever of the language being spoken. A phonemic transcription, however, is impossible unless the transcriber is fluent in that language, at least to the extent of knowing which sounds are meaningful in that language and which not.

By convention, if IPA symbols are being used for a phonetic transcription they are surrounded with square brackets, for example [pʰɪn], while the same symbols used for a *phonemic* transcription of 'pin' are surrounded with slashes, /pɪn/. Notice that in this example the phonetic transcription includes the [ʰ] which is often heard in the pronunciation of 'pin', but which in itself has no phonemic significance in English.

Most of the transcriptions in this book are phonemic. Of course, English societies have different 'pronunciations' in different parts of the world, and it would be impossible for me to include all the phonemic variants of these regions. What I have aimed at is a general transcription sufficient to show the patterns of most English poetry. In most cases, regional shifts of pronunciation have usually been consistent enough for a pair of words which rhyme in Scotland, for example, to rhyme also in California, Tasmania or Newfoundland.

## Phonemic Alphabet

### Consonants

/p/ as in pit   (oral bilabial voiceless stop)
/b/ as in bit   (oral bilabial voiced stop)
/f/ as in fat   (oral labio-dental voiceless fricative)
/v/ as in vat   (oral labio-dental voiced fricative)
/t/ as in ten   (oral apico-alveolar voiceless stop)
/d/ as in den   (oral apico-alveolar voiced stop)
/θ/ as in thin   (oral apico-dental voiceless fricative)
/ð/ as in this   (oral apico-dental voiced fricative)
/s/ as in hiss   (oral prelamino-alveolar voiceless fricative)
/z/ as in his   (oral prelamino-alveolar voiced fricative)
/tʃ/ as in char   (oral prelamino-alveolar voiceless affricate)
/dʒ/ as in jar   (oral prelamino-alveolar voiced affricate)
/ʃ/ as in mesh   (oral lamino-palatal voiceless fricative)
/ʒ/ as in measure   (oral lamino-palatal voiced fricative)

/k/ as in call   (oral dorso-velar voiceless stop)
/g/ as in gall   (oral dorso-velar voiced stop)
/m/ as in mail   (nasal bilabial resonant)
/n/ as in nail   (nasal apico-alveolar resonant)
/ŋ/ as in sing   (nasal dorso-velar resonant)
/w/ as in wink   (oral bilabial resonant)
/l/ as in link   (oral apico-alveolar resonant)
/r/ as in rung   (oral prelamino-alveolar resonant)
/j/ as in young   (oral lamino-palatal resonant)
/h/ as in hung   (fortis)

The technical descriptions following each example refer to the way in which the noise is produced. In oral sounds, breath is expelled from the mouth as the sound is made; in nasals it comes from the nose. The second term of the description refers to the two parts of the mouth involved in the production of each sound:

bilabial – both lips
labio-dental – lower lip and upper teeth
apico-alveolar – tip of tongue and ridge behind upper teeth
apico-dental – tip of tongue and upper teeth
prelamino-alveolar – front edges of tongue and ridge behind upper teeth
lamino-palatal – back edges of tongue and roof of mouth
dorso-velar – back of tongue and soft palate

The distinction between voiced and voiceless consonants is explained on pp. 40–1 above.

A stop is a consonant sound which is not prolonged but made with a single release of breath. A fricative sound is produced by the friction of escaping breath against different parts of the mouth. An affricate is similar, but is preceded by a stop.

'Fortis' is a special term used to describe the voiceless sound of /h/. This sound requires significantly more energy to produce, involving the expenditure of a relatively strong (Latin, *fort*, *fortis*) exhalation; hence, /h/ sounds are frequently dropped or minimized in rapid or informal pronunciation.

Vowels

*Front*

/i/ as in b̄eat
/ɪ/ as in bit
/ɛ/ as in bed
/æ/ as in bad

*Central*

/ɜ/ as in bird
/a/ as in bard
/ʌ/ as in but
/ə/ (schwa) as in wanted

*Back*

/ʊ/ as in book
/o/ as in bore
/ɒ/ as in pot
/u/ as in boot

*Diphthongs*

/ɛi/ as in bay
/ai/ as in buy
/oi/ as in boy
/aʊ/ as in bough
/əʊ/ as in beau

The sound **schwa** (/ə/) needs special explanation. It is the 'colourless', neutral sound frequently used in the pronunciation of unstressed vowels in a word or a phrase, as /tʃɪl.drən/ ('children') or /kʌm ən gɛt ət/ ('come and get it'). It is *never* found alone in a stressed syllable.

Vowel sounds are apt to cause the most difficulty in any attempt at phonemic transcription. Not only are the symbols more difficult to learn, as most of them are unfamiliar-looking, but regional and national accents usually differ mainly in the pronunciation of vowels rather than of consonants. For example, a Canadian attempting a phonemic transcription of the word 'here' will probably write

/hir/; an Australian, on the other hand, will probably write /hiə/. Nevertheless, the rhyme 'hear – beer' will sound equally acceptable as either /hir – bir/ or /hiə – biə/.

# Appendix B
## Pronunciation of Old and Middle English

### Old English Pronunciation (AD 700–1100)

In general, consonants in Old English have roughly the same pronunciation as they do today. Occasionally the following pronunciations are used.

**c** is pronounced /tʃ/; for example, 'cild' (child) is pronounced /tʃild/

**f** is pronounced /v/; for example, 'wefan' (to weave) is pronounced /we.væn/

**g** is pronounced /j/; for example, 'dæg' (day) is pronounced /dæ.j/

**sc** is pronounced /ʃ/; for example, 'scip' (ship) is pronounced /ʃip/.

The modern pronunciation of many words will often serve as a clue as to when such special pronunciations should be used.

Vowels are pronounced nearly as they are in Latin or Italian. All vowels and consonants are pronounced in every word, with the stress usually falling on the first syllable. So, the **c** of 'cnawan' (to know), the **w** in 'writan' (to write), and the **h** in 'hlaford' (lord) should all be heard.

For further guidance, see *Sweet's Anglo-Saxon Primer* (Oxford University Press). Listening to recordings of Anglo-Saxon by modern scholars can also be most helpful. Remember, though, that our views on Old English pronunciation are the result of modern reconstructive research; it is impossible to be absolutely certain about such matters, though most scholars agree on the main features.

For the Old English selections in this book, I have changed the runic letters ð (eth), and þ (thorn), to their closest modern equivalent, **th**. It should be noted that in Old English spelling ð and þ were used interchangeably for either /ð/ or /θ/.

**Middle English Pronunciation** (AD 1100–1500)

Consonants in Middle English have roughly the same pronunciation as they do today. Vowels are pronounced nearly as they are in Latin or Italian.

Generally speaking, all vowels and consonants are pronounced in every word, even if they are not in the modern equivalent. The k is pronounced in 'knowe', the g in 'gnawe', the l in 'half', and so on. Final e which is silent in Modern English is usually pronounced in Middle English. For example, 'age' is pronounced /a.dʒə/, 'crepe' (to creep) /krɛ.pɜ/, and so forth.

For further guidance see *An Introduction to Chaucer* (Cambridge University Press), or *A Chaucer Reader* (Harcourt, Brace and Co.). There are many excellent recordings of Middle English readings, which will help you develop a feel for the sound of Middle English poetry.

For the Middle English selections in this book, I have changed the letter þ (thorn) to 'th' and ʒ (yogh) to either 'g', 'y' or 'z', depending on context.

# Appendix C
## Quantitative Metre

*Poets that lasting marble seek*
*Must come in Latin or in Greek.*
>                                    – *Edmund Waller*, Of English Verse *(1687)*

The notion of 'quantity', or time-length, was central to the perception of Classical Latin metres. As quantitative metre was for centuries the basis of English metrical theory, it is a good idea briefly to outline it.

The two units of quantitative prosody are the *long* (longus) and the *short* (brevis) syllable. The short syllable was the basic unit of time (Greek, *chronos*; Latin, *mora*), and a long syllable was perceived as being exactly equivalent to two short ones.

Here is a typical hexameter, or 'six-foot' line, the main vehicle for serious poetry in Latin, with – marking each long syllable and ˘ each short:

| 1 | 2 | 3 | 4 | 5 | 6 |
|---|---|---|---|---|---|
| – – / | – – / | – – / | – – / | – ˘ ˘ / | – – |
| Ibant | obscur | i so | la sub | nocte per | umbram |

Various combinations were possible – for example, in each foot two shorts could be used in place of the second long. Moreover, an extra-metrical caesura (pause) could fall in the middle of either the second, third or fourth foot.

Many English poets, among them the Briton Robert Bridges, have attempted to write poetry in English making use of quantitative rather than stress metres. Here is Bridges' version of the Latin line above, in which he seeks to duplicate the effect of the original, using another familiar variant of the Latin hexameter:

| 1 | 2 | 3 | 4 | 5 | 6 |
|---|---|---|---|---|---|
| – ˘ ˘ / | – – / | – ˘ ˘ / | – – / | – ˘ ˘ / | – – / |
| They went am | id the | shadows by | night in | loneliness | obscure |

Longfellow's *Evangeline*, with its well-known opening line

> This is the forest primaeval. The murmuring pines and the
>   hemlocks

is also cast in hexameters. Nevertheless, the general feeling among poets and others who have attempted the conversion is in accord with that of Tennyson (itself expressed in hexameters):

> These lame hexameters the strong wing'd music of Homer!
> No – but a most burlesque barbarous experiment.

For historical information, here are the names of the classical quantitative feet most often applied to English metre:

> iamb (adjective: iambic) – short–long
> trochee (trochaic) – long–short
> dactyl (dactylic) – long–short–short
> anapaest (anapaestic) – short–short–long
> spondee (spondaic) – long–long
> pyrrhus (pyrrhic) – short–short

Feet beginning with a short are commonly described as 'rising', those beginning with a long as 'falling'.

These terms are usually combined with another which merely states the number of feet in the line:

> monometer – one foot
> dimeter – two feet
> trimeter – three feet
> tetrameter – four feet
> pentameter – five feet
> hexameter – six feet
> septameter – seven feet, and so on

In the sixteenth century and later, attempts were made to link English metre to the quantitative metres of classical Sanskrit, Greek and Latin. Such attempts may have been the product of a generally high regard in England for the cultural models of antiquity. It may also have been the result of low cultural self-esteem in England; the influence of the English grammar schools, and their emphasis on 'classical' education, is also important. So is the fact that classical poetry was largely associated with the culture of a great power (Rome), a model for British, and later American, imperialism in the centuries which followed. Whatever the cause, from the sixteenth century on, poets were enjoined to duplicate the effect of classical metres in English.

In fact, the perception of long and short syllables is alien to the English ear. We are simply not accustomed to hearing or even to listening for such patterns. This is not to argue that they do not exist – simply that they will not be perceived as such by an English ear. A way round this was proposed by the theorists, however: the long syllable of classical metre was taken as equivalent to the stressed syllable in English, and the classical short as equivalent to the English weak syllable. So the Latin pattern of short–long (the iambic foot of classical prosody) was taken as equivalent to the English pattern of weak–strong. In this way, it was argued, all the classical metres could easily be duplicated in English, and all the techniques and terminology of the ancient Greeks and Romans could be taken over holus-bolus.

The problem is that the two prosodies are not equivalent at all. A line of Latin iambic (short–long) feet sets up a pattern of duration, one which could be rendered in traditional music notation as ♩♩♩♩ ♩♩ ♩♩ ♩♩. Stress has nothing to do with this pattern: it is set up by the relationship between the lengths of the syllables – the second syllable lasts twice as long as the first, the third half as long as the second, and so on. In contrast, a 'musical' representation of an English 'iambic' line would have to use bar-lines to show where the stresses fall; the syllables, on the other hand, would be taken as of equal duration: ♩|♩♩|♩♩|♩♩|♩♩|♩.

Even in the most influential periods of eighteenth-century English neo-classicism, some writers were disagreeing about the relevance of quantitative metre to English prosody. In *An Essay on the Power of Numbers and Principles of Harmony in Poetical Composition* (1749), John Mason compares the stress in English poetry with the accent in music, arguing that in poetry the stressed syllable should always be taken as marking the beginning of the 'measure'.

Another theorist, Joshua Steele, in *Prosodia Rationalis* ('Rationale of Prosody'; 1779), suggests that something like the musical rest (a fixed period of silence) would be of great use in accounting for rhythmical effects in English poetry. (I have called this the 'silent stress' and symbolized it with an asterisk.) So none of the principles presented in Chapter 2 is particularly new, though in the past they have not been methodically applied.

The transformation into English terms was made by taking the longs of classical metre as equivalent to the stressed syllables of English, and the shorts as equivalent to the weak syllables. But, as is explained in Chapter 2, they are only occasionally equivalent and, more important, the stress-based nature of English makes possible certain rhythmical effects which are impossible in quantitative metres. On the other hand, the inversion of a foot (for example, replacing a trochee with an iamb) is an effect impossible to duplicate in the isochronic stress-based metres of English. Let's see why. Here is an English 'iambic' line, marked off in the 'feet' of Classical prosody ( ˘ is weak and ′ strong):

```
    1     2     3     4
/ ˘  ′/ ˘  ′/ ˘  ′  / ˘    ′ /
```
The farmer left his horse and plough.

Now let's follow this line with one in which the second 'foot' is inverted, from weak–strong to strong–weak (a 'trochee'):

```
    1         2        3       4
/˘    ′ /      ′  ˘/ ˘ ′/  ˘ ′ /
```
And screamed: 'Give him the gold and run!'

This looks fine on paper, but is an effect the English ear will not perceive. What would be perceived, instead, in this second line is something closer to

```
    1        2       3      4
/˘    ′/      ′   ˘ / ′ ˘   ′ /
```
And screamed: 'Give him the gold and run!'

which is quite different. This is because, whatever else we may perceive in English metre, we will hear the stresses of its rhythms as isochronous. So instead of an 'inverted foot' we have the substitution of a triplet measure in the second position. The effect can be more clearly conveyed by the notation which is described in Chapter 2 and used throughout the book:

<pre>
The    farmer left his horse and plough
       ●o      ●o       ●o        ●/o
And    screamed: 'Give him the gold and run!'
       ●        ●oo            ●o         ●
</pre>

which makes clear the main variations to the regular rhythmic pattern which occur in the second line: first, a single-syllable measure, then a triplet.

The extent to which classical metrical terminology has been misapplied in English may be demonstrated by a short extract from Paul Fussell's *Poetic Meter and Poetic Form* (Random House, 1965; 1969). Seeking to illustrate 'the sort of perception that scansion makes possible by translating sound into visual terms', Fussell quotes two lines from Edward Fitzgerald's rendition of the Persian poem, *The Rubaiyat of Omar Khayyam*, giving them the following scansion markings:

<pre>
     ˘  /   ˘  /   ˘  /   ˘  /   ˘  /
That ev / ery Hy / acinth / the Gar / den wears /
     /  ˘  ˘  ˘   ˘  /   /   /   ˘  /
Dropt in / her lap / from some / once love / ly head.
</pre>

'By giving us a clear visual representation of the metrical status of the words,' he writes, 'the scansion of these two lines makes apparent the substitution of a trochee for the expected iamb at the beginning of the last line. This variation, which reinforces the shocking suddenness and rapidity of the fall of the drops of blood, constitutes a moment of high, although perhaps not the highest, technical accomplishment. It is to learn to appraise such accomplishments accurately that we scan at all.'

Let's see if we can be any clearer about the rhythms which are actually perceived. (I assume Mr Fussell's markings for the second and fourth feet of the second line must be misprints.) If we lay the two lines out in rhythmic measures instead of feet, we see:

| That | every | Hya- | cinth the | garden | wears |
|------|-------|------|-----------|--------|-------|
|      | ●○    | ●○   | ●○        | ●○     | ●     |
|      | Dropt in her | lap from | some once | lovely | head. |
|      | ●○○   | ●○   | ●○        | ●○     | ●     |

which better reflects their effect: first, the surprise of a singlet measure at the end of the first line; second, the speeded-up delivery of a triplet at the start of line two; third, a return to normal duplet rhythms after that. It is the speeding-up of 'Dropt in her lap' which 'reinforces the shocking suddenness and rapidity of the fall of the drops of blood', together with the fact that no weak syllable follows 'wears' at the end of the preceding line – and this effect will be noticed by any attentive English ear.

Some commentators have argued that English poets have always been able to convey the notion of quantity by the judicious placing of vowel sounds – /ɪ/, for example, is taken as being 'short' and /u/ as 'long'. R. F. Brewer, in his *Orthometry: The Art of Versification and the Technicalities of Poetry* (London, 1950), argues that it would be wrong to regard quantity as having no bearing upon our versification. 'It is an important aid to metrical perfection, and is sedulously cultivated by all our poets as an embellishment, though not as the foundation of rhythm . . . Quantity cannot be altogether neglected without manifest and great injury to the verse.'* Brewer gives lines from Milton's 'L'Allegro' and 'Il Penseroso' to demonstrate predominantly long quantities:

> Come, pensive Nun, devout and pure,
> Sober, steadfast, and demure;
> All in a robe of darkest grain,
> Flowing with majestic train . . .

and predominantly short ones:

> Haste thee, nymph, and bring with thee
> Jest and youthful jollity.
> Sport that wrinkled Care derides,
> And laughter, holding both his sides . . .

* Brewer, *Orthometry*, pp. 24–5.

The reader may like to try reading these aloud to someone else to test whether the notion of quantity is really conveyed. The semantic content of the first lines, of course, has to do with slowness (and thereby, perhaps, length), just as the second is about speed (and thereby, perhaps, brevity); but whether the vowels in isolation can convey this information is doubtful.

Most older books about English poetry use the quantitative 'foot' terminology for describing all metre, whether pure stress, stress-syllabic, or syllabic. If you are using such a book, the conversion from such terms as 'tetrameter' and 'pentameter' to the ones used in the text of this book is easily made. Classical 'feet' may be converted to rhythmical measures as follows:

| | |
|---|---|
| spondee → | singlet |
| iamb | |
| trochee | } duplet |
| anapaest | |
| dactyl | } triplet |

So a line of dactylic tetrameter is equivalent to four-triplet, iambic pentameter is equivalent to five-duplet, and so on. The pyrrhic foot, (two shorts) of classical prosody is not found in English metres, where isochronous stress is always present, or at least (as in silent stress) implied.

I'm aware that some readers will not wish to give up the old quantitative terminology – for many, the very sound of a term like 'trochaic hexameter' has a kind of magic about it, giving the impression that in poetry one is dealing with an occult art (which – to a large extent – one is, of course). But for the many others who have only felt confusion and vexation over the notion of 'scansion by feet', this book offers a simpler alternative, one based on English speech-sounds.

The very real objection may also be made that in using the rhythmic measure as the basis of metre, one is losing the important classical distinction between 'falling' and 'rising' feet – that is, in English, between lines which open with a stressed syllable:

'Take my hand and walk with me!'

and those that do not:

   'Oh,   no, my Lord, that cannot be!'

but I do not believe that the difference is particularly noticeable to the average reader. The stress-column alignment of the anthology selections makes any larger patterns visible, in any case. Compare no. 21 (all stressed openings) with no. 29 (all unstressed openings) and no. 30 (a mixture of the two). The old terms are still there if you feel the effect *is* significant, however: 'falling' for lines which begin with a stress, 'rising' for those which do not. The essence of the old quantitative term 'iambic pentameter' can thus be conveyed by 'rising five-duplet'.

# Appendix D
## Glossary of Technical Terms

**accent**  Used in this book to denote the strong beat in music; comparable to *stress* in language. May also be used in linguistics to refer to the stress patterns of groups of words; for instance, in the phrase 'two and two are four', the first, third and fifth words are accented.

**action poetry**  Poetry written for performance by two or more voices; a type of *concrete poetry*.

**alliteration**  One of the phonemic patterns of poetry and other forms of speech, in which one or more of the opening consonants of a stressed syllable are repeated in other stressed positions in the line. The phrase 'slippery and slimy sludge' alliterates. Alliteration may also be **partial**: some, but not all, of the leading consonants are repeated; as, for example, in the phrase 'tall travellers'.

**allitero-assonance**  See *assonance*.

**anthropomorphism**  Giving human shape or characteristics to a god, an animal or an inanimate thing. 'The house crouched waiting' is an example. See also *personification*.

**assonance**  One of the phonemic patterns of poetry featuring repetition of the stressed vowel sound(s). The phrase 'trade a plate of steak' is an example of assonance. Other types include **allitero-assonance**, in which both the opening consonants and the vowels are repeated in other stressed syllables (an example is 'playful plaintiff'), and *rhyme*, in which both the vowels and the closing consonants are repeated.

**ballad**  The 'traditional ballad' is a narrative song or poem characterized by short stanzas and simple words. 'Lord Randal' (no. 14) is an example. The word 'ballad' also refers to modern songs, often about love. Although all ballads may be seen as types of literature, the term 'literary ballad' is generally used in our time to describe a nineteenth- or twentieth-century poem written by a literary poet in imitation of the form and spirit of the 'traditional ballad'.

**ballade**  A fixed form of poetry of French origin, consisting of three stanzas of eight or ten lines each and an *envoy* (an additional section directed to a particular person) of four or five lines. The last line of each stanza and of the envoy is the same. An example is Chaucer's 'Ballade to Rosamund'.

**blank verse**  Unrhymed five-stress lines, of principally duple rhythm. Milton's *Paradise Lost* and most of Shakespeare's plays are written in blank verse.

**bouts rimées**  A game, popular in Victorian times, in which contestants write verses using groups of rhymes agreed on beforehand.

**burden**  A repeated line or group of lines occurring between the stanzas of a *carol*. Often called the 'chorus', probably because it was sung by all participants in the song, with the intervening stanzas being sung by a solo leader.

**caesura**  An extra-metrical pause in a line of poetry. The caesura in Old English poetry was dictated by the metre, and always divided the four stresses of the line into two groups of two stresses each. In more recent poetry, the caesura is dictated by the sense of the line, and is usually indicated by some strong punctuation mark. In the line

That was no trouble. Soon the wheel was fixed,

there is an evident caesura between 'trouble' and 'soon'.

**carol**  A fixed form of song, of popular appeal, which originated in

France as a kind of round dance. Typically, the last line of a four-line stanza rhymes with the lines of the *burden*, which is sung between the stanzas of the carol. 'Bring Us in Good Ale' (no. 11) is an example of a carol, though its three-line stanza form is not typical.

**chanson**   A medieval *lyric* type, a song whose chief interest has to do with some manifestation of romantic or courtly love.

**chanson d'aventure**   A *chanson* characterized by an opening line such as 'As I rode out the other day', in which the narrator describes a series of happenings, typically culminating in an encounter with the beloved.

**circumlocution**   A rhetorical figure of speech in which something is expressed in a roundabout way: 'Fourscore and seven years ago . . .'

**closed couplets**   Pairs of rhymed lines (usually *heroic couplets*) in which the lines end with some kind of punctuational pause. Extremely popular in eighteenth-century poetry. See also *end-stopped*.

**closed rhyme**   Forms with a *rhyme-scheme* such as *abba*, in which the same rhyme opens and closes a stanza or part of a stanza.

**concrete poetry**   A general term which covers *ear poetry*, *eye poetry* and *action poetry*.

**connotation**   The range of secondary or accompanying meanings suggested by a particular word or phrase, as opposed to its *denotation*, or 'dictionary meaning'.

**consonance**   A phonemic pattern in poetry and other speech featuring repetition of the final consonant sound(s) of stressed syllables. The phrase 'take the doctor back' is an example of simple consonance. Other types are:
   **partial**   Some but not all the final consonants of stressed syllables are repeated; for example, 'Dot has Pete's hatchet.'
   **full**   Both the opening and the closing consonants of the stressed syllable are repeated; for example, 'tap the top'.

**reversed**   Both the opening and the closing consonants of the stressed syllable are repeated, but with their positions reversed; for example, 'tip the pot'.

**reversed with assonance**   All the sounds of the stressed syllable are repeated, but the opening and closing consonants of the first are reversed in the second; for example, 'top of the pot'.

Generally speaking, the term 'consonance' may be understood to include any or all of these effects.

**consonant**   Any speech-sound made by stopping and releasing the air stream (/p, t, k, b, d, g/); by stopping it at one point while it escapes at another (/m, n, ŋ, l, r/); by forcing it through a loosely closed or very narrow passage (/f, v, s, z, ʃ, ʒ, θ, ð, h, w, y/); or by a combination of these means. See also *vowel*.

**corona**   A sequence of *sonnets* in which the last line of each sonnet reappears as the first line of the following one. Popular in Elizabethan times.

**couplet**   Two lines of the same *metre* which have a common *rhyme*.

**curtal sonnet**   An abbreviated *sonnet* of ten and a half lines.

**cynghanedd**   A set of phonemic patterns commonly found in Welsh poetry and occasionally imitated in English. Hopkins's phrase 'fall, gall, and gash', in which the first stressed syllable rhymes with the second and the second alliterates with the third, is an example of one of these, **cynghanedd sain**.


**deictic**   Words which particularize either themselves (for instance, 'John Conklin' is a particular individual) or general nouns with which they are associated ('this street' is a particular street). Often used unconventionally (that is, apparently without adequate information) in poetry and other forms of literature.

**denotation**   The 'dictionary meaning' of a word, as opposed to its *connotation*.

**diphthong**   Two vowels sounded one immediately after the other; for example, the sounds of the word 'eye'. See Appendix A.

**douzain**  The opening twelve-line section of an English *sonnet*.

**duplet**  A two-syllable rhythm in which the first syllable is stressed and the second is not; for example, 'empty' and 'drink it'.

**ear poetry**  A form of *concrete poetry* in which phonic patterns are the dominant effect. An example is Louis Zukofsky's 'Julia's Wild' (no. 79).

**elegy**  A formal poem of lament, often for a particular person.

**end-stopped**  Refers to a line of poetry in which the end of a syntactic and semantic phrase coincides with the end of the line. Couplets with frequent end-stopping are called *closed couplets*.

**enjambment**  The effect caused when the semantic content of a phrase carries on beyond the end of the line and this is accompanied by opening weak syllables in the following line. Often shown by an absence of any punctuation at the end of the line. See also *run-on line*.

**envoy**  The concluding stanza of a *ballade*, in which the poem is directed to a particular person.

**epic**  A long narrative poem on a great and serious subject. Traditional epics, such as the Greek *Iliad* and *Odyssey* of Homer, or the Old English *Beowulf*, were shaped over generations of telling, and made much use of fixed verbal formula. 'Literary epics' – such as Virgil's *Aeneid*, Dante's *Divine Comedy* or Milton's *Paradise Lost* – imitate some of the aspects of the traditional form. The most ambitious of all poetic genres.

**epic simile**  An extended simile, in which the object of comparison is described at great length. See *simile*.

**epigram**  A short, and often witty, poem. May also be applied to neat and witty statements in prose.

**epigraph**  A quotation placed at the beginning of a poem or other piece of writing.

**epithalamion**  A poem written to celebrate a marriage. The first

English epithalamion was written by Sir Philip Sidney *c.*1580, and Spenser wrote his great 'Epithalamion' fifteen years later. The Latin name **epithalamium** is also used.

**etymology**   The origin and development of a word or other part of speech.

**exemplum**   A tale which carries a moral message; common in medieval times.

**eye poetry**   A type of *concrete poetry* in which visual appeal is of predominant interest.

**eye rhyme**   A pair of syllables which look as though they should rhyme but do not; for example, 'love' and 'move'. Sometimes called 'courtesy rhyme' because its use, though strictly incorrect, is conventionally allowed. Note that some rhymes which appear to fall under this category today may have rhymed at the time the poem was written.

**fabliau**   A short comic or satiric tale in verse. Chaucer's 'Miller's Tale' and 'Reeve's Tale' are good examples.

**feminine rhyme**   See *rhyme.*

**figurative language**   The use of non-literal expressions to convey certain ideas or things more vividly; includes all varieties of *simile, metaphor, hyperbole,* and *personification.*

**fixed forms**   Types of poetry which use a metre, rhyme-scheme, or stanza fixed by convention. The most prevalent type in Engish is the *sonnet;* other fixed forms include the *ballet, carol, rondeau, rondel,* and *villanelle.*

**form**   The physical appearance of poetry on the page; also, the structural units of the poem – couplet, quatrain, and so forth – and their arrangement.

**format**   The physical lay-out (margin sizes, type style and size, line arrangement, pagination) of a book of poetry or any other printed material.

**found poem**   A piece of pre-existing written language (perhaps a newspaper article, an advertisement, written instructions) presented in the format of a poem.

**free verse**   Poetry of no regular metre. Also called **non-metrical poetry**. Many of the poems of Walt Whitman are in free verse.

**genre**   A literary type. Examples of literary genres are the novel, the short story, the play, the poem. Examples of poetic genres are the epic, the elegy, the lyric, and the like.

**grammar**   In the past, used prescriptively to mean 'the rules of correct diction'; now used descriptively in reference to the ways in which we combine elements of language to communicate.

**grammatical words**   Words which have little or no independent meaning, but are used to show how the meaningful (or *lexical*) words in a phrase are related. Articles ('the', 'a', 'an'), auxiliary verbs ('to be', and 'to have' when used in combination with other verbs), and prepositions ('to', 'from', 'over', 'under') are examples. Grammatical words tend to be unstressed when used in a phrase with lexical words.

**heroic couplet**   Form using rhymed pairs of five-stress lines, of predominantly duple rhythm. Introduced by Chaucer (*The Legend of Good Women* and most of *The Canterbury Tales*) and popular ever since. In the eighteenth century, the great age of the heroic couplet, they were usually *end-stopped*, or *closed*; that is, the units of meaning coincided with the line, and were nearly always marked with some punctuation (comma, semicolon, colon, full stop). The nineteenth century saw the development of *enjambed* and *run-on* heroic couplet lines.

**hyperbole**   A type of *figurative language* characterized by exaggeration or overstatement: 'I died of embarrassment.'

**iconic language**   A newly coined term to describe the notion of poetic language *being* its own reality, instead of merely symbolizing some other external reality. Contrasted with *referential language*. See also *performative language*.

**imagery**   Vivid description of a visible object or scene. Also used loosely to mean *figurative language*.

**interlaced rhyme**   An arrangement of lines in a stanza or part of a stanza so that rhymes are interwoven; as in the rhyme-scheme *abab*.

**irony**   The speech convention that allows for an interpretation of meaning which may be quite different from the surface appearance; for example, one might ironically remark, 'You look happy today!' to someone wearing an obviously woebegone expression. Appreciation of irony depends mainly on context and (to a somewhat lesser degree) tone of voice. Another common meaning of the word refers to a happening which is the opposite of what one might have expected; for example, 'It's ironic that their nuclear-bomb shelter collapsed and killed them all instantly.'

**isochronism**   A phenomenon central to all English metres and observable in most declamatory speech, in which stressed syllables are perceived as falling at more or less equal intervals of time. The adjective is 'isochronous'.

**kenning**   An Old English poetic convention, a type of *metonymy*, in which one thing is represented by another which is usually associated with it. The expression 'whale's road', meaning 'sea', (no. 1) is an example.

**lexical words**   Words which carry independent meaning: nouns, main verbs, adverbs. Opposed to *grammatical words* which mainly state the nature of the relationship between the lexical words in a phrase. In the sentence, 'Joan and John have eaten their dinner', 'Joan', 'John', 'eaten', and 'dinner' are lexical words; the others are grammatical words. In English speech, lexical words tend to be stressed, while grammatical words tend not to be, except in cases of unusual emphasis (often in print conveyed by the use of italics).

**limerick**   A comic, often bawdy, poem, usually printed as five lines rhyming *aabba* (though metrically better understood as four lines rhyming *aaba*, with the b-line containing an internal rhyme). 'Invented' by the Victorian Edward Lear, though much improved on since.

**literal language**   Language which means what the sum total of its words denote, as is usually the case in everyday speech. Opposed to *figurative language*, where meaning may be quite different from what the words denote.

**litotes**   A type of *figurative language* in which understatement is used to heighten the reader's or listener's sense of reality. A good example occurs in *Beowulf* when one of the characters, after describing the horrors of a monster's den, comments: 'It is not a pleasant place.'

**lyric**   The word derives from Greek, and means literally 'of the lyre'. The **medieval lyric** is a short rhyming poem, often about secular or sacred love. (The term was first applied to such poems only centuries afterwards, it should be noted.) Later ages, particularly the nineteenth century, extended the meaning of lyric to include personal statements, or revelations of the poet's innermost feeling. In the twentieth century, 'lyrics' often refers to the words of a song.

**masculine rhyme**   See *rhyme*.

**measure**   The basic unit of metre, made up of one stressed syllable and any weak syllables which follow it. The most common measures in English are *duplet* (one stressed and one weak syllable) and *triplet* (one stressed and two weak syllables), though *singlet* (a single stressed syllable) and *quadruplet* (one stressed and three weak syllables) measures are not unusual.

**metaphor**   A type of *figurative language* in which one thing is described in terms of some other thing: 'Beauty is but a flowre' (no. 17). Literary critics, from Aristotle on, have seen metaphor as the most distinctive type of poetic language.

**metonymy**  A type of *figurative language* in which the name of one thing is replaced with that of another commonly associated with it.

**metre**  Literally 'measure', this word refers to the abstract regular pattern of strong and weak syllables realized through the rhythms of successive lines of a poem. Although we may characterize the metre of a poem as, for example, five-duplet (that is, lines with five measures each, each measure being made up of one strong and one weak syllable), it may be that few lines in the poem actually conform to such a regular pattern. *Rhythm* is the phenomenon which we actually perceive, whereas metre is a regularized abstraction derived from the rhythms which are perceived.

**Middle English**  The various dialects of English spoken and written between the beginning of the twelfth and the end of the fifteenth century, abbreviated ME.

**Modern English**  The various dialects of English spoken and written since the beginning of the sixteenth century, abbreviated Mod.E. Sometimes subdivided into Early Modern English and Later Modern English.

**non-metrical poetry**  See *free verse*.

**octave**  A *stanza* or group of eight lines; the opening eight lines of an Italian *sonnet*.

**Old English**  The various dialects of English spoken and written from the first half of the fifth to the end of the eleventh century, abbreviated OE. Sometimes called **Anglo-Saxon** (AS).

**onomatopoeia**  A word whose sound symbolizes its meaning; for example 'hiss'. The meaning of a truly onomatopoeic word should be evident to speakers of every language. True onomatopoeia is extremely rare, and is often confused with *phonolexis*, in which the sound of a particular word recalls the meanings of words with similar sounds in the same language.

**ottava rima**   An eight-line *fixed form* consisting of five-measure lines rhyming *abababcc*. Byron is one of its greatest exponents.

**oxymoron**   An apparently self-contradictory phrase; for example 'happy sorrow'.

**paradigm**   The list of all possible words or forms which may be used at any particular position in a speech utterance. The paradigm for the first position in the utterance, 'The house is white', would contain not only 'The', 'Some' and 'Every' but also possessive forms such as 'Tom's, 'Dick's', 'Harry's', and so on. Often we are not so much interested in the conventional members of a paradigm, but in the poet's insertion of a quite unconventional member, such as 'grief' in Dylan Thomas's phrase 'a grief ago', which the poet makes part of the 'Nouns denoting fixed periods of time' paradigm. A paradigm may be seen as a list of variants of an invariant heading. Paradigm, the vertical axis of language, contrasts with *syntagm*, the horizontal axis, denoting the combination of words and parts of words into meaningful speech expressions.

**paradox**   A statement or observation which seems self-contradictory, but which usually has a logical explanation.

**pastoral**   A poetic and literary form in which the countryside and its people are celebrated.

**performative language**   A term often applied to poetry, conveying the idea of language that works inherently – first and foremost – as performance, and only secondarily as a bearer of some external reality. Contrasted with *referential language*.

**personification**   Often loosely used as equivalent to *anthropomorphism*, but more usefully limited to describing the convention of addressing an inanimate object or an abstract quality as though it were a living person: 'O Moon, look down from thy silver sphere', or 'Happiness, too long you have been away.'

**phoneme**   The smallest meaningful unit of sound. The concept is an abstraction derived from the actual sounds of language, which vary from speaker to speaker. Phonemic symbols (see Appendix A for a list of those needed to transcribe English) are written between two slash marks: /g/ for the first sound in 'get'.

**phonemic patterns** The repetition of certain sounds in stressed syllables. This repetition must be relatively close and obvious (rhyme conventionally occurs at the metrical close of a line, for example) if the listener is to perceive it. Common phonemic patterns in English are *rhyme* and *alliteration*.

**phonolexis** Meaning conveyed through the invocation of the meanings of other words with similar sounds. For example, the word 'clump' may recall the meanings of 'stump', 'thump', 'rump', 'plump'. Works only in the context of a single language. Often confused with *onomatopoeia*.

**pleonasm** A phrase containing redundant words; for example, 'unmarried bachelor'.

**prose** Any kind of non-poetic literary work. The sound of prose is usually of minimal interest, and most attention is given to the referential content.

**prosody** The systematic study of versification, mainly concerned with the principles and practice of *metre*, *phonemic patterns*, *stanza* forms, *figurative language*, and the like. The main focus of interest of this book. (Nothing to do with *prose*.)

**quadruplet** A rhythmic measure containing a stressed syllable followed by three weak syllables: 'dictionary' is an example.

**quaestio** A rhetorical convention; the asking of a question whose answer is evident to all: 'Are we going to put up with this idiocy?' Often called **rhetorical question**.

**quatrain** A four-line stanza or group of lines, usually rhymed.

**referential language** A term used to describe everyday language, in which words are taken as referring to some external reality. Contrasts with the *performative* or *iconic* nature of the language of poetry.

**reverdie**   A medieval *lyric* type celebrating the joys of the return of spring.

**reverse sonnet**   A comic form of *sonnet* invented by Rupert Brooke, in which the normal English sonnet form and content are reversed: the climactic concluding *couplet* comes first, and is followed by a long, discursive *douzain*.

**rhetoric**   A codification of different types of heightened expression and their use. Derived from the practices of classical Greek and Latin, and important in medieval and Elizabethan times. Rhetorical 'colours' are still used in effective writing and speech, but their use today is less mannered.

**rhyme**   The main phonemic pattern of recent English poetry, in which the vowel and closing consonant sounds of a stressed syllable are repeated, together with any weak syllables which may follow. Rhyme may be **one-syllable** ('house/mouse'), **two-syllable** ('cooking/looking'), or **three-syllable** ('tricycle/bicycle'). One-syllable rhyme was traditionally called *masculine rhyme* and two-syllable rhyme *feminine rhyme*.

**rhyme-scheme**   A conventional way of noting how rhymed line-endings are arranged in a *stanza* or group of lines. The letter *a* is used for the first rhymed sounds, *b* for the second, and so on. The letter *x* denotes lines which do not rhyme with any others.

**rhythm**   The recurrence of groups of stressed and unstressed (or strong and weak) syllables in speech. In poetry, the rhythmic unit is the *measure*, which opens with a single stressed syllable and may conventionally include up to three weak syllables after the stress. *Metre* describes the typical line in terms of how many rhythmic measures it contains, and what the dominant rhythm of these measures is.

**rime royale**   A late-medieval *fixed form* consisting of a seven-line stanza rhymed *ababbcc*, in five-stress lines of duplet metre. Chaucer's greatest completed poem, *Troilus and Criseyde*, is in *rime royale*, as are some of *The Canterbury Tales*.

**rondeau**   A *fixed form* consisting of ten or thirteen lines, with only two rhymes, and an unrhymed refrain of the first two lines, partially repeated in the middle and at the end of the poem.

**rondel**   A *fixed form* similar to the *rondeau*, but with fourteen lines, two rhymes, and with the first two lines used as a refrain in the middle and at the end of the poem.

**run-on line**   Lines in which meaning and syntax lead the ear quickly past the end and on to the beginning of the next line. Often reinforced by *enjambment*, in which run-on syntax is combined with opening weak syllables in the next line. An example of a run-on line without enjambment is:

> It's  sweet to write upon the sandy
>     shore the thoughts you find too handy . . .

An example of a run-on line reinforced with metrical enjambment is:

> It's  funny how the things you're told
> Can  never lead to pots of gold . . .

**semantics**   The aspect of language which involves meaning.

**sestet**   A six-line *stanza* or a group of six lines, usually with some sort of *rhyme-scheme*. Often refers to the concluding section of an Italian *sonnet*.

**silent stress**   A moment of silence which occurs where a stressed syllable is expected; indicated, in this book, with an asterisk.

**simile**   A figure of speech in which an explicit comparison is made between two things, using either 'like' or 'as': 'the stars glittered like frost', or 'as empty as a drum'.

**singlet**   A measure containing one stressed (or strong) syllable, and no weak ones. The phrase 'Dear John' at the opening of a letter consists of two singlets.

**sonnet**   A *fixed form*, usually of fourteen lines, each consisting of five measures of duplet metre. The two principal types are the

**English sonnet** (also called the **Shakespearean sonnet**), consisting of a *douzain* and a concluding *couplet*; and the **Italian sonnet** (also called the **Petrarchan sonnet**), consisting of an *octave* and a concluding *sestet*. Sonnets typically follow a preset rhyme-scheme, and develop an idea in a way which parallels the major structural divisions of the poem.

**sonnet redoublé**   A sequence of fifteen sonnets in which the last line of each sonnet is the first line of the following one, the last line of the fourteenth sonnet is the same as the first line of the first sonnet, *and* all fourteen linking lines are then used in order to make up the fifteenth sonnet.

**Spenserian stanza**   The stanza form used by Spenser in *The Faerie Queene*, consisting of nine lines rhymed *ababbcbcc*. The first eight lines have five duple measures each; the concluding line has six measures.

**stanza**   A group of lines forming one of the divisions of a poem. A stanzaic poem commonly uses the same stanza form throughout, repeating its *rhyme-scheme* (if any) and *metre*.

**stress**   A feature of all English speech, referring to the prominence given to certain words or syllables in an utterance. The components of stress are loudness, raised pitch, and prolongation of the stressed syllable. Loudness is the chief of these; the other two may be entirely absent, and yet stress will still be perceived. In the phrase, 'I've **told** you **o**.ver and **o**.ver', the bold letters indicate the three stressed syllables of the phrase. In poetry, stress occurs at roughly equal time intervals and, in English culture, is perceived as *isochronous*. Stressed and weak syllables combine (one stress with zero to three intervening weaks) to form the *rhythms* of speech. The above example contains three rhythmic *measures*, each beginning with a stress: an opening *duplet* ('**told** you'), a *triplet* ('**o**.ver and') and a concluding duplet ('**o**.ver'). Any weak syllables opening a line (such as 'I've' in the above example) are ignored in an isolated line or phrase. In a line of poetry, any weak syllables coming before the first stress are associated with the measure which ends the preceding line. The more weak syllables there are between the isochronous stresses, the more rapidly the syllables are perceived to occur. In reality, significant departure from strictly equal timing of stresses is a continual part of the performance of poetry; nevertheless, our underlying cultural perception of English metre is based on the concept of equally timed stresses.

**strong syllable**   Same as a stressed syllable. See *stress*.

**syllable**   The smallest combined form of English speech sounds (*phonemes*), a syllable must include a central *vowel* or *diphthong* (a few words, such as 'I', 'a' and 'oh', contain no more than this), and may be preceded by as many as three and followed by as many as four *consonant* sounds. The word 'tree' contains one syllable, 'acorn' two, and so on. In multisyllabic words, one syllable receives the main *stress*, though other syllables may receive secondary stress (these may be considered either as strong or weak syllables, whichever seems to meet the demands of the poem's metre best). The rhythms of stressed and weak syllables in particular words or phrases cannot be changed – they are set by usage, and the poet must fit them to the metrical pattern of the poem.

**syllable-stress metre**   A type of metre, usually said to have followed the pure-stress metres of Old English. In syllable-stress metres, not only must the number of stresses per line be metrically regular, so must the total number of syllables in each line. In actuality, most English poets have felt perfectly free to depart from this strict limit whenever it suited them. It is unlikely that an English audience is much aware of the total number of syllables, weak or strong, in a line – one is much more struck by the number of stresses and the amount of rhythmic variation (mainly between *duplets* and *triplets*).

**synecdoche**   A figure of speech in which a part is used for a whole, an individual for a class, a material for a thing, or the reverse of any of these. For example, in 'Many hands make light work', 'hands' is used in place of 'helpers'.

**syntagm**   The horizontal axis of combination in speech; the way in which word choices (made from *paradigms*, or lists of available variants) are combined according to certain rules. See also *paradigm*. In the phrase, 'He hit the ball', the syntagm is a particular variant of the invariant model Subject + Transitive Verb + Deictic Word (here, an article) + Object. The same syntagm would also underlie the phrases 'Sue cooked her omelette' and 'Winds blew the curtain'. The choice of a word for each position in the invariant model is understood as being made from independent paradigms: the first, headed 'Subject', containing many thousands of variants, the second, 'Transitive Verb', also containing many thousands of variants, and so on.

**syntax**  Closely related to *syntagm*, the term refers to the arrangement of words in a sentence to show their semantic relationship to one another. Disruption of normal syntax is common in poetry, where we find adjectives following nouns ('a pleasure rare'), inversion of verb and subject ('where was heard the mingled measure'), and so forth.

**tautology**  A statement which says something more than once: 'His empty phrases were devoid of meaning.'

**tercet**  A three-line *stanza* or group of three lines within a stanza. The concluding *sestet* of an Italian *sonnet* is usually divided into two tercets, and in *terza rima* tercet stanzas are used. Sometimes spelled 'terzet'.

**terza rima**  A three-line stanza form in which the middle line of each stanza rhymes with the first and last lines of the stanza which follows: *aba bcb cdc*, and so on.

**triplet**  A rhythmic measure containing a stressed syllable followed by two weak syllables: 'relative' is an example.

**unvoiced consonant**  A *consonant* which is spoken without any vibration of the vocal cords. Examples of unvoiced consonants are /p, t, s, k/, and so on. See also *voiced consonant*.

**villanelle**  A *fixed form*, usually containing five three-line *stanzas* and a final four-line stanza, with only two rhymes throughout.

**voiced consonant**   A *consonant* which is spoken while the vocal cords vibrate. Examples of voiced consonants are /b, d, z, g/, and so on.

**vowel**   A prolonged speech-sound made using the mouth simply as a resonator and allowing the vocal cords to vibrate as air is exhaled. A rapidly sounded combination of two vowels is called a *diphthong*. See Appendix A for a list of meaningful English vowel sounds.

**weak syllable**   An unstressed syllable. As many as three weak syllables may occur between successive stressed syllables in normal English speech. See *stress*.

This is by no means intended to be an exhaustive list of all terms that may be useful in a discussion of different aspects of poetry, particularly the more literary ones. For information on such general topics as 'allegory', 'courtly love', 'symbol', 'tragedy', and so forth, look at any good guide to English literature, or one of the many glossaries of literary terms in English.

# Further Reading

Abercrombie, David, *Studies in Phonetics and Linguistics* (London, 1965). See especially 'A Phonetician's View of Verse Structure'. The rest of the book, although not limited to poetry, is quite entertainingly written, offering an interesting sampling of recent language studies.

Berry, Francis, *Poetry and the Physical Voice* (London, 1962). A fascinating, though inconclusive, book, which argues that all poetry is conceived in terms of the limitations of the poet's own voice and breath.

Bessinger and Kahrl, eds., *Essential Articles for the Study of Old English Poetry* (Hamden, Conn., 1968). See especially Marjorie Daunt, 'Old English Verse and English Speech Rhythm', and C. S. Lewis, 'The Alliterative Metre'.

Brooke-Rose, Christine, *A Grammar of Metaphor* (London, 1958). A study of the grammatical structure of metaphor. Extracts are quoted in Chatman and Levin, listed below.

Chatman, Seymour, *A Theory of Meter* (The Hague, 1965). An important book, though not easy reading. Includes findings of a number of experiments to test audience perception of English metrical effects.

— and Levin, Samuel, eds., *Essays on the Language of Literature* (Boston, 1967). A collection of technical articles, mainly by linguisticians. Includes extracts from Brooke-Rose's *A Grammar of Metaphor*, as well as articles on metre, stylistics and other aspects of poetic language.

Copley, James, *Shift of Meaning* (London, 1961). An account of the changing meanings of a number of important literary words from Shakespeare's time on.

Crystal, David, *The English Tone of Voice* (New York, 1976). Highly technical, though Chapter 7, 'Intonation and Metrical Theory', presents a useful summary of recent linguistic studies of metre.

Culler, Jonathan, *Structuralist Poetics* (London, 1975). A way of examining all linguistic and literary levels of a poem simultaneously. Somewhat demanding; frequently illuminating.

Dixon, Peter, *Rhetoric* (London, 1971). A useful little guide to patterns of usage which play a part not only in poetry but in all literature.

Fowler, Roger, ed., *Essays on Style and Language* (London, 1966). See especially ' "Prose Rhythm" and Metre', pp. 82–99.

Fraser, G. S., *Metre, Rhyme and Free Verse* (London, 1970). Interesting material, but unfortunately marred by some misprints among his metrical markings, particularly in the chapter on quantitative metres.

Fuller, J. L., *The Sonnet* (London, 1973). An extremely useful guide to this most important poetic form. Source of some of the examples quoted in this book.

Fussell, Paul, *Poetic Meter and Poetic Form* (New York, 1965; 1969). Lively, thought-provoking, but occasionally flawed (see Appendix C).

Gimson, A. C., *An Introduction to the Pronunciation of English* (London, 1962). A good all-round account of speech-sounds.

Groom, B., *The Diction of Poetry from Spenser to Bridges* (Toronto, 1955). A literary approach to poetic language; wide-ranging but inconclusive.

Gross, Harvey, *Sound and Form in Modern Poetry* (Ann Arbor,

1964). Much of this book is good, but the author's views on rhythm and metre at times seem unrealistic.

Halliday, M. A. K., *Short Introduction to Functional Grammar* (London, 1983). A section on prosody discards notions of quantitative metre as irrelevant to English poetry, and concentrates on speech rhythms and intonation as the basis of metre.

Hamer, Enid, *The Metres of English Poetry* (New York, 1930). Based on stress, but uses the quantitatively derived 'foot' as the basic unit of metre.

Hawkes, Terence, *Metaphor* (London, 1972). An excellent summary of views from Aristotle and Plato to the most recent linguistic theories. Helpful bibliography.

Langer, Suzanne, *Philosophy in a New Key*, 2nd edn (Cambridge, Mass., 1951). One of the seminal books of our time, accounting for the aims and effects of different artistic forms. Especially good on poetry and music.

Leech, Geoffrey, *A Linguistic Guide to English Poetry* (London, 1969). Perhaps the best single guide to a multitude of different poetic effects possible with our language. Possibly a little vague on the subject of rhythm and metre, but extremely informative on most other aspects. Technical, though not dauntingly academic.

Legman, Gershon, *The Limerick* (New York, 1964; 1969). An exhaustive guide to the various manifestations of a lively oral tradition. Legman (better known for his lively *Rationale of the Dirty Joke*) points out that the appeal of the limerick is chiefly to the well-educated. Legman's real interest is the bawdy limerick, but his introduction deals perceptively with all types. My only quibble is with his characterization of English metre as quantitative: he describes the metre of the limerick as 'anapestic trimeter rising . . . from its short syllables to an accented long syllable'. (p. lvi). (See pp. 104–5 for a more idiomatic account of the metre of this form.)

Leishman, J. B., *Translating Horace* (Oxford, 1956). A noted scholar and poet explains the difficulties of 'translating' classical quantitative metres into equivalent English forms.

Levin, Samuel R., *Linguistic Structures in Poetry* (The Hague, 1962). A short but fairly technical account of the phenomenon of 'coupling' in the language of poetry.

Lord, Albert B., *The Singer of Tales* (Cambridge, Mass., 1960). An account of the practice and performance of twentieth-century epic poets in Yugoslavia which has important implications for what we know of the origins and development of similar forms in Old English.

Lotman, Yury, *Analysis of the Poetic Text* (Ann Arbor, 1976). One of the most illuminating books of our times, dealing with all linguistic and cultural aspects of poetry. It is fairly technical, however, and its examples are taken from Russian poetry. (English transliterations are provided in this edition.)

McIntosh, A. and Halliday, M. A. K., *Patterns of Language* (London, 1966). A collection of articles on various aspects of linguistics in literary studies. See especially Chapter 2, 'Linguistics and Literary Studies'.

Miles, Josephine, *Eras and Modes in English Poetry*, 2nd edn (Berkeley, 1964). A statistical approach to the examination of poetic language of different periods from the sixteenth century on. (See Chapter 4 above for an account of her main findings.)

Muecke, D. C., *Irony and the Ironic*, 2nd edn (London, 1982). Covers poetry, drama and various aspects of the novel. A fascinating account of this most subtle of effects.

Nowottny, Winifred, *The Language Poets Use* (London, 1962). A literary–critical approach to poetic language, including metaphor, diction and ambiguity.

Opie, Iona and Peter, *The Lore and Language of Schoolchildren* (Oxford, 1959). Most of the rhythmical and phonemic effects of English poetry may be seen emerging in children's rhymes and other word-games. A fascinating account of what had earlier been a hidden culture.

—, *The Oxford Dictionary of Nursery Rhymes* (London, 1951). The standard collection of children's rhymes, an excellent guide not only to every rhythmic effect possible in English, but also to the most basic effects of even the most sophisticated poetry in our language.

Preminger, Alex, *The Princeton Encyclopedia of Poetry and Poetics*, enlarged edn (Princeton, N.J., 1974). A useful general reference text.

Scully, J., ed., *Modern Poets on Modern Poetry* (London, 1966). Interviews with contemporary poets on the nature of their work and their views on technical and philosophical aspects of poetry. A good read.

Sebeok, T. A., ed., *Style in Language* (New York, 1960). See especially Seymour Chatman, 'Comparing Metrical Styles'; Roman Jakobson, 'Concluding Statement, Linguistics and Poetics'; and Edward Stankiewicz, 'Linguistics and the Study of Poetic Language'.

Shapiro, Karl and Beum, R., *A Prosody Handbook* (New York, 1965). A general reference work, but based on traditional quantitative terminology.

Solt, Mary Ellen, *Concrete Poetry, A World View* (Bloomington, Ind., 1970). A very full treatment, with copious examples from the fields of both ear- and eye-poetry.

Valéry, Paul, *The Art of Poetry* (New York, 1958). A statement of aesthetics from one of the leading poets of our time; useful as a universal philosophy of poetry.

# Index

This lists references to poets and other writers of fiction, as well as the titles of their works, given significant mention in the text, anthology, and appendices. Other writers (for example critics, scholars) are cited by name only; you should see Further Reading (pages 292–6) for information on their titles. Technical terms and general subjects (for example, limerick, metaphor, rhyme) are also included; but first check the Glossary (pages 274–91). First-line references to poems in the anthology have been given when it seemed this might be helpful.